The Happy Lagoons

*ADVENTUR

by Jørgen Andersen-Rosend

The Happy Lagoons

F A SOUTH SEA WANDERER

TRANSLATED FROM THE DANISH
EILER HANSEN AND J. F. BURKE

lt, Rinehart and Winston ✳ *New York*

This book is dedicated to

ANNEMARIE SELINKO

as a small token of gratitude to
a great author
for a still greater friendship

He who has not a thousand friends
has not a friend to spare
and he who has an enemy
will meet him everywhere

OMAR KHAYYÁM

Contents

The Happy Lagoons

Tea and flying saucers

Mrs. Hanson obviously pitied me for having to go all the way to the South Sea Islands. She was sitting opposite me on the train from Copenhagen to Esbjerg, a splendid Danish matron who looked as well filled as her cupboards at home. She was going to Sonderho on the island of Fano to attend her niece's confirmation.

"It's a long trip," she assured me, "and very expensive. But after all, one can't count pennies. Girls are confirmed only once and this one, you know, is an only child. And such a nice, good girl, just the kind you'd want. Not like a lot of others I could tell you about, getting in trouble and bringing misery on their parents like that awful girl next door. Oh, she was just terrible. Let me tell you, be glad you haven't got a child like that. Imagine, she got mixed up with the local dairyman, and he a man in his fifties and married, too. Although I must say he has the best cheeses in the

3

neighborhood. You can't get them better anywhere, not even in Nakskov." Mrs. Hanson rambled on and on, telling me everything she could think of about herself. However, she finally had to stop to catch her breath, and so at last asked me where I was headed.

"Oh, I," I said, shrugging my shoulders and trying my best not to smile. "I'm just going as far as Tonga." I felt as smug as a bridge player trumping his opponent's ace. I went on to explain to her that Tonga was a kingdom of little palm-tree islands right in the middle of the Pacific Ocean. "I am going to London, and from there to Marseilles," I continued, delighting in the impression I was sure these exotic names were making, "and there I will take a boat through the Panama Canal to the Fiji Islands, and from there a plane to Tonga. Altogether it will take me only about two months."

A look of infinite astonishment filled Mrs. Hanson's eyes. Success, I thought; this woman was really impressed. But no, not my Mrs. Hanson. The look in her eyes changed quickly from shock to pity.

"Poor boy," she said, "so far away! Oh, I feel so sorry for you. Do you really have to?" She sank back in her seat, looking as though she were trying to find the proper words of consolation. Naturally, she found them. "Perhaps," she said, with a smile that was meant to encourage me, "perhaps you are going there to join your family, some loved ones whom you haven't seen for years. Ah yes, I can see that, that's a different matter of course." Then, more practical, she asked, "Isn't this going to cost you an awful lot of money?"

I told her the price, and she was aghast at the thought of it. "Good God," she said, "that's outrageous! Why, for that money, my husband and I could have central heating. That's been the dream of our lifetime, you know. We've been saving for it for years, but we've nowhere near enough yet." Thinking about the expense made her feel so sorry for me that she invited me to share her lunch, and it was only with the taste of her own homemade sausage in her mouth that she was able to summon up the energy to wish me a good trip and a happy return. "You're never happy until you're home again," she commented, punctuating her thought with another bite of the fresh bread and cheese.

It may seem odd that I remember Mrs. Hanson so clearly. Hers was only the first of many faces I saw on my long jaunt halfway around the world, yet it stands out to this day in my mind. For it was to Mrs. Hanson that I first tried to explain where I was going and why. Not that my explanation did any good: in spite of all my pretty phrases about the sunshine of the tropics, the children of nature, a paradise on earth, Mrs. Hanson remained unconvinced, still sorry for me, still asking me, even as we said good-by, "But why on earth do you have to go so far away?"

All right, why did I have to go so far away? The answer's a fairly simple one. No lost relatives, no secret mission for the Danish F.B.I.: I happen simply to be one of those odd cranks you always hear about who travel around with typewriter in hand, peering into all the world's hidden corners and scribbling down tales of what's hidden in them. In the old days, we were called "globetrotters"; now it's been reduced to "travel writers." But although the profession's been shorn of its glamour, the ranks have somehow or other been fantastically increased. I don't know what the statistics are on the number of travel writers active today. But I do know that the number must be uncomfortably large. Writers all over the world have suddenly dug out their suitcases in search of new places to put in print. Naturally, all this competition makes for a fairly tight situation.

I had been sitting in one of my lonely hotel rooms, poring despondently over my map and wondering where on earth I could go to next. The South Sea Islands stood out as an enormous hole in my travels, a place whose idyllic reputation had intrigued me for years. In the past, that reputation had deterred me. Too many travelers had gone there, looking for paradise in the romantic vision of palm trees, sun, and lagoons, and had come home with nothing more than a sense of disappointment and a bad case of sunburn. I did not intend having that happen to me. Discarding all romantic illusions, and armed with a plentiful supply of suntan lotion, I decided to see for myself what the South Pacific really looked like. Perhaps it was because I set off not expecting to find a lagoon of happiness that I found one. For there is indeed an earthly paradise in the Pacific, but only the lucky ever find it, or see it so. To many travelers I met, that paradise was hell. And for each happy lagoon on the coral islands, there is another full of pain.

Map in hand, I set off for the South Seas. Oddly enough, once I got there, I found myself in possession of another map, and a very unusual one at that. The places on my new map had never been visited by any human being. In fact, it was questionable even whether the places existed. It's a curious map, and the story behind it, as Alice would have said, is even curiouser.

I was given the map, with strict instructions never to show it to another living soul, by a strange couple named Theophile and Marcelle Tellier. The story of how I came to meet the Telliers is strange enough in itself. It had something to do with a murder. Not a plain old ordinary murder, the kind you wouldn't think about twice; no, this was one of the more complicated kind. Two of the stewards on my ship had been fighting with each other throughout the course of the trip. One had finally whipped out a knife and killed the other. The difficulty was that the one who had done the killing had not started the fight. The poor fellow had been simply minding his own business while the other one, a villain at heart, had tried to egg him on. The victim had really gotten no more than he'd asked for, but try explaining something like that to the police.

I went ashore with the supposed criminal in the hope that I might be able to help in his case. I was sure that if the authorities knew something of the situation, they would be more lenient toward the defendant. After all, he hadn't *planned* on murdering his colleague. He'd been pretty much forced into it, and in my book that spells manslaughter instead of murder. But murder was what the people wanted. They hadn't seen a good hanging in years, and they were raring to have one now. It was a hopeless affair. My defense of the man resulted only in casting suspicion on myself. The case was lost, and the defendant committed suicide. This naturally pleased all the good citizens on the island, for it proved—in their eyes, at least—that their verdict had been correct. I was thoroughly depressed and embittered by the whole matter, and wanted nothing more than to get away from that island as fast as possible.

As it was too late to follow my original itinerary, I simply went down to the harbor and hopped the first small schooner in sight. It was headed for an island named Monuafefafa, a peaceful-sounding place which I'd never before noticed on my map. I had decided to let the wind blow me wherever it would, but that it should have blown me right into the arms of the Telliers was a coincidence even I had no right to expect.

I liked the Telliers from the first. They were intelligent and unconventional, and I was desperate to escape the atmosphere of mindless conformity which had deemed it criminal of me to defend an accused murderer. M. and Mme Tellier were as solid and conventional-looking as could be; but underneath, they were quite different.

They had managed to survive for ten years on the island without joining in any of the organized social life surrounding them. It was the only way they knew of maintaining privacy in a colony where gossip was regarded as the main form of entertainment. I myself lived on Monuafefafa for only a few days before everyone knew more about me than I did. For example, on my first night on the island, I went for a midnight walk along the shore. Being basically a romantic soul, and thinking I was quite alone, I made up my own little moonlight serenade and sang it to myself as I walked. By noon of the next day, the entire island was humming with news that a "Danish singer" had arrived in town. But that was life on Monuafefafa.

Life among the natives was just as open; but with them it was quite a different thing. Built like bronze statues, the islanders lived in palm huts without doors or windows and performed the dance of life in full view of the world. They had even less privacy than the Europeans, but for the missing walls they substituted an innate discretion which we Westerners have not yet achieved. They were happy, carefree people, with not the slightest desire to become "civilized" as we know it.

In only one respect did they envy Western life, and that was in their desire for a bit of private property. The natives on Monu-afefafa dwell in one of the few totally communal societies in the world. Everything is share-and-share-alike, with no buts about it. Pity the poor islander who returns from New Zealand sporting a fine foreign suit, a wrist watch, and a pen. Unless he is exceptionally lucky, he will be stripped of all his treasures the minute he sets foot on home ground. A relative need only point to the wrist watch, the pen, or even the trousers, say that he likes them, and immediately they must be handed over with a smile. To protest would be worse than an insult. As a result, the smart native hides what few possessions he has. The best possible present you could give to one of the islanders would be an enormous chest with a strong lock.

It was in a chest of exactly that kind that the Telliers were hiding their most private possession—the secret which, for ten long years, had evaded all the prying attempts of their fellow Europeans. The governor's wife and her cronies, all stuffed into their imported corsets and crowned by their somewhat outlandishly chic Parisian hats, spent hour upon hour discussing the Telliers and trying to guess what their mystery might be. For there was no doubt about it, the Telliers were involved in something very mysterious, if not downright *peculiar*, and the good ladies had been trying diligently for years to find out just what it was. Their suspicions were endless: Why, for example, did Mme Tellier stand outside the house at night talking to herself? Why did they leave their lights on all night long? And *why*, above all, did they refuse to tell anybody else what they were doing?

I was the first person on the island to be let in on their secret.

Why they picked me, I don't know; but I imagine it was because I listened to them and seemed interested in what they had to say. I took them seriously, and that was all they asked.

I first met the Telliers at a cocktail party given by the Governor. Mme Tellier stood out immediately as someone different from all the rest. I soon realized why: she was the only lady there who was dressed sensibly, in a plain cotton print of the same material the Polynesians use for their loincloths. That, of course, was absolutely taboo among the other European ladies, who were all decked out in their vintage Paris originals. No matter how hard they tried, the European ladies on the island were always a few years behind the styles. But since there was nothing to be done about it, they staunchly carried on, outmoded but still determined to maintain good form.

Mme Tellier was a bit strange-looking altogether. Her long, sharply pointed nose made her look somewhat like a field mouse, and she moved about so timidly that she seemed to be apologizing to the floor for walking on it. She seemed too frightened to walk about on her own, and preferred instead to hitch herself onto her husband's sleeve and let him tow her around. He had both feet on the ground, and could navigate well enough for both of them.

It was hard to tell how old they were; the late forties I'd guess, although I never asked them. Tellier was as friendly-looking as his wife was shy. While he laughed broadly at the Governor's jokes, she tried to hide her smile by holding an apologetic hand to her mouth. I particularly noticed her eyes. They were filled with a glow that did not at all match the rest.

When I arrived at the party, the Telliers were standing, as they always did, off in a corner by themselves. I immediately felt the woman's eyes on me, and wondered uneasily why she was staring at me so intensely. She whispered something to her husband, then hooked on to his sleeve and allowed herself to be towed—apparently by request—across to me. They introduced themselves without formality, sounding a little bit like old friends wanting to know whether I still remembered them. Everyone in the room turned to stare at us. Apparently the Telliers' forwardness was as much a surprise to the others as it was to me. "He must have a way with them," I heard one lady whisper to another from the sidelines.

The Telliers invited me, then and there, to come to tea. By "tea," I had already been informed, they meant tea and nothing else. "You'd better eat before you go there," one of the ladies told me, "for you'll get nothing at *her* table. Why, she's so cheap she won't even serve cookies! Oh, they're not poor, not by any means. He's an engineer with a big international firm, and you know what *they* pay. No, she's just cheap, and that's all there is to it. I think it's an insult to the colony!"

As it turned out, I found myself glad that the colony was insulted. I became a steady teatime guest at my friends' cottage, and so found a wonderfully easy escape from the boring cocktail-party conversation of the rest of the Europeans. Curiously enough, the other colonists were not annoyed, or even suspicious, at my spending so much time with the local outcasts. That's one advantage of being a "travel writer." People expect you to do odd things and to go around mingling with peculiar types. The ladies simply smiled, full of understanding for me. "*Voilà*," they said to one another, "our author is looking for material. How interesting."

"Poor man!" one of them commented, "I'd no idea these travel writers had to go through so much trouble. Imagine, spending all that time swilling tea," she added, feeling very sorry for me indeed.

But they needn't have wasted their sympathy. I'm sure that tea is as harmless a drink as any around. And as for food, well, Mme Tellier did occasionally serve a bit of cake. Sometimes even a sandwich as well. But more important than food, my hostess served me something I had never experienced before, and probably never will again: *tea with flying saucers*.

It took a little time before the saucers started flying across the kitchen table. On my first few visits we just talked—not about clothes and servants, the way they did at the cocktail parties, but about the problems concerning the stars and the universe. My new friends did not regard the stars simply as pretty decorations hung up on the sky for the exclusive use of lovelorn poets. Like me, they felt that the universe was an awe-inspiring reality, challenging us on earth with the mystery of its existence.

The Telliers had risen to that challenge. Whether their ideas about the universe were right or wrong did not matter. Their suggestions could not, at least, be disproved. Their theories were fantastic, but so is the universe itself. M. and Mme Tellier were not the least bit mad. Different, perhaps. But different only in that they had found something important to live for, while the rest of the Europeans on the island were simply killing time.

It was quite a while before I actually got my mystery map. One evening before tea I was told that I was very "electric." "I'd estimate you at about 300,000 volts," Marcelle said with a smile.

This information about my electric power came as quite a surprise. I had never before thought I was all that dynamic. But more surprises were to follow. My electric voltage was like nothing compared to my sunbeam. That's right, I said sunbeam.

"You have an exceptionally good sunbeam," Marcelle said, "and now that we've finally charted it, we can't wait for you to see it." I could scarcely wait either. Marcelle and Theophile bent down and opened the great locked chest that had so mystified the other islanders, and extracted a batch of papers containing strange drawings and complicated geometrical patterns. These papers were the results of ten years' work.

As I later found out, it had all begun with a divining rod. Once, many years ago, Marcelle had tried just for fun to see if she could use one. And she could: the divining rod went wild every time she touched it. The only odd thing was that the rod, which is supposed to point out where there's water, would always point straight up to the sky. To Marcelle and Theophile, it was obvious that they were on the verge of making some great discovery; just what it was to be, they found out only gradually.

Marcelle never spoke about it. She was, as I have said, very modest. But Theophile was quite proud of his wife's great powers.

"Marcelle is one of the chosen nine," he told me. "You see, throughout time there have always been nine people on earth in contact with the universe. Each of these 'chosen nine' has been born with five elements in his brain, while the rest of us have only four. That's how Marcelle is able to be in contact with the universe and to receive its messages through electromagnetism." Her system of communication, he went on to explain, had nothing to do with mental telepathy or anything like that. Hers was a purely technical phenomenon, which worked somewhat like a television set. Since Theophile was an engineer, they made a perfect team. She received cosmic pictures on her television screen, relayed the information to him, and he in turn worked it all out on maps and graphs. In this way they had created a detailed map of the universe.

The largest of the maps was like a surrealist painting which would have made one of Dali's wildest nightmares look pale in comparison. The space map was so large that it filled a whole wall when it was unfolded and put up. I had often taken mental trips across a map, but never one like this. With Marcelle and Theophile I traveled up, down, and sideways through nebulae, cosmic vibrations, neutron spirals, and heaven knows what else. How two people could have dreamed up all these fantastic details was beyond my comprehension, and I said so out loud. "But we didn't make them up," Marcelle laughed. She frowned for a moment, apparently trying to think of the proper analogy. "Ah, I know" she exclaimed, with a cheerful snap of her fingers, "this is a stenographic report on infinity, dictated to me by the universe." I nodded sagely, only wondering who the typist was going to be.

There was one detail on the map that particularly disturbed me, and that was the fact that God had been drawn on it as a triangle. I never found out why, though. One simply doesn't question triangular gods.

Like God, I too was on the map, or rather my sunbeam was. You remember my sunbeam, of course. It's very important.

To talk about sunbeams is incorrect. Actually, there is only one sunbeam, and from this all life originates. On its way through the universe this ray of light absorbs electromagnetic waves and cosmic vibrations. The sunbeam, together with all its waves and vibrations, is attracted by the earth's radioactivity and is drawn relentlessly toward the Equator, where it explodes and splits into eight electromagnetic-cosmic currents. Four of these go north, the other four go south. A lot of tension is created and, presto! out of this tension comes you and me and just about everybody else. What's left of the sunbeam has split up into a jillion parts, each of which has its own precise personality: and there we are.

If you think this is hard to follow in English, you can imagine the trouble I had trying to understand it in French. My knowledge of the French language has always been limited, to say the least. At school we only learned French for everyday use. I still remember the excellent lessons. Useful phrases like "the friend of my uncle has lost his left rubber shoe," "the hairdresser of my mother has jumped off the top of the Eiffel Tower," and "the hunchbacked gardener suffers from tapeworm" have stuck firmly in my memory. The cosmic phrases which Marcelle and Theophile rose to were simply not included in my textbook. My one consolation was the knowledge that I myself was on that map, no matter what else might be lurking there. When we got to the sunbeam matter and I learned that I was an explosion, I merely nodded agreement. I'm sure that my friends have suspected that for years.

We had to roam over hundreds of miles of the universe before we found me. I was hiding behind a nebula, shyly hoping that no one would ever find me. But leave it to Marcelle and Theophile. "There you are!" both shouted at once, and proceeded to drag me out into the open. Theophile slapped a happy finger on the map. "You started here, in a cosmic vibration," he said. "We can't find out which explosion it was, but it's been there since the world was created. Since you started that far back, you must have many extra brain cells. Marcelle estimates you at about 9,000,000, isn't that right, dear?" Marcelle nodded, and Theophile continued. "One can also tell from your vibration that you have uranium in your brain. Not much, but it's there, and you should be grateful for it. You're really quite powerful, you know. You use your vibrations instinctively. Marcelle received them at once, that first day we met you." I listened in stunned silence, awed at all I had been through.

When Theophile had finished his brilliant lecture, I realized that I had understood next to nothing of what he had said. I was about to admit my ignorance when Marcelle offered me one of her beautifully introspective smiles. "Really, it's all so incredibly simple," she said dreamily.

It was at moments like this that I found myself wondering seriously if the Telliers might, after all, be mad. Or if not exactly mad, perhaps suffering from that form of insanity which the French call *"la folie douce."* But they were not fanatics at all, for they both admitted that all their theories might be wrong. For example, way up at the top of the universe, beyond the planets and stars, Marcelle had located an enormous void which she called the Great Snake and which she described as a sort of invisible wall separating human perception from the Great Unknown. In other words, she wasn't too sure what the Great Snake was. She thought it represented the end of explorable space. But she was willing to admit that if either the Americans or the Russians were to send manned rockets beyond it, her theory would be incorrect. They were really very broad-minded, you see.

For the time being, however, they decided to take it for granted that the Great Snake existed. They were even thinking up ways of breaking this barrier, and it was on that problem that they were concentrating most of their energy. They weren't working in the dark, either, for they were being helped by friends who knew the secret of the Great Snake.

These friends often came visiting at teatime. They didn't come to drink tea, so out of politeness they stayed outside the house. Marcelle would go out and chat with them. Theophile and I were never allowed out to join her, as it was feared that we might frighten the guests away. Besides, Marcelle was the only one they really wanted to talk to, and since she always reported the conversations verbatim, Theophile and I were content to wait inside. It was in this way that our get-togethers turned into tea with flying saucers.

One evening, Marcelle stopped in the middle of a sentence and listened intently. "I thought I heard something," she frowned. She picked up her divining rod, and it vibrated instantly toward the ceiling. "Yes," she whispered, "it's a flying saucer. Please excuse me for a moment. You go on and drink your tea."

Theophile and I sat stirring our tea, anxiously awaiting her return. I could see that he was fairly bursting with excitement. "Well?" he asked, when she finally came back.

Marcelle's eyes were shining. "It was from Mars," she said, "and lower than any we've had before. It touched the roof. And imagine, it was green. All the others," she explained to me, "have been orange."

"The details! Did you get the details!" Theophile interrupted.

"Yes, this time they brought them. They asked at top level, and the way you've drawn it is perfectly correct, incredible as that seems."

Theophile leaped out of his chair and embraced his wife in a wild burst of enthusiasm. In their happiness, however, they did not forget about me, still sitting and stirring my tea. They decided that since I had been present on the great occasion, I might at last be let in on their most cherished secret. Theophile plucked a colored drawing out of the locked chest, and unfurled it before my eyes. It was the plan for a flying saucer they themselves were going to build. Pilots of other flying saucers were giving them the exact specifications.

"All they want is more concise and clear questions," Marcelle told me.

"You realize, of course," said Theophile, "that these are scientists they're sending down to earth. The best brains they've got.

You see, our H-bomb experiments have made them nervous. They've been watching earth for quite a while, and they know our lack of control even better than we do. They know we're capable of blowing up the whole universe. They're prepared, naturally, to intervene, but they'll do it only as a matter of self-defense. No sir," Theophile shook his head sternly, "you won't find them attacking unless we ask for it."

Theophile's drawings of the flying saucers were as amazing as they were convincing. They were to be made of a metal which could withstand heat up to 7,000 degrees without glowing. Marcelle had been told how this extraordinary metal was made, and Theophile planned to take out a patent on it. The spacemen were far beyond us in engineering ability, and Marcelle and Theophile hoped that with their advance information, Earth's conquest of space would be drastically speeded up.

Once they had completed their plans for the flying saucer, Marcelle and Theophile planned to go to the United States to publicize the project. They had saved enough money (largely by offering their tea guests nothing but tea) to finance a few years of travel around the country. They were sure they would have no difficulty finding a few rich backers interested in investing in their enterprise. After all, think of the fortune to be made in the manufacture of flying saucers! Detroit would be revolutionized overnight.

But the production of flying saucers, Marcelle modestly assured me, was still a dream. A soon-to-be-realized dream, but nonetheless a dream. "Now, getting back to reality," she said, "you'll be interested to know that all our visitors so far have been only from the planets Venus and Mars. The Venus saucers are always piloted by women."

One evening when Marcelle had been outside for longer than usual, she came running back to us glowing with excitement. "Guess what," she said, "there was a little girl among the passengers tonight. A sweet little girl from Venus. I wonder why they brought her along; I suppose just to give her a treat. Isn't that lovely?"

Theophile told me that once they had also been visited by a flying saucer from Jupiter.

Marcelle glanced at him reproachfully. "Theo!" she protested, "you mustn't say things like that. You're just pulling our friend's leg. How do you expect him to believe anything we say if you tell him such ridiculous things?"

"But it might have come from Jupiter," ventured Theo.

"*Might have.* Might have is right. But we have no way of *knowing.* Unless we're sure, we have no right to make any such statements!" Theo looked properly cowed.

So many remarkable things happened that in the end I almost believed their theories myself. The one thing holding me back was the fact that the only saucers I'd seen so far had been those on the kitchen table. I'm a suspicious guy; I wanted proof.

As though she had been reading my mind, Marcelle quickly explained that it would be too dangerous to take me outside to meet the spacemen. "You'd only frighten them away," she said, "and then all our work would come to nothing." She had another, more practical, solution to offer. "The flying saucers can be seen from other parts of the island, you know. Monuafefafa is a sort of magnet drawing them. As a matter of fact," she smiled, "that's why Theo and I decided to come here. We think they use the island as a kind of filling station. There's a spot near the shore where they come very often. Anyway, there are lots of them, and I can easily show you some that are not here to visit us. Then if you scare them away, it won't matter."

That evening instead of having tea we drove out to see the flying saucers. Marcelle said the weather was ideal. We would undoubtedly see a lot of them.

We chose a spot near the beach where the road wound its way through low rocks, and there we sat in absolute silence for what seemed like hours. Suddenly Marcelle pointed to a star shining more brightly than any of the others. "There! Do you see it?" she said. "Now watch!"

I watched, and sure enough, the light from space was coming slowly toward us. Suddenly the entire beach was bathed in a blinding light, while our silence was shattered by the roar of an engine thundering upon us. I even fancied that I could hear the sound of voices. This was too much. I closed my eyes and nearly fainted from sheer excitement.

When I dared look around me again, I found myself face to face with the biggest anticlimax of the year. The engine we had heard belonged to a very mundane Renault which had just pulled up alongside us on the shore. The blinding light came from the car's headlights, and the voices, sad to say, belonged only to the Governor and his wife.

The Governor's wife peered out the car window at us. "What on earth are you doing out *here* at this time of night?" she demanded.

"Just looking at the stars," I replied, as amiably as I could.

"Well, I insist you come home with us for a drink," Madame announced, and opened the car door for me. I saw no choice but to accept the invitation, and so climbed in. Madame smiled triumphantly at the Telliers and we were off.

Of course I never did find out whether I had really caught a glimpse of a flying saucer that night. These things are so hard to tell. We never repeated the experiment. Too risky, Marcelle decided, and Theo thoroughly agreed.

As a parting gift, Marcelle and Theophile gave me the mysterious map and an invitation. Their flying saucer, when completed, would have room for three; and I might, if I cared to, make up the third party on their first expedition into space. That first trip would be to Mars via the moon, a small-scale flight but nonetheless important. Naturally, I accepted.

Don't laugh when I tell you I've already given serious thought to the new travel books I'll be writing once the Telliers take off. I might even try my hand at a novel for a change. There was certainly plenty of material for one in some of the things Marcelle told me. Like the story of Rudolphe, for example. Marcelle had one day pointed to a photograph on her desk and said, "I've never told you much about him, have I?"

As a matter of fact, she had told me nothing about this handsome young man. I had often been tempted to ask her who he was, but had hesitated for fear of opening some old wound. I had noticed that there were fresh flowers placed near the picture each day, and had assumed that the young man had been someone closely attached to Marcelle, perhaps even a son. "Is he dead?" I asked.

Marcelle smiled. "Yes, I suppose he's what is called dead. Although I prefer to think that instead he has found another and better form of life. Let me tell you about him." She motioned for me to sit down, and then began her story. "Rudolphe was one of the many wandering souls who come to Monuafefafa looking for an answer."

"Trying to find a paradise?" I asked.

"Yes, in a way," she said. "But he wasn't one of those naïve victims of travel books, who come thinking they can find happiness just by sitting underneath a palm tree. No, Rudolphe wasn't looking for sunshine and native girls; he came instead looking for *me*. You see," she smiled modestly, "he had heard about me, and wanted desperately to find out what I knew of the Great Snake. He'd had a strange experience, and he felt that I was one of the few people on earth who might hold the explanation for it.

"Rudolphe, as you can see, was very handsome. And like many handsome young men, he had found and fallen in love with a girl who fitted all his dreams. Her name was Aimée, and their love was as beautiful and as pure as any you have ever read of. It was almost as though their meeting and its fulfillment had been ordained since the beginning of the world. They were like Adam and Eve in Paradise. But every paradise has its snake; and theirs was Rudolphe's airplane.

"Rudolphe was obsessed with flying. He wanted to get higher and higher in the sky than anyone else had ever been. He volunteered for all the most dangerous test flights, and naturally drove Aimée nearly out of her mind with worry. One day, the inevitable happened. Rudolphe's plane exploded in mid-air; it was assumed that he had gone up in flames with it. What Aimée did not know was that Rudolphe had parachuted to safety and was stranded, very much alive, on the side of a mountain. It took several days before he could make his way to the nearest village, and by that time it was too late. Aimée was dead. She had committed suicide, leaving behind a letter in which she wrote that she hoped to be reunited with Rudolphe somewhere in the great beyond.

"Rudolphe disappeared then, and was not heard of again for a long time. People forgot the story, and so, years later, very few connected him with the reckless young test pilot in the United States who was breaking all altitude records. But that was Rudolphe all right, trying to soar higher and higher in search of his Aimée. And one day he stepped down out of the clouds with a strange, transfigured smile, and asked for leave to come to Monuafefafa.

"He came, as I said, not looking for palm trees, but to ask me if it could be true that up there beneath the stars he had come so close to paradise that he had seen Aimée in the distance, beckoning to him across the sky. He had tried to get closer to her, but each time he drove the plane upward he had been stopped by an invisible wall. Was that the Great Snake? he asked me. I wish that I could have answered him. We talked for a long while, and I told him all that I knew; but I think he was disappointed when he left. He was fiercely determined to keep trying, though, and I think that explains what happened to him later. He returned to the States and to his record-breaking flights. And one day, while up on a test flight, he simply disappeared. Not a trace was ever found of the plane. Of course, an extensive investigation was held; but they found nothing, and it was finally dismissed as just another hopeless mystery, one of those odd disasters which no one can ever explain. I thought of offering my own information, but then decided against it: they would never have believed me. The farewell letter Rudolphe wrote me would have been regarded only as proof that he was insane."

Marcelle opened one of her desk drawers and took out a letter. "Here," she said, "you may read this. In it he says good-by to me, and explains what he planned to do." I picked up the letter and examined its few brief lines: *Dear Marcelle, Thank you for your understanding and friendship. I don't think you will ever see me again. I am flying up to Aimée. I know this time I will reach her, for if science and technology can't help me, then surely my yearning—and hers—will bring us together again. Yours, Rudolphe.*

"But Marcelle," I asked, "surely you don't believe . . ."

"Yes, I *do* believe," she interrupted. "That's exactly what I think happened. You'll say it's impossible for a human being to get into an airplane and fly up to paradise. All right, I know it does sound absurd. But there are other powers besides technology and science for conquering the universe. Rudolphe didn't fly to heaven by jet power. He flew on the wings of eternal love and divine longing. And he flew so high that he saw something, something very beautiful that he wanted and dreamed of seeing. Perhaps what he saw was some sort of divine mirage, created out of his own longing; and perhaps it was something else. I don't know. How is anyone to know for sure. I don't think that what Rudolphe saw was heaven itself; what I *do* think is that he saw something like it, yet less distant, something, oh, like the bottom rung of the ladder to paradise. Do you know what I mean?" She glanced at me and I shook my head sadly.

"Well," she went on, trying to explain, "you know that the spacemen who come to visit in the flying saucers all look exactly like us. I mean they're not grotesque monsters with antennae and tails and all the other things science-fiction writers would have us believe. No, they look for all the world like perfectly normal human beings, like people you've passed again and again on the street. And I think that the reason for this is that they *are* those people on the street—after death! I'm convinced that our one short life on earth is not enough to purify the soul, and that we are all therefore reincarnated, not on earth as the Hindus would have it, but on the other planets instead. I think we start on the nearest planet, then move on to a higher orbit, and so on from there until we've reached the highest place of all, up above all the galaxies there are.

"Rudolphe, they say, committed suicide somewhere up in the sky. I'd rather believe that he found a way, up there, to reach the first way-station on our long upward journey, the station where Aimée was still waiting, close enough to earth for him to see her. Now don't look at me that way," she scolded. "I know you're going to say that he couldn't possibly fly all that high. Well, there are things we don't know, secrets we can't even guess at. Who knows, perhaps she was allowed to fly down and fetch him in a flying saucer. That would make the most plausible explanation."

"But Marcelle," I began, leaning desperately across the table and so knocking a saucer to the floor, where it smashed into smithereens.

And before I could utter another word of protest, Marcelle had switched off the mystic glow and returned to her down-to-earth housewifely self. "Oh dear, there goes another saucer," she said cheerfully. "But never mind, you'll still get another cup of tea."

Full-rigged ships
and a seductive
submarine

I was pursued by flying saucers throughout the Pacific. My first run-in with them, however, was actually long before I'd ever laid eyes on Marcelle and Theo. It was during the time of the great "*Joyita* mystery," when everyone on the islands was trying to guess what had become of the missing ship. The *Joyita* had simply disappeared one day, together with its cargo and twenty-five men. When the ship was found five weeks later, there was not a sign on it of any of the men who had been on board. No one had the faintest idea what had happened, and so, of course, the rumors flew fast and furious. One of the most popular theories was that the men on the *Joyita* had been kidnaped by flying saucers.

I was staying at the time in Suva, on the Fiji Islands, and was trying to calm down a picturesque friend of mine named Polly Thompson. Polly was convinced that spacemen had swooped down on the *Joyita* and made off with all her poor men—or rather (as Polly saw it) with *one* especially delectable young man and twenty-four of his friends. In spite of all my reasoning, Polly clung to the spacemen theory with all her might. It was the only way in which she could comfort herself that she was not to blame for dear Rudy's death, for it was through her maneuvering that Rudy had gotten a place on the *Joyita* at all. If Rudy had been kidnaped by men from Mars, she felt, then at least he would only have vanished, not died.

Polly loved dramatic situations, and she was bent on making the most of this one. She summoned me one day to discuss the tragedy with her. When I arrived, I found her all decked out in what she called "improvised semi-mourning." It was a costume that defies description. All I can say is that even for Polly it was a bit unusual.

"Oh, what on earth am I going to do," she cried out the minute I appeared. "Here, take a seat, I think we could both use a drink." And with that bit of hospitality taken care of, Polly returned to her role. "Oh, this is all so terrible, if only I knew whether he were alive or dead. But I think I know." Her voice dropped to a whisper as she pointed to the sky. "Do you see that star? I think he's up there. It never twinkled that way before. I think he's been trying to get a message through to me. Do you know the Morse code?"

"Yes," I answered, trying to hide a smile. "But I'm sure Rudy didn't."

"Even so," Polly continued, her voice still hushed, "I'm convinced that he's been taken up there by those spacemen. Then, you see, he's both alive and dead, dead to us, yet alive to himself. It's sad, don't you think?"

If you've caught a slight similarity between this dialogue and that of Marcelle and Rudolphe, don't worry. It's not the same story. For while Marcelle deeply believed in her Rudolphe's afterlife, Polly was only play-acting. She knew it and enjoyed it. Yet when I think of what later happened to Rudy, I find myself remembering what Polly said that evening. Oddly enough, without realizing it, she had predicted his fate. Rudy today is dead to all of us who knew him; but unlike most of the dead, he is forced to go on living.

But before I get too far ahead with my story, let me go back a bit and explain what made me wind up in the lap of a middle-aged Polly Thompson on the Fiji Islands. I was headed, if you remember, for the Kingdom of Tonga. My interest in Tonga was not purely academic. I had come, specifically, to visit the Queen of Tonga, Salote of the internationally famous beautiful smile.

My first brush with Queen Salote had been at the coronation of Queen Elizabeth, some years back. Before the coronation I had never heard of Queen Salote. For that matter, I had never heard of Tonga. But by the time the ceremonies were over, I doubt that there was anyone in Europe who had *not* heard of the radiantly smiling Polynesian queen. While everyone else in the royal procession had hidden inside their nice dry cars, Queen Salote had sat outside in the rain, waving to all the wet subjects as she drove by. She nearly stole the whole show.

So when I decided to set off for the South Sea Islands, I made Tonga my number-one destination. I wanted to know what the everyday life of a great queen out there would be like.

The capital of Tonga, where Queen Salote lives, is called Nuku'-alofa; it means "love's place." And Tonga itself is located in a little area called the Friendly Islands.

Now, finding the Friendly Islands on a map is a fairly simple thing to do. Finding them on a travel agency's itinerary is nearly impossible. I have never in my life encountered more unfriendliness than when I tried to buy a ticket to the Friendly Islands.

"Nuku-*what?*" was the enraged cry wherever I went, mildly asking for a ticket. Most clerks seemed to think I was insulting them, and would energetically proceed to tell me where I *could* go if I didn't stop wasting their precious time. In London I was informed there was an expert on things Tongan; naturally, he was away—probably in Tonga himself. I was about to give up and go to Baden-Baden instead when I finally came across a shipping company in Paris able to transport me to Suva in the

Fiji Islands. Of course, Fiji and Tonga are quite a distance apart. But by that point I was too anxious to quibble over details. I would simply have to find a boat leaving from Fiji to Nuku'-alofa, and arrange to change ships at the Suva station. Besides, as the shipping company had already pointed out to me, going to Nuku'alofa via Suva would save me a lot of money, in spite of the added distance. The Suva-bound ship was an ancient vessel named the *Lalona*, which compensated for its lack of modern conveniences by offering an exceptionally low fare. I was, as the saying goes, sold.

But my troubles were not yet over. Armed with a ticket to Suva, I now had to find the missing links that would get me to Nuku'-alofa. The same "Nuku-*what?*" chorus was repeated, but this time with complications. I would smile wistfully at the travel agent, and recite my litany: "I want to go to Nuku'alofa-the-capital-of-Tonga-in-the-Friendly-Islands. I have a berth on a boat to Suva in the Fiji Islands. Can you please tell me how to get from Suva to Nuku'alofa?" But nothing worked. The French travel agents looked hurt, while the British ones just looked bored. One heavily made up Parisienne insisted on questioning my motives. After she had carefully examined my map, she leaned across the counter and glared at me with all the sinister suspicions of a Gestapo spy. "What is the purpose of your journey, Monsieur?" she asked, staring deep into my soul.

"That's *my* business," I said stuffily. "Can you help me or can't you?"

This reply sent the lady agent into an ecstacy of despair. She lurched away from me and lifted her arms to the ceiling, like a Wagnerian soprano preparing for the rape scene. "Monsieur," she clamored, "if you are on a secret mission, I *will* not help you, and, what is more, I will ask you to leave, *immédiatement!* Go!" And before she could get in another clamor, I went.

The fact that I left for Hamburg the same night did not mean that I was on the run. I was just off to see one of my publishers. After telling my editor-friend about all my troubles, I was sent trundling off to a German travel agency, where, with typical German efficiency, my itinerary was mapped out and sealed in a matter of minutes. From Suva I would fly to Nuku'alofa by TEAL—Tasman Empire Airways Limited—one flight a month except in July. Tickets were issued and reservations confirmed, while a heavy sprinkling of *bitte sehrs* and *danke schöns* went flying across the room.

After the Germans had helped me, the British tried to sabotage the good work. I nearly wound up finishing my trip to the Pacific on Hyde Park Corner in London. When I left my hotel on the grand morning of my departure, I thought I had plenty of time to spare to get to Victoria Station and catch the express for Marseilles. What I had not counted on was one of the worst traffic tie-ups in years. Cars were jammed up from one end of London to the other, and I, my luggage, and the cab driver were jammed up in the middle of them. The three of us sat together, admiring the view, for over three-quarters of an hour, while my train to Marseilles—the only one, I had been told, that would get me there in time for the boat—went chugging off without us. I accused the driver of not caring whether I ever made it to Nuku'alofa. He agreed with me entirely; he didn't give a damn whether I got anywhere, and told me so without the slightest hesitation.

When we finally did get out of the traffic jam, I rushed over to the travel agency to see if I could possibly fly to Marseilles. When the travel agent told me that there actually *was* a later train, and that they had deliberately withheld this information in order to get me there on time, I blew up. In Danish, fortunately. But there was no mistaking the meaning of my torrent of words. The British agent simply looked bored, and I, not so simply, caught my boat.

It was on board the *Lalona* that I met both Polly Thompson and Rudy. We were assigned to the same table in the dining room, and a lady named Madame Bijou made up our fourth. As the *Lalona* was slow for even an old ship, we had plenty of time to get to know each other. The trip took nearly a month and a half, and in that time we all became close friends.

Polly Thompson and Eugenie Bijou were wealthy South Sea widows, returning from their yearly holiday in Europe. They were friends from way back, and could not stand the sight of each other. They outdid each other trying to criticize each other's charms. Both ladies were enormous, but Mrs. Polly was a bit more shapely. At least you could see what was what, while Madame Bijou's body was so covered with fat that you couldn't tell where one part ended and another began.

When they were tired of attacking each other, they would launch out at the younger generation. Both felt highly complimented by the current use of falsies and padded bras. "Those young chicks have nothing," Mrs. Polly would announce. "Look at me, I've got enough to distribute spare parts to at least a dozen of these flat-chested things!" and she would roar with laughter, giving me a few meaningful pokes to make sure I'd gotten the point. Or points. "Have you taken a good look at 'La Rasputine'?" she asked me. "Why, that woman is built like an ironing board. She has to decorate herself with a brooch so you can tell which side of her is the front."

"La Rasputine" was Polly's pet name for Mademoiselle Raspail, the Protestant missionary with whom she shared a cabin. The choice had not been her own. Poor Polly had booked on the *Lalona* too late, and so had been thrown into a two-berth cabin with a woman she couldn't stand.

"Mind you, it's not her deafness I mind," Mrs. Polly said. "I'm not one to blame people for their troubles. What burns me up is that the woman's too cheap to replace the batteries in her hearing aid. I've been yelling my lungs out ever since I got on board. Even though the cabin's so small she nearly knifes me with that pointed nose of hers, having a conversation with her is like calling long-distance from Paris to New York. '*Please speak a little louder*,'" Mrs. Polly mimicked, "'*my batteries are running down.*' She might at least stop calling me when her phone is out of order. But no, not *her*, she's got to know everything. Sometimes I think she must be a Russian spy," and with that Mrs. Polly was off into wild laughter again, delighted with the idea of "La Rasputine" being a Mata Hari in disguise.

Polly's face was still very pretty, and it was not hard, looking at her, to see that she had once been one of the most beautiful girls on the islands. She had been born in Suva of an English father and a Samoan mother, and the combination had made her a strikingly attractive woman. So attractive, in fact, that she had managed to run off with one of the best matches in the tropics. Her marriage to Archibald Thompson, the uncrowned Coca King of Samoa, had earned her the full-fledged hatred of every colonial lady on the islands. When "dear Archie" died after only fifteen years of married life, the ladies all twittered "I told you so's" and assured each other that it was Polly who had led him to an early grave. "Dear Archie" became "poor Archie," and Polly slipped even lower in colonial eyes.

It was a very different Polly who moved back into the damp sixteen-room villa in Suva left her by her parents after her husband's death. Like most Polynesian girls, her season had been glorious but brief. Within fifteen years of her spectacular marriage, Polly had become not only a widow, but a large economy-sized one at that. Her girth, although noticeable enough as it was, was decked out even more lavishly with layer upon layer of colored necklaces, shawls, and flowers. She sailed about in her finery like a full-rigged ship on its last voyage. Her season might be over, but Polly was not one to give up easily. She loved dwelling on the memories of her Samoan golden age. "Those were such wonderful days," she told me. "During the war our house was always full of American soldiers. Oh, they were so much fun!"

Madame Bijou sniffed. "I'll bet *Mr.* Thompson, rest his soul, didn't find them much fun."

"That's none of your business, you fat tub," Polly growled. "A lot you know about having fun! At least *my* husband didn't die of boredom."

Behind all her sarcasm and her roaring laughter, Polly Thompson was a lonely and disappointed woman. "I've become a has been," she said bitterly. "While Archie was alive, no matter how I looked, I was still the belle of the ball. Now nobody even notices me." This, as I have already indicated, was not quite true. One would have to be blind and deaf to avoid noticing Polly.

Madame Bijou was on her way to Tahiti, where she would be taking a schooner off to the tiny island where she lived. Although she resembled Polly in size, the similarity ended right there. Madame Bijou was a lady of indisputable morality. Without waiting to be asked, she would invariably offer her pat dictum on sex: *"Moi, je flirte, mais je ne couche pas."* I flirt with men, but I don't go to bed with them. This, of course, was always delivered with a sneer in Polly's direction. The sneer was wasted, however, for Polly made it well known that she thought of flirtation as a waste of time. "Life is short," she would say. *"Moi, je couche,* period."

But Polly's forthrightness only added fuel to Madame Bijou's coquettish fires. Eugenie was as thoroughly French as her name, and, when so moved, as coy as a lovesick hippopotamus. For example, her flirtation with me consisted mainly of telling me all about the pollination of vanilla flowers. "Did you know," she would ask wistfully, "that the little vanilla flowers are so delicate they must be pollinated by hand? And," she would add with a deep sigh, "if a flower is missed during the pollination, it dies." With that she would look soulfully into my eyes, as though to make it clear that she herself was a missed vanilla flower, but one that, nonetheless, might still be saved. Somehow, I never felt quite moved to rise to the challenge.

Madame Bijou had gained all this intimate knowledge of the vanilla flower from long personal experience. Her husband, you see, had been the uncrowned Vanilla King of Tahiti. The islands were simply swarming with uncrowned kings. And all their queens seemed to come equipped with built-in thrones. After Monsieur

Bijou's death (whether from boredom or not I never found out)
Eugenie had turned over the management of the plantation to a
splendidly attractive young man who, she said, blushing furiously, was a master at pollination by hand.

When she discovered that her flirtation with me was pretty
much a lost cause, Madame Bijou decided to devote all her energy
to young Rudy. This made things a bit difficult, as Polly had
already appropriated Rudy for herself. The two ladies gave up
fencing over relative weight and ex-husbands and turned to
more intimate topics. "It's a disgrace for a woman of your age to
carry on the way you do," said Madame Bijou.

"Then it's my disgrace," answered Polly most amiably. "You
shouldn't waste your time worrying about me."

"I'm not worrying about you, I'm thinking of the rest of the
people on this ship. It's dreadful for those of us who have led
respectable lives to have to watch your shameful behavior."

"Try closing your eyes for a change," Mrs. Polly said, and then
added, with a burst of laughter, "you won't miss much that way."
Which was the truth, for Polly, in spite of her many open
invitations, had gotten no further with Rudy than had Madame
Bijou.

The object of all this passion was a young Englishman named
Rudolph Zellensky. He was very handsome and quiet, with the
kind of half-innocent face that most women find unbearably
attractive. Polly said that Rudy had the hair of an angel and the
eyes of a devil, and in a way she was quite right. His boyish blond
hair seemed totally out of place above those probingly serious coal-
black eyes. It was as though his eyes were much older than the rest
of him, and had seen too much.

Polly had just taken up the subject of psychoanalysis, and
Rudy's refusal to talk much about himself gave her ample material to practice on. Some of her guesses, as it turned out, were
quite accurate. "Now let's see," she said, "we know his parents
are divorced. That's as good a place as any to begin, don't you
think? Children from broken homes are always so neurotic.

"His mother's English, I think; London address and British passport, he's probably been living with her. And Zellensky sounds like a Russian father. Terribly Asiatic and brutal. Perhaps a member of the MVD. Oh, I know Rudy had a terribly unhappy childhood. You can just see in him the hurt soul of a child who has longed for love, yet never found it." Polly paused to sigh over that last part. "Of course, now he's *afraid* of love, that's what. Why, you just can't get near that boy! Oh well," she went on, "I know I'm not the first to complain about that. No woman, between fourteen and eighty could possibly resist that smile. Why, even 'La Rasputine' has been smitten," she guffawed, "and that really takes some doing!"

Rudy managed to take all this adoration with surprising patience and good humor. The only one who really irritated him was "La Rasputine," and that wouldn't have surprised anyone. We were all impressed with the restraint he showed whenever she'd been particulary annoying. He growled at her, of course. But if I'd been in Rudy's shoes, I'd have thrown the missionary lady off the boat.

Polly also had a theory about that. "He's got a mother complex," she announced one day. "You see, he really hates his mother deep down inside, but he doesn't dare show it on the surface. So he walks around feeling guilty, and takes it out on 'La Rasputine.' He identifies her with his mother, and so gives vent to his resentment by being as nasty to Rasputine as he'd like to be to old Mama. And it works, too. He's been looking happier every day."

"Could be all the charming female company," I murmured.

Polly beamed. "Why of course. I never of thought of that. Or rather I did, but——" She stopped and stared thoughtfully out at the horizon. "I wonder what he sees in Madame Veyrier. That's a peculiar thing, isn't it? Must be a madonna complex, the dream of an immaculate love or some such nonsense. You know," she turned to me, "there's something strangely immature about Rudy, something that has nothing to do with his age. I worry about him sometimes. He needs someone to teach him what life is about, because I don't really think he knows."

"Oh, come now," I said. "You're just inventing masses of complexes in Rudy so you can convince yourself that he really needs you."

"And why not?" Polly demanded. "Believe me, there's nothing better for a mixed-up young man than an experienced old hand like me. I'd be damned good for him, I assure you."

"Well," I said, "Madame Veyrier seems to be pretty good for him from what I can tell."

Polly laughed. "But I'd be good for him in a much more interesting way!"

Madame Veyrier was the wife of a minister, and one of the kindest, gentlest women I have ever met. Like Rudy, she too met her nemesis in "La Rasputine," but unlike Rudy (or for that matter all the rest of us), she managed never to show the intense dislike she felt for the woman. One day, after a particularly long ordeal with Mademoiselle Raspail, Madame Veyrier confided to me that she just couldn't take it very much longer. "I hate that woman so, you can't imagine," she said. "And being a minister's wife, I really shouldn't feel this way toward *anybody*. But I hate *missionaries*. All of them. And especially *female* missionaries. I'd never have married Monsieur if he were anything but a plain and simple parson. Of course, he'd kill me if he knew I were telling you this. He hates missionaries, too," she smiled, "but he feels it's *most* unseemly ever to say so."

Monsieur and Madame Veyrier were on their way to their first post abroad, and they were both very nervous about it. "We've heard such terrible things about church rule on the islands," she explained. "Pierre has a lot of very modern beliefs, and I'm not sure they're going to like that at all."

Polly called Madame Veyrier "the madonna," and as usual, the nickname was appropriate. If ever I met a woman with what is called a pure heart, it was she. I could well understand why Rudy loved being near her. She radiated warmth and human understanding, and although she was not beautiful, her face was always lit up with a kind of beauty coming from within. She worried about her own impulsiveness, which she thought somehow improper in a good minister's wife. "I should try to be more sedate," she said, "like the Chaste Joseph."

"The Chaste Joseph" was our shipboard name (designated, of course, by Polly) for Mr. Joseph Cook-Bennett, a very proper young British barrister taking a trip around the world. He was as *comme il faut* as a king of England, and was apparently doing his tour because it was the thing to do. He was so much the gentleman that he was hopelessly taken advantage of by all the unattached ladies on board. He strolled with them on deck. He chatted with them. He played bridge with them. He paid for their drinks and danced with them, each in turn. He did everything they asked, simply because it was his duty as a gentleman. I don't think it ever occurred to him that he was being criminally exploited.

"That idiot," said Polly with a sneer. "Why he could go to bed with half of them, for all the effort he's put into it. But no. He doesn't do a damn thing about it. I'll bet that poor oaf is still a virgin. If I were twenty years younger, I might sacrifice myself and try to give him some lessons. He'd probably be pretty good once he found out how to go about it." Fortunately, the Chaste Joseph wasn't around to hear that. He would probably have expired on the spot. Even Madame Bijou, overhearing this bit, turned white around the gills. "*Really!*" she announced, "these native women have *no* morals whatever. And the half-castes are even worse," she added stiffly, then marched indignantly away.

Madame Bijou had seen nothing, however, before Moana came aboard at Panama. Moana was a South Seas siren, the likes of which Madame Bijou despised. The girl was from Tahiti, and as young, beautiful, and uninhibited as Tahitian girls are supposed to be. In a way, Moana looked as though she had just stepped out of one of those incredible picture books people are always collecting. She had cascades of coal-black hair and an open, natural smile. Her skin was golden brown and amply exposed. And to make things worse, she too had set her cap for Rudy.

"*Mois, je flirte, mais je ne couche pas,*" came the old refrain from Madame Bijou, each time sung a bit more desperately than the last as Moana continued on her merrily pursuing way. Rudy looked like a doomed man.

Like Madame Bijou and Polly, Moana too was a merry widow of sorts. The distinction being that both of Moana's ex-husbands were still alive.

Moana was only sixteen when she married her first husband, a young French poet seeking paradise and divine inspiration. He thought he had found both when he met Moana. His only mistake was that he expected Tahitian girls to be like their European counterparts, equating love with fidelity. This, as Moana explained to me, was pretty silly. It turned a simple thing like love into a complicated problem. Moana's marriage became fraught with complicated problems, and after many a stormy battle over Moana's little "adventures," her jealous husband demanded a divorce.

At twenty-two, Moana had experienced more of life than most women twice her age. She had only one regret, and that was that none of her countless lovers had provided her with a child. Polynesian families don't worry about their unmarried daughters having babies. To them, it's simply proof that the girl is capable of having others. Men on the islands are very much concerned with having large families, and so they like having some sort of guarantee against their wives being childless. A girl who can produce samples stands a much better chance of marriage than one who has nothing to show for her shape. And poor Moana had nothing but that to show. Fate had indeed been cruel.

But Moana was a very practical girl. Since she had been denied the prestige of motherhood, she decided to concentrate on gaining another kind of status. Namely money. And to get that, she would simply manage to marry somebody rich, preferably an American. Her family agreed that this was a good idea, and they decided that financing her trip to the United States would be a wise investment to make.

Well, Moana sailed off to New York and there, just as predicted, she met and married her rich American, a baby-carriage manufacturer. He was a sly old chap, and kept plying Moana with free baby carriages in the hope that she would do something about it. She did. Ten of the most expensive models were shipped off to the family in Tahiti, with specific instructions for having a certain Chinese merchant send them on to Australia if they could not get a high enough price on the islands. But this was not what the baby-carriage maker had had in mind; he was deeply grieved that Moana didn't need one of his carriages herself. Moana was fond of her rich husband, and in her great desire to satisfy his wish, she decided to seek assistance from outside. This assistance took the form of a Cuban jazz drummer, whom she established in their elegant Park Avenue apartment while her husband was away on a business trip. The musician was a man of fiery passion, and Moana hoped he'd be able to produce the proper results.

All might have gone well had the lovelorn manufacturer not decided to surprise his little hibiscus flower by returning before he was expected. He popped his graying head into the bedroom one morning, and roared with dismay. The drummer leaped out of bed, stark naked, and tried to attack the intruder with a pair of nail scissors. But the husband, who had seen quite a few Hollywood movies in his time, saved himself and his honor by knocking out the Cuban with a flower vase. Then he turned to Moana (who had been standing naked all the while, cheering the combatants on) and announced that their marriage was kaput. Finished, he said. He didn't care that the drummer had only been trying to help. That kind of help he didn't need. And with those words, the baby-carriage manufacturer quickly whipped out his suitcase and began to pack. He was leaving, he said, never to return. He would call his lawyer immediately, and see that Moana left the apartment as naked as she had come.

In his anger, the deceived husband completely forgot Moana's habit of taking everything he said literally. She took him at his word, and silently tiptoed out of the apartment after him without a stitch of clothes on.

He refused even to look at her until they were in the elevator. And by that time it was too late. As the elevator reached the ground floor and Moana stepped out after him, he was seized with panic. His reputation would be ruined if he didn't do something about her, quickly. He dragged her back into the elevator and made her promise to put some clothes on. She agreed, only on condition that he pay to have the Cuban's skull riveted. The baby-carriage manufacturer knew a good business deal when he saw one. He offered Moana money to cure the Cuban, plus a nice fat sum in addition for keeping her mouth shut. And so it was that on that famous day in June of 1955, Moana upset the precedents of a thousand years by putting *on* her clothes in order to get rich.

Now Moana was sailing triumphantly home, suitcases crammed with the spoils of victory. The investment had paid off. There were expensive presents for every member of the family, plus enough extra cash for Moana to play the rich relative for the next few years. After the money ran out, she would allow fate and her family to take over again.

I got this touching story from the lips of Moana herself. One evening I had been strolling along on the foredeck when I came across her curled up on top of a coil of rope. In the flickering moonlight she looked like something out of a Charles Addams drawing. "I'm very glad you came," she whispered, so suggestively that I was sure she had mistaken me for somebody else. But no, it was me she wanted all right. It seemed she needed to open her heart to a good friend. At that stage we had known each other for about four days. But I'm an obliging fellow, so I settled myself alongside her on the rope and prepared to hear her sad tale.

When she had finished her confession, she took my hand and pressed it to her cheek. "You are so sweet to listen to my foolish story," she purred. "I would like very much to pay you back, but unfortunately I have another appointment just now." And with that she rose and glided away, turning only once to wish me good night and add softly, "You know, you're much better-looking in the dark than you are in daylight." I thanked her for the compliment, but I don't think she heard me. By that time she was already on her way down to the crew's quarters, where her next appointment would be waiting.

Moana had sailed the *Lalona* on both her trips across the Pacific and she knew the ship as well as she did the palm of her hand. As it happened, that was one of the few attributes she shared with the rest of the passengers. Most of them had been traveling back and forth on the *Lalona* for as many years as they had been in the colonies, and the old-fashioned ship had become as much a part of their lives as the islands they left and returned to each year. The "regulars" regarded the *Lalona* as a very dear, if eccentric, old friend. They could not imagine another crossing without her.

Yet this was the *Lalona's* last voyage. She had put in many faithful years on the high seas, and now she was to be retired for good. Her old friends sat around each evening and exchanged memories of her former glory, of the births and deaths she had watched over, of the wars and love affairs she had seen. All that, and now she was to be hacked up for scrap simply because she had passed the age limit. Not even a decent burial for her, or at the very least a place in some old ship's home. No, nothing but the scrap heap. It was a degrading way for a ship to end, and all of *Lalona's* old friends bitterly resented it.

It was easy to see that *Lalona* had been a *grande dame* in her time. Out of date she might be, but she still possessed the elegance and charm that had marked her as a lady. She was all plush and tassels, chandeliers and mahogany. Eating in her great domed dining room was like attending a royal banquet. While we dined in armchair comfort, cupids and goddesses smiled benignly over us from their tapestries and marble pillars.

Those who loved *Lalona* tended to be hypersensitive in their loyalty to her. They were quick to take offense at even the slightest criticism. When a few grumblers complained that the cabins were as cramped as prison cells, the *Lalona*'s defenders immediately leapt to her aid. At their insistence, the shipping company thenceforth refused to dock in at the complainants' port. Passengers destined for that narrow-minded city could swim there for all they cared.

Of course, there was a bit of truth in the grumblers' complaint. The *Lalona*'s cabins were not large. But space isn't everything. In the case of the *Lalona*, comfort was deemed the highest consideration and we enjoyed the most tightly compressed comfort conceivable. The rooms were not cramped; they were simply well-filled. So well-filled that they were a little bit difficult to walk around in. But that was all right, for cabins are not made for walking around in. You have the deck for that. Looked at in the proper light, those cabins were really quite luxurious. Both ceilings and walls were lined with shiny Madagascar mahogany, which made the floating bedrooms look like neatly closed cigar boxes. Lying on my berth in the evenings, I felt like an expensive Havana cigar in a private box. Such luxury is not to be taken lightly.

Moana loved the intimacy of the cabins. She said she couldn't resist them. And we were all well aware that indeed she couldn't. Moana appreciated the bathtubs too. She informed me with a giggle that they were as roomy as double beds. They were like double beds in other ways too. For one thing, there was no running water to be had in them. And for another, the tubs stood on huge lions' paws, looking too elegant to be in any way associated with such mundane matters as washing. But for all that we did have our baths, filled with warm sea water set out for us each morning in decorated tin buckets. And with our baths we had a view. The engineers who built the *Lalona*, nearly a century ago, were men of rare sensitivity; they knew that portholes were more important than pipes in a ship's bedroom. These windows on the sea were situated at eye level, and anyone climbing into the tub was treated to a splendid view of the Pacific Ocean and its inhabitants. Polly swore that each time she dropped into her bath she had only to look out the porthole at all the sea creatures passing by in order to imagine that she herself was out there with them, a well-endowed mermaid happily wiggling her tail with all the rest.

Whether in the bathtub or elsewhere, it was hard to ignore the Pacific Ocean for more than a few minutes at a time. Magellan made one of the biggest mistakes in history when he labeled this expanse of water "pacific"; the Pacific is many things, but peaceful it is not. By comparison, the Atlantic is as safe as a child's wading pool, and about as dull. For the Atlantic has nothing to offer but gallons of sea water; no more than a handful of islands, not a single volcano, and fish that do nothing but swim. It's a deadly bore for the traveler, and I suspect it's equally dull for the fish.

The Pacific, on the other hand, offers a constant program of events for the interested viewer. And unlike television, the stations don't sign off on the hour or disappear just when you're ready to start watching. There's always something on the screen. For example, there are some four hundred odd active volcanoes in the Pacific, nearly all of them likely to erupt without a moment's notice. From the ship's deck on a clear day you can often see smoke wafting gently away from one of the pressure-cooking islands. Many of the islands in fact, are the products of volcanic explosions—underground ones which have boiled over, solidified, and thus created another brand-new island for the geographer to map. Sometimes the process works the other way around. An island that has been sitting peacefully in its place for a few hundred years will one day decide to move over, or even disappear entirely. Falcon Island, in the Kingdom of Tonga, has been playing around that way throughout the ages. It comes and goes as it pleases, leaving everyone thoroughly confused in its wake. And Bogoslov Island, in the Aleutians, is even odder. It never disappears, like Falcon Island, but it moves around so much that sailors can rarely find it; when they do come across it—several miles from wherever it was last seen—it's often hard to recognize, for Bogoslov not only shifts position, it changes shape as well. One day it's round, another day it's oblong, and the next day it's decided to split itself in two.

Aside from its volcanoes and islands, the Pacific offers some of the most talented fish in the world. Take the flying fish for example: they soar over the waves like low-flying planes, seeming scarcely ever to touch the water at all. Unfortunately, I'm told that their flight is just an illusion. According to scientists who've studied up on these things, the flight of the flying fish is really a glide. The fish, who apparently grow tired of simply slugging along under water, every once in a while feel impelled to rear up on their tail fins and, flapping them madly, go coasting along on top of the water in a nearly vertical position. Try to imagine a fish on water skis and you'll have the picture; it *looks* like flying, and makes a delightful performance to watch.

One of the sea's top entertainments was staged on a morning when I and most of the other passengers were sitting in the bar trying to teach a little Englishwoman to drink absinthe. Mrs. Jollyheart was a shy and very provincial lady who had lived all her life in the English countryside. Her farthest journey before this had been to London. She was now on her way to New Zealand to visit a married daughter, and since it was her first long trip away from home, she spent all her days worrying over how her family would ever manage without her there to take care of them. The house would fall apart, she knew; the children would live on taffy and no one would remember to close the windows when it rained. To balance her perpetual homesickness, Mrs. Jollyheart was determined to get every penny's worth out of her trip. She was simultaneously naïve and eager for experience; separated from her family's watchful eyes, she was anxious to do nearly all the exotic things she had read of before in books. And drinking absinthe was one of those very exotic things. Everybody in French novels did it; so too would Mrs. Jollyheart.

We all gathered in the bar early one morning to witness the

great experiment. To our disappointment, Mrs. Jollyheart downed two large glasses of absinthe without showing the slightest effect. The third drink, however, made her feel the need of a bit of air. She stood up very carefully and announced that she would just step out on the deck for a moment or two. We watched her make her way to the door while smiling very smugly among ourselves.

Mrs. Jollyheart had been gone for only a minute when suddenly she came rushing back into the bar, shouting, "There are *animals* on that ocean, *animals, hundreds* of them, *sea monsters!*" We all burst into laughter and pulled poor Mrs. Jollyheart into the nearest chair. "Tsk, tsk, tsk," Polly said, "imagine, drunk at nine o'clock in the morning. That's the trouble with trying to start these things late in life. Three drinks and you're seeing sea monsters."

"Oh dear me," sighed sad Mrs. Jollyheart, and she would have gone on feeling sadder still had not one of the ship's crew come ambling in just then to tell us there was a school of several hundred dolphins playing right beside the ship. Those were Mrs. Jollyheart's "animals," and the joke, as it turned out, was on us.

We hurried out on deck so that we all might get a look at these extraordinary inhabitants of the sea. We were able to study them at close quarters, for the dolphins had decided this particular morning to amuse themselves by racing against the ship. Dolphins are not afraid of either people or ships. They are fantastic swimmers and great show-offs as well. Not only could they swim faster than the *Lalona*, but they were able to perform somersaults while swimming too. It was clear to all of us on deck that the dolphins had won their race hands (or fins) down.

I met a particularly gifted dolphin some time later while I was staying in New Zealand. The dolphin's name was Opo, and his story was written up in papers throughout the world.

The story took place in a sleepy little town called Opononi, situated on the northern tip of North Island. In spite of its beautiful surroundings, Opononi had rarely seen a tourist. Scarcely anyone outside the town knew of its existence.

One day two playful dolphins swam into the town's bay. The people of Opononi were delighted, for the dolphins were quite tame and seemed overjoyed at being able to perform their acro-batics before an audience. The two dolphins cavorted happily to-gether until the day a stupid would-be hero, bent on showing off his marksmanship, put a rifle bullet through one of them and killed it.

The surviving dolphin swam around alone, and eventually—I suppose out of sheer loneliness, for dolphins are very social-minded creatures—it began to seek company by following all the motor boats it met. And soon it began following the boats all the way in to shore, where it mingled happily among the bathers near the beach. It was not at all afraid of humans and, indeed, loved nothing more than being played with in the surf. The dol-phin soon became Opononi's official pet, and in their own honor the townspeople named him Opononi Jack. "Opo" for short.

Opo was really just a playful child. He could not bear to be left out of the children's games, and would come swimming happily to shore the moment he saw a child approaching the water. The chil-dren in turn loved Opo. He would swim in and out among them, inventing new games as he went. He didn't mind being pinched in the dorsal fin or pulled by the tail fin. And in the end, he was so tame that he permitted the children to be seated on his back for rides back and forth along the shore. In return, Opo liked nothing better than to be scrubbed with a stiff broom. He was like a kitten curling up to be scratched; whenever he saw a boat coming his way, he would swim merrily up alongside, then close his eyes complacently while waiting for someone to scratch his back with an oar.

One day Opo discovered some children playing in the water with a large colored beach ball. Before the children could quite understand what was happening, Opo had snatched the ball away and begun to swim around with it in large circles. He tossed it high up in the air with his snout and then caught it again, and be-haved for all the world like a trained sea lion in a circus. When his little act was finished, Opo elegantly returned the ball to the children and thanked them for lending him their toy.

Opo was not only playful, he was discriminating too. For all his fondness for beach balls, he would play only with those that were brightly colored, sniffing his snout disdainfully whenever anyone tried to tempt him with something dull-looking. Gray or white balls were simply not worth his time. Empty beer bottles, however, were another matter. Whenever he spotted one floating in the water, Opo would charge enthusiastically toward it, then swim around with it balanced on his snout.

The story of Opo and his wonderful tricks spread quickly across New Zealand, bringing thousands upon thousands of tourists to the once lonely little town. Both the town and the dolphin were delighted; Opononi found itself turned overnight into an internationally famous resort, while Opo had found for himself an ever-increasing audience for his lively water ballets.

As the crowds in Opononi increased, the town began to look more and more like a seaside Disneyland. Milk bars appeared on the beach and a host of "dolphin signs" lined the streets, requesting visitors to treat the dolphin with consideration and restraint. So widespread was Opo's fame that even the New Zealand Parliament unbent in order to pass a special law for the protection of the dolphin. And the dolphin, well-protected by national law, seemed to grow happier every day among his many two-legged friends.

Opo liked everything about humans but their food. No matter what delicacies were tossed out to him, he would inevitably turn his snout away in frank disgust. When Opo was hungry he would swim out to sea for a decent meal. Occasionally he would get so carried away on his foraging excursions that he would forget to come back. Disappointed tourists, having come all that way just to see him, would stand waiting in vain on the beach, then give up and move on to another resort. The hotel owner and the restaurant keepers, worried over losing what had become a splendid source of income, finally came up with a solution to Opo's absent-minded disappearances. They discovered that Opo would gladly come back if reminded. All that was needed was the distant sound of a motorboat chugging through the waves, and Opo would come splashing furiously toward it, happy to follow it home.

It's difficult to say where Opo's popularity would have led him had it not ended so soon in his death.

The tragic event was discovered one Friday, on the very day of the arrival of American film producer James Fitzpatrick, who had come with an army of technicians to turn Opo into a Hollywood star. Cameras were set up along the beach, directors and prop men stood at their posts, everyone, in short, was on hand except the star. Opo made not a single appearance that day. This had happened before: occasionally Opo would cancel a performance and take the day off. The townspeople weren't the least bit worried. As a matter of fact, they thought it a good joke on the Hollywood crew and announced maliciously that it served them right: the Americans ought not to have expected Opo to be at their beck and call.

The joke quickly wore off, however, when an alarming message arrived that evening. A fisherman had found a dead dolphin in the bay. Apparently it had gotten caught among the rocks when the tide went out, and had gashed itself to death in a desperate struggle to get free. Townspeople and tourists alike waited anxiously in the hope that it might not be Opo.

But Opo it was, and on Saturday morning the thousands of people crowding the beach dropped their circus-audience smiles and silently stood in mourning for the dead dolphin.

The funeral was postponed until a group of scientists had had a look at Opo. They established that he was two years old and regretfully announced that he was a she. Aside from those few facts they were able to contribute little to what was already known about the dolphin. Why Opo had been so fond of people was something they dared not venture more than a guess at. Perhaps the dolphin had simply been lonely, and had not had the faintest idea of where to go to find other more compatible friends.

All the townspeople of Opononi mourned the dead dolphin, but none missed him quite so much as the hotel owner and the restaurant keepers. Now that Opo was gone, Opononi's one claim to the tourist's dollar had gone with him. The town passed once more into quiet oblivion, as sleepy and as desolate as it had ever been before. Its dolphin days were over and so its fairy tale was ended.

People in Opononi would have regarded me as mad if I had ever dared mention whom the dolphin reminded me of. But when I first saw Opo splashing happily in the bay, I was immediately struck with the dolphin's resemblance to Father Cicero, floating in full canonical dress in the swimming pool of the *Lalona*. The happy little Catholic priest was by far the most popular passenger on board the ship, and in a way he looked somewhat like a dolphin in his neat little clerical frock. Like Opo, he too took pleasure in amusing others; when the *Lalona* held its Over-the-Equator celebration, Father Cicero agreed, to everyone's delight, to play ship's clown and let himself be thrown into the swimming pool in full clerical attire.

Polly Thompson, who, like all large women, had a predilection for everything small, called Father Cicero a religious knickknack. "He's so sweet, our little padre," she said. "I almost want to take him on my lap and stroke him, but that would never do. I suppose when you've taken a vow of chastity, it becomes a mortal sin even to be cuddled. By the way," she turned suddenly to Father Cicero, "how do you *ever* manage to live without . . . I mean, isn't it awfully boring in the long run?"

The little priest laughed so hard he nearly toppled over. He always laughed that way, no matter what you said to him. Thus everything became screamingly funny just because, once Father Cicero had begun to laugh, nobody else could help laughing with him. His laughter was contagious, and it acted like a mirror, reflecting back on him all the happiness he sent forth. Father Cicero smiled at life, and life smiled right back. All of life, that is, except for the Protestant missionaries. On behalf of the Reformation they felt obliged to look surly before Rome.

I often wondered why Father Cicero was so happy. There seemed little in his life to explain it. His lot was a poor one, for he was priest (and sole European) on a small, lonely island so remote that it rarely had any contact with the outside world. The allowance he received was too small even to be called a pittance: it came to a little bit less than ten dollars a month, out of which Father Cicero had to manage both his own necessities and the expenses of his church work. His wardrobe consisted of two clerical frocks, one for daily wear and the second for state occasions. He was returning now from his first visit in fifteen years to his old parents in France, and it was likely that he would never see them again. Try as I might, I could not for the life of me see any bright spots in his poor and lonely life. Yet he was the most radiant and cheerful man I have ever known.

I often discussed Father Cicero with Madame Veyrier. The minister's wife and the Catholic priest had immediately become good friends, and that, of course, infuriated Mademoiselle Raspail. "Here we go again," sighed Madame Veyrier. "Sometimes I think these missionaries care more about hate than love. Can't she see that he's a delightful little man with a heart of gold?" Madame Veyrier paused thoughtfully and looked out at the sea. "And you know, I believe he has some wonderful secret that he keeps all to himself. I've no idea what it is, but I can read it in his eyes."

One day I asked Father Cicero whether it was true that he had a secret. "No," he answered, "I'm just a melancholic." Then he burst once again into his thundering laugh, while a gleam in his eyes affirmed that there was, indeed, a secret, but one that he would not soon be giving away.

He was young—in his late thirties, I would say—and had come of good French peasant stock. His hair, which was always hopelessly disordered, resembled nothing so much as a nice but hastily put together thatched roof. His vain attempts at combing it only made the roof look somewhat awry, as though some great bird had been building a nest in the straw. But Father Cicero was both stubborn and vain. His idea of dressing for dinner consisted mainly in trying to part his hair differently each night; the style varied, but the effect remained much the same.

Moana, too, went in for offbeat hair styles. She would appear each evening in a different role, her headdress announcing what part she would play. So far she had been an Indian goddess, a madonna, an equestrienne, a South Sea Island girl and an American divorcée. But all her previous accomplishments were shadowed the night she decided to be a submarine. Her hair intricately modeled to form a periscope, Moana sailed into the ship's dining room and immediately torpedoed all the ship's French officers. Submarines they had seen before, but never one in a strapless gown.

Moana was a master at showmanship. She knew exactly how long to delay before making a grand appearance. She would wait until all of us were seated, then glide proudly in, each night wearing (in addition to her sensational hairdos) a different one of the many exquisite gowns the baby-carriage maker had paid for but never seen. Her taste in clothes was a bit extreme, but well calculated to show off her charms. When she was not décolleté to the brink of the precipice—front or rear, depending on her mood —she would appear in a skirt slit up to her hips, or wear a silk so tight that she might almost not have worn anything at all.

Her most attentive admirers at these nightly displays were the young French officers who sat at the neighboring table. Half of them sat with their backs toward her, and so were obliged to twist three-quarters of the way around in order to enjoy the view. They had suffered from backaches ever since Moana had boarded at Panama, but they all nearly broke their necks on the evening of the periscope. Not a one of them could keep his eyes off her.

"Elle est ravissante, la périscope," one of the officers exclaimed, so loudly that everyone in the dining room turned and smiled.

From that evening on, Moana was "La Périscope" to all of us. When she went strolling along the deck in a revealing pair of shorts, the officers whistled and called, "*Très périscopique!*" Every bit of strategy they had learned at officers' school was applied to their effort to capture the seductive submarine. Their failure was not due to Moana's being invulnerable; far from it. She was simply rationing her adventures in order to keep things from getting too complex. Ever since the attack on Rudy had turned out to be hopeless, Moana had stuck to just two lovers on board and had refused to cope with any more. One of her lovers was the nice young radio operator, an old flame of hers from Tahiti and, moreover, the gentleman who had been kind enough to carry all her luggage on board ship; Moana would not think of allowing such kindness to go unrepaid. The second lover was a handsome youngster of French-Tahitian descent. He had thrown himself at her feet with such wild abandon that Moana could not find it in her heart to resist.

Young Jean-Pierre had romantic almond eyes and the body of a young god. He preferred passion to poetry, and made no secret of the fact that his only interests in life were wine, women, and song. Song he considered an adjunct of dancing, and at our Equator celebration he demonstrated just what a Polynesian dancer can do. He performed one of the most sensual acts I have ever seen, the minute chastity belt underneath his grass skirt making his swaying body even more provocative than if he had danced for us completely nude. Which he would gladly have done. Jean-Pierre had not a single inhibition in his bones.

And in this he was a chip off the old block. The most enthusiastic spectator at Jean-Pierre's performance was a lean, thin-legged Frenchman who looked like an ostrich. Glancing at his enormous bird's nose and the few tousled feathers on his pate, you would not have guessed that he was the *Lalona*'s most distinguished passenger. But indeed he was; and if you wanted to find the illustrious Count de Tresor—for that was his title—at any time of the day or night, you had only to look in the bar. He would be there from dawn until long past dark, holding court while slaking his permanent thirst. With him, and even thirstier, would be the wild almond-eyed youth. The ostrich count paid the bills, and did so proudly; for the divinely handsome young man, incredible though it seemed, was his son.

"Count Ostrich," as we naturally christened him, was a paradise-seeker who had been paid in full by the South Sea Islands. He was just as girl-crazy as he was ugly, but thanks to his sardonic intelligence and a rather sizable inherited fortune, he had always been able to get all the girls he wanted. But beautiful women, like good cars, are expensive to run. Moreover, they were only after his money and not even tactful enough to pretend they felt otherwise. So the smart French count one day decided to take a little trip around the world in order to see what things were like in other places. One look at Tahiti, and he knew that that was the place. For there a fat bank account could buy both the favors of a beautiful woman and her affection. A Tahitian girl who conquers a rich white man has made the greatest coup of all, and she knows how to show her gratitude for it. In return for the money and social status she has received, she gives all that she can—her fiery beauty and her most tender adoration. And there are none of the complications that accompany similar situations in the West. If the girl gets tired of the arrangement and walks out of her own free will, she demands not a penny. After all, she feels, it was her choice. If, on the other hand, she is fired, then she expects a reasonable amount of money in the form of severance pay. It's all very simple and everyone winds up pleased.

Count Ostrich had settled on Tahiti, and in the past twenty-five years he had enjoyed six so-called marriages to as many beautiful South Sea girls. It was the old ugly duckling story all over again, but with a new twist at the end: the duckling stayed as ugly as ever, but surrounded himself with an unending supply of swans. The swan countesses grew younger and younger, but the discarded ones were installed in comfortable houses with such generous pensions that the ostrich count was always welcome to visit them—overnight if he wished. Each of the reigning countesses had presented her benefactor with several golden-brown children, and these had all, by some strange miracle, inherited their mothers' beauty and their father's intelligence. The changing of wives had taken place so harmoniously that now and again they all gathered together for happy family parties. These affairs were always an enormous success. The predecessors smiled at their successors. The successors smiled at their predecessors. Nobody had anything to complain about, and there was not a trace of jealousy or bitterness. Count Ostrich sat at the end of his table and flirted with all of his six lovely wives, his bird-like face beaming with paternal pride over his wonderful garden of children.

I was amused by the count's account of his *ménage*, and this made Madame Flaubert ask me with an acrid smile if I really found Count de Tresor's family life so diverting. "I'll have you know," she had me know, "that I find it disgusting."

"But why——" I began.

"Because I regard men who let themselves be fooled by these native girls as imbeciles," she said in a high, sharp voice. "Those girls are the most scheming bitches in the world, and they can smell a European's money ten miles away. They pick a white man to his bones, then throw him away and start looking for another victim."

"Well," I tried to smile, "at least the men don't seem to mind."

"No. But ask their wives."

Madame Flaubert was a faded Parisienne who had lived on Tahiti for over twenty years. She was always talking about how perfect her marriage was. "When I'm in France," she told us at least a thousand times, "I write to my husband every day. Every single day, mind you. We simply can't bear to be apart." She called him her *petit bonhomme* and told us that he still called her his *cherie*.

But the bitter lines around her mouth grew deeper whenever the rest of us raved about the South Sea paradise. Madame Flaubert hated the islands.

"When you come to Papeete, of course, you'll swoon over the beauty of the scenery. But when that's been your only entertainment for twenty years, you can do without it. Or at least *I* can," she added, turning away.

Madame Bijou confided to me that Madame Flaubert had good reasons for hating Tahiti, and the biggest of those reasons was her husband. "I have it from a reliable source," she whispered maliciously.

Those reliable sources gushed from morning till night on board the *Lalona*. We were on our way across the Pacific, the largest ocean in the world, with over ten thousand separate islands. There are large islands and small islands, inhabited islands and desert islands. Only a few of them are grouped so that they have a view of each other. Most of them are totally isolated, with only the sea and the horizon to form their view. Nowhere in the world do people lead more isolated lives. Yet they know all about one another. Rumors fly from island to island faster than jet planes. The news somehow or other arrives ahead of the ships, not in their wake.

And that is Pacific gossip. What happens on Raratonga is known on Bora-Bora within a week. The French lady in Papeete may not yet have found out that her husband is deceiving her with a Tahitian girl; but they know all about it on Eromango, hundreds of miles—and stormy sea miles at that—from the scene of the crime. How it happens is a mystery that no one yet has solved.

"There you have the material for a new and more exciting *Kon-Tiki* theory," said Count Ostrich one evening as we sat in the bar. " 'Trying to trace the route of a rumor across the high seas.' " He laughed his hoarse laugh and washed it down with more whisky.

"Take a seat on a rumor and follow it around the Pacific," he continued. "Then write a book about where the rumors of gossip can take you. It will be a best-seller, I assure you. Much more dramatic than *Kon-Tiki*. And ever so much more intriguing."

Rudy, who had been sitting all the while in a corner of the bar, suddenly interrupted. "You can't tell me that Pacific gossip is just as malicious as gossip in Europe."

The boy looked almost desperately frightened. Count Ostrich dipped his beak pensively into the whisky glass before replying.

"Yes and no," he began. "There are two wave lengths, you see. One European and one Polynesian. The European rumor line is the most gossipy. It's mainly concerned with divorces, adultery, and sex scandals. Who's sleeping with whom, you know, all that sort of thing. The important point is that the Europeans consider these things secrets." He looked up and stared thoughtfully at Rudy. "And because they regard these matters as secret and sensational, the Europeans take a particularly vicious spite in retelling the news. They do it to hurt people, and there you have the main difference between the two systems.

"The Polynesians, you see, are interested in this sort of news too, but their attitude toward it is entirely different. They regard it simply as news. Their open-mindedness about sex makes secretiveness unnecessary, and they see nothing sensational about events which are to them the inevitable facts of life. They tune in on the rumor line because it keeps them informed of what's going on. It interests them about as much as Stock Exchange quotations would interest us. There's no excitement, and there's no spite. Besides," the count smiled, "the Polynesians see no harm in having their love affairs talked about. It simply increases their prestige among the others. It proves they've been around and gotten some know-how in the game."

Rudy's face brightened into a smile that smoothed the taut fear-lines away. He looked like a small boy who had just received an unexpected birthday present.

"Then it is a completely different world," he said happily.

I looked at Rudy and for the first time caught a glimpse of what he had been hiding behind his silence. He had told us he was traveling to the Pacific to visit a brother, and I suppose that was true. But with this one remark he revealed that his journey had another purpose as well. I was quite sure that evening that in Rudy I had come across another of the Pacific's wandering souls. I was quite sure that evening that he too was looking for an island on which he hoped to find a new and different world.

The dream of an island lives in all of us. I'm sure you know it as well as I do. Suddenly you feel like getting away from it all, far away from office hours and corporate politics, from taxation and corrupt government, from gossip and trouble, from lukewarm wars and hydrogen bombs. You trudge to work in the snow and imagine a place where every day is a sunny Sunday. You dream your dream of an island—for it must be an island, how else then would you be safe?—and you paint it pale green with the evergreen of palms, reflected in the clear blue of a lagoon. You brush in the final touches: the flowers and beautiful girls; and then you open your eyes just in time to escape being hit by a car, you punch the time clock, pay the taxes, and finally, after office hours, you drown the dream in the bottom of a pint of beer.

But some don't let go of a dream that easily. Some pack up their suitcases and go out in search of that island, assuming it exists. You hear about them, these brave "I'm-going-to-find-it" boys, perhaps you envy them, and you forget them. You never hear whether they've found their island or not.

I thought of those island-seekers that pink Pacific morning when we stood on the *Lalona*'s deck and watched our first coral island rise into view. For weeks we had seen nothing but sea and horizon. And suddenly it was there, even more beautiful than we had dreamed, the first pearl in the chain of South Sea islands that would tell us whether the dream of an earthly paradise ever comes true.

The island itself is like a dream, for it appears out of the sea like a mirage. It stands alone and proud on the deck of the sea, with the surf thundering down against white palm beaches. The origin of a coral island is itself a dreamlike affair. Billions of small coral polyps worked day in and day out, for thousands of years, to build that island. They worked and they died, leaving their shells behind to form a magnificently colored coral reef. The reef glows in the sunlight, proving that death here was no end, but rather a beginning. A more beautiful churchyard cannot be found.

Year after year the coral reef grew, until one day it reached up above the sea into daylight and sun. Sand washed ashore, and fertile ashes came flying with the wind from distant volcanic eruptions. A bird dropped a seed as it flew by, and a coconut drifted up onto the beach. And so the island was born. Now it closes its small circle of palm beaches protectively around the quiet, happy lagoon it has stolen from the angry sea. Triumphantly the island turns its back to the sea and reflects its own beauty in the sky-blue mirror of the lagoon. The dream is realized, and a miracle has been done.

That first coral island we saw was named Puka-Puka. It marked the beginning of the French insular kingdom in the Pacific, a small world of only 55,000 souls, yet at the same time a world so large and so widely spread apart that the island to the south, Rapa, was visited in 1919 by a schooner bringing two sensational pieces of news. One was that a world war had broken out in 1914, and the other was that peace had been declared four years later. The entire tragedy was over in a single peaceful afternoon for the residents of Rapa.

The radio has now brought the world and its news much closer, but mail and supplies still arrive a couple of times a year. A large ship sailing past is still a rare sight, and so the inhabitants of Puka-Puka were gathered out on the beach to watch the *Lalona* float by. We stood on the deck and waved to them, wondering whether they saw their island as we did, as a dreamlike lagoon of happiness. Or did they stand there, under their almost impossibly beautiful palm leaves, envying us on this great wide-world-traveling ship? Did they yearn for our world as much as we longed for theirs? Or were they actually, as so few of us ever are, content with what they had. I turned to Father Cicero for an answer. "You, if anyone, ought to know," I said. And for once he did not laugh. "Yes, I ought to know," he answered quietly.

And then he began, for the first time on our long journey, to speak to me seriously about what he knew of life on a little island. He told me of the happy unpretentious existence that knows no difference between work and play. Of the peace that comes with the eternal roar of the surf and lives in the flickering colors of the reef. Of the happy dances and the childishly joyous songs, sung as part of an ovation to life. He told me of the light-green days that demand little of man beyond pleasure, and of the dark-blue nights where what we call entertainment is less an escape than a loving embrace of nature. He spoke of a small, water-insulated world where life is man's only profession, and where the cares of civilization are all but unknown.

Father Cicero, I knew, was not speaking of Puka-Puka at all. Of yes, he pretended he was, and he used its name, but I knew—and I'm sure he did too—that what he was really telling me about was his own little island, Tukutuku. It was there, I knew, that he lived his happy secret. But Father Cicero was a priest, not a Polynesian. . . .

The gong, sounding its warning that we were to lunch in half an hour, interrupted our talk and gave me a chance to tease him a little. Father Cicero had been preaching on the simple pleasures of the simple life, but he certainly seemed not to despise the far from simple pleasures of the *Lalona's* dining room. Father Cicero attacked his meals with gusto. And his approach to the ship's supply of free red wine was even heartier.

"There's no red wine on Puka-Puka, Father," I said.

The little priest smiled broadly. "No . . . importation of wine is forbidden. But . . ." The happy secret gleamed all over his face.

"But what?" I asked.

He coughed gently and looked away. "They make their own wine. Palm wine and orange wine."

"Well, isn't that forbidden too?"

"Ye-es, but . . ."

"But what?" I asked again.

Father Cicero collapsed with laughter. "It tastes wonderful!"

Our conversation was interrupted then by the Chaste Joseph, who also wanted to know something about the coral island.

"What do they *do* in there?" he asked.

Father Cicero looked at him with a puzzled frown. "What do they *do*?"

"Yes," explained the sober-faced Chaste Joseph, "what's their principal occupation? What do they do?"

The happy little priest sent a smile into the sunshine over Puka-Puka. "They don't *do* anything," he laughed. "They just *live*."

The song of Papeete

Although the voyage was not yet over, we held a big party on board just before our arrival at Tahiti. The *Lalona* was sailing on to the Fiji Islands, the New Hebrides, and New Caledonia, but since most of her passengers disembarked at Papeete, it was logical to hold the farewell banquet there.

We were treated to the most luxurious dinner of the journey, complete with champagne and music for dancing beneath the stars. There was even an improvised show, featuring many of the same performers who had entertained at the Equator celebration. On a stage set up over the hold, Moana danced her last dance for us. It was not a sad farewell waltz, but a joyously gay one instead, a dance that bid us all welcome to the South Sea paradise that awaited us. In a grass skirt decorated with flowers and conch shells, Moana looked even more beautiful than she had before.

After Moana's number, young Jean-Pierre took over the stage

and danced his wild Bacchanalian tribute again. And six-year-old little François followed suit, showing that on Tahiti they learn these things early. Together with a four-year-old grass-skirted beauty François enacted for us a South Sea version of *Nymphs and Shepherds*. Both of them shyly and with childish eyes guessed at life's loveliest secrets in their imitation of a grownup's dance.

I asked François one day why he had gone to France with his parents and brothers and sisters. His answer was both brief and typically Polynesian. "First Mommy and Daddy were married at home on Tahiti," he explained. "Then we went to France to visit grandma."

As a featured performer, François was invited to the captain's table to drink free lemonade out of a champagne glass. This was quite an honor for him, but he abandoned both lemonade and honor when he heard the young Polynesians on board begin singing their South Sea songs.

We had heard these songs many times before during the long trip. In the evenings the young Tahitians sat with their guitars and ukuleles out on the quarter-deck, singing soft murmuring serenades in a language we could not comprehend. But when we approached Tahiti they began to sing a song we understood. Only one word was necessary: *"Papeete . . . Papeete . . . Papeete. . . ."* It was the song of Tahiti, calling out the names of the town they would soon be seeing again. It was a song so full of longing that even we, the strangers who had never been there, began yearning for the unknown town. "Papeete" is a song in itself, for its name is full of music. When sung by a homesick Tahitian, it sounds like a passage from an Italian aria. *"Pape-ete . . . Pape-ete . . . ,"* pronounced as though it were two words, gently linked in the middle.

We stood on deck before sunrise on the solemn morning of arrival, our pulses beating in staccato Papeete rhythm. As our boat sped in toward shore, we became slowly aware of the island rising majestically out of the dawn, its coral reefs reflected in lagoons even bluer than forest lakes. Tahiti has been called the

"Pearl of the Pacific," and it's easy to understand why. The Pearl has attracted many paradise seekers, and those seekers, who found what they had hoped to find, in turn lured on others in their wake. Among the most famous of the first group were Pierre Loti and Paul Gauguin, the American Frederick O'Brien and the French poet Alain Gerbault. Following them came a host of artists, globe-trotters, vagabonds, and idlers, all hunting for the paradise they had glimpsed in the lines of Loti's poems. They came and they painted, they wrote and they reported. And each one disagreed violently with all the others about what he saw. Every odd migratory bird who came to Tahiti had his own idea of what paradise ought to be like, and each was convinced that all the others were wrong. But about the island itself they all agreed: for Tahiti is by far the most beautiful of all islands. It is, indeed, the closest thing to a paradise on earth.

Not so the city. Papeete has been called the "Paris of the Pacific" and, in a rather depressing way, I suppose that description is accurate. For Papeete, in becoming a city like those of the West, has lost much of the charm those early paradise-seekers once knew.

Our arrival in the capital was, to put it mildly, a sensation. Half the town seemed to be on the dock, waiting to greet us.

Nowhere else in the world will you find so overwhelming a reception as in Papeete. When a large passenger vessel pulls into town, every other care is momentarily forgotten. The whole town goes wild. Everyone who can make it to the harbor comes bearing flowers with which to welcome the new arrivals. Fat Tahitian women stand bulging on the dock beside equally bulging mounds of flowers, offering them to everyone passing by. The flower women are all ladies of colorful pasts. Once they too were beautiful, seductive Tahitian girls, and that not too long ago: for both flowers and girl wilt quickly in the tropics. Unlike their Western counterparts, Tahitian women don't lament their lost youth, nor do they waste precious time trying to recapture it. They accept the change as part of life, and offer passersby flowers once their own beauty has passed. Flower-selling is a fine profession, and they take it up with pleasure. The flower ladies may no longer dance in the front row, but never mind, they say; in their own time they did enough living to make up for all that's now lost. With a full life behind them, they can smile contentedly at youth and sit back to watch new participants play the game.

The wharf at Papeete is like a teeming sea of people. There are many Europeans, but they are far outnumbered by the variety of other people who, though Polynesian by birth, represent the cross-breeding of nearly all the races on earth. In old log books you will often find entries saying that the captain had the ship call in at Tahiti "to let the sailors refresh themselves with fresh fruit and in other ways." The results of the "refreshment" can be seen in nearly every face. But it is all to the good. The Tahitian girl with French blood in her veins has become just a bit more chic. The girl with a strain of China in her has acquired the delicate little feet of a Chinese maiden to replace the usual Polynesian hoofs. And a touch of black Melanesian blood in a milk-chocolate girl will not embitter the taste, but only sweeten it.

The *Lalona* was nearly stampeded, and we were all welcomed with so many flower chains around our necks that we looked more like floral centerpieces than decked-out human beings. Madame Bijou looked like a hanging garden too extravagantly planted. Her struggle to get some fresh air amid the profusion of flowers was almost pitiful.

Far from pitiful-looking was my friend Polly, who, to mark the grand occasion, had washed her hair in gin. Yodeling with enthusiasm she danced wildly around the deck, nearly overturning her friends with embraces and assuring us one and all that Papeete made her feel sixteen all over again. "But not sweet sixteen and never been kissed," she shouted, distributing smacking kisses left and right, and carefully making mistakes in order to kiss the youngest and best-looking men several times over. When one of the gentlemen tactfully pointed out that he'd been done, three times in fact, Polly simply shrieked, "My God, how in the world do you expect me to keep track! You're all so sweet and handsome, all of you!"

Even I was declared sweet, and I got a big wet kiss in passing. Rudy avoided this fate by sensing the danger in time and managing to slip away quietly.

Nearby, Count Ostrich stood distributing his own kisses. With his bird's beak and piano-key teeth he struck his relatives so energetically in the face that he looked like a cross between a lovesick vulture and a woman-hunting rattlesnake. There was no doubt that his welcoming committee consisted of the six wives—the present countess and the five pensioners—plus all their incredibly beautiful children. Festooned with flowers and gobbling with cock-a-hoop reunion cheer, the ostrich count strutted off with all his cackling brood behind him, headed toward the cortege of waiting cars which would drive him in triumphant processional down the streets to the family estate.

The rain of flowers and kisses also dripped down on us, the friendless strangers. When you land on Tahiti, you're never left standing alone on the dock like a homeless puppy. Complete strangers will embrace you and, if you're not too careful, take you home with them. The Chaste Joseph was standing in a corner, watching the fray with fearful eyes, when he was suddenly pounced upon by a beautiful Tahitian girl who clearly wished to offer him more than flowers. Cornered, Joseph managed a chaste "My goodness!" and appealed hopelessly to us for help. Moana came rushing over, a fiery hibiscus flower flashing like a red light on top of her periscope. "What's the matter with you?" she cried. "This is my friend, she likes you and wants you to have her. Now stop being rude!"

Poor Joseph was dragged out of his corner and pushed into the girl's arms, still mumbling that he hadn't been introduced, that he still didn't know her name. "No matter," Moana said briskly, "you can get to that later. Meanwhile come along, my family's arranged a big welcome party and all of you are invited." Like a seduced innocent the reluctant Joseph was pushed down the gangway to his two Mrs. Potiphars and brutally thrown into a car full of giggling Tahitian girls.

We were shoveled into the garden of a large villa, where we were again embraced and beflowered by hordes of people we had never seen before. Before long I was decorated with flowers from top to toe and felt like a cross between a flame dancer and the hero of a musical in the finale of the last act. Under the circumstances, I felt strongly tempted to hop up on a table and sing "*O Sole Mio*" or the flower aria from *Carmen*.

The setting for this spectacular—which would have made a Hollywood musical look paltry by comparison—was a palm-leaf festival-pavilion erected in the garden for the occasion. No expense had been spared, for Moana, as her old grandmother explained to me, had returned from America with splendid gifts and lots of American "*moni.*" The entire family had turned up to cheer her return and to get their share of the profits.

I was placed at the head table with grandmother on one side and Moana's ravishingly beautiful sixteen-year-old sister on the other. Little sister talked a charming tropical French, while grandmother worked like a steam shovel filling my plate.

The food was Polynesian and heavy, the wine French and light. And the conversation was free from any kind of inhibition. Even grandmother cracked some pretty risqué jokes. We ate and drank for several hours nonstop: whole fried suckling pigs decorated with flowers, unidentifiable salads that slipped down the throat like chilled lava, half golden-browned chickens, grilled breadfruit, and boiled bananas; the two local vegetables, yam and taro, which look better than they taste; scarlet fish and tadpoles from the lagoon, which, oddly enough, tasted more like French-fried potatoes than anything else. There were plump-tailed lobsters, overweight shrimps, and succulently fried flying fish. The *pièce de resistance*, though, was Tahiti's own favorite dish, raw fish. Raw shrimps are even more popular; they are served *au naturel* and eaten with the fingers, with a bright hibiscus flower behind the ear.

I had forgotten that the hibiscus flower was still behind my ear when I took a walk later that day around the city. I may have looked rather odd, but nobody stared. On Tahiti everyone dresses as he pleases. When I removed the flower, finally, it was not because I felt foolish; I just didn't think there was anything to feel flowery about. The "Paris of the Pacific" was even worse close up than it had seemed from the ship. There is a Pierre Loti Street and there is a Paul Gauguin Street. But what great difference does that make when the rest of the city is a shambles of corrugated iron roofs, ramshackle shops, and houses as badly looked after as those of any Western slum? None. If Pierre Loti were not already dead, he would die at the sight of his statue. The decaying columns of the Governor's residence echo a far-gone past when officials tried, without much success, to bring Western ideas of beauty into the then umblemished islands. The so-called palace of the Archbishop is moldering slowly but surely in a park full of weeds and rubbish. The old palace of the ex-queen, Pomare, is nothing but a sad, termite-eaten memory behind the post office, which is in turn an edifice far too fine for stamps. There is something wryly amusing in the fact that on Tahiti, the only well-kept structure is the post office; it is so grand-looking that, by contrast, all the rest of Papeete looks even more hopelessly downgraded.

The only sight I found worth seeing that day was the brass plate of a lawyer, a Monsieur Damiansky, who, in order to translate a matter-of-fact idea like "Legal Counselor," had had to resort to a delightful Polynesian equivalent—"*Haamaramarama-raa.*" Once you've seen a sign like that, you give up any idea of looking for a Berlitz school in Papeete. Besides, learning Polynesian is unnecessary. Nearly everyone on the island speaks French.

There are hotels too, of course, but few that would be likely to be recommended by your AAA. There is one brand-new hotel, right in Papeete. It's an overgrown concrete box unsuccessfully trying to live up to its name—the Grand Hotel—and it is totally out of place on the Tahitian landscape. How one books into that hotel is a mystery to me. When, out of sheer curiosity, I ventured inside, I could contact no living being other than a moth-eaten old cat lying asleep on the desk. Apparently the cat acted as receptionist. It peered at me out of bleary eyes, and clearly announced that it couldn't care less whether I was coming or going, so long as I helped it to shift the fleas in its fur. And that I did, for underneath it all I have a heart of gold.

If you want to stay at a hotel and live comfortably, you have to go outside the town to Les Tropiques or The Royal Tahitian. Both of these are infinitely grander than the Grand Hotel, and both of them have receptionists who, if they don't really care, at least don't seem to have fleas. At either of these two luxury spots you can have your own little cabin with all modern conveniences, including a fresh nightly supply of Tahitian girls. You can go native in the most delightful way, and it costs no more than an average hotel in New York. Of course, it's not exactly against the regulations to bring your wife, but the process is frowned on. You will find yourself sneered at by all the bus boys. If, on the other hand, you appear with a chick-looking doll who looks positively illicit, you'll get the glad hand everywhere you go. The waiters will hover and the management will smile, and you'll have gone up at least five notches in everyone's opinion.

As I lived on board the *Lalona*, which was scheduled to stop in Papeete for a week or so, I did not need a hotel. I went out tramping in search of other sights, but they were hard to find. The local museum takes about fifteen minutes of study, and the local library even less. The little shops—all run, strangely enough, by Chinese—were even more disappointing. Their selection of South Sea souvenirs was uniformly drab and commercial.

Feeling tired and depressed, I settled down for a drink at a small sidewalk café. Sipping a cool aperitif, I tried to figure out what on earth the Polynesians on board the boat had seen in this town. Fragments of the song, *"Papeete, Papeete,"* ran through my mind, and I wondered what I might have missed.

A street sign told me that I had again wound up in the Rue Paul Gauguin, and that made me think of something I most definitely *had* missed. Where were Gauguin's South Sea girls? The brown half-naked goddess sitting under a palm tree was nowhere in sight. Had the beauty seen by Gauguin in the serene eyes of a tropical Venus also perished under iron roofs and concrete boxes?

I had scarcely finished the thought when suddenly she was there. A Tahitian girl looking as lovely as though she had just stepped out of a Gauguin frame appeared before me in Gauguin Street. Her smile was soft, her skin chocolate brown, her hair loose and flowing about her. She was Gauguin's dream girl, all right, but without the palm tree. For that lovely maiden, God help me, was seated on a motorcycle.

It was only the first of many shocks to come, as I soon discovered. Life on the islands has changed since those romantic early days.

I sat still, staring in disbelief, as other, equally beautiful Tahitian girls went speeding by. The fat Chinese bartender stepped outside, summoned by the explosive sounds of motorcycles roaring down the street. "Damned noise," he muttered, "every day after office hours. It's so bad you can't even hear the radio proper."

It was almost more than I could take. Tahiti and office hours! Gauguin girls and motorcycles! I leaned back in my chair and wondered if it might not all be a horrid dream, brought on by sunstroke or some such thing. But no, it was real all right. Two hibiscus girls proved their reality by parking their engines in the gutter and settling themselves for a drink at a nearby table. They stuffed bubble gum into their mouths and guzzled Coca Cola, gabbling like golden geese all the while.

There was—and is—nothing to be done about it. One has to face the facts. Civilization has come to Tahiti.

Gauguin's dream girls were anything but dreamy. They chattered a mile a minute, bombarding me with giggling glances. Each armed with a lipstick, they were apparently planning an attack. But their ability to paint with lipstick was such a bloody insult to Gauguin's brush that the alluring maneuvers of the two artists put me to flight. I got up and, since they say water is soothing to the nerves, fled automatically toward the harbor.

Little did I realize as I went loping off down to the bay that I had unknowingly hit upon the best place to go in Papeete. Oddly enough, in racing unhappily away, I had not noticed that I was walking toward a different harbor from the one I had seen on arrival. Papeete has two harbors, and the second one, I discovered, is the Papeete of the moonlight songs. It's a small dock, made for honest ships; no floating luxury hotels stop in at this entrancingly hidden port. Yet for all its modesty, Papeete's second harbor is a harbor of the world, where ships from every land arrive laden with goods and where sailors sail for the love of the sea and adventure.

The ships lie in neat rank and file, but otherwise there's a wonderful chaos everywhere. A copra schooner arrives from Mangareva, an island far to the south, and the full-bellied copra sacks are carried ashore. Or rather they are sung and danced to shore, for the muscular Polynesian longshoremen regard this as no chore. What is work, they seem to ask, when one can sing? Alongside the copra boat sits a small frigate full of fragrant vanilla—grown perhaps on Madame Bijou's own plantation—while its equally fragrant steerage cargo is set ashore undamaged. How undamaged the steerage cargo will be tomorrow is another question, for the steerage here consists of happy brown Bora-Bora girls who have come to Papeete to see the big world and who will probably have found their first big-city lovers by evening.

Passengers swarm aboard the small vessels that serve as the commuting system of the local islands. There are Tahitian girls of all ages and shapes, bustling little Chinamen, and bulging tourist ladies who have gone South-Sea-crazy in flowered shorts and hats. And seated on every fishing smack, lording it over the entire tumble of confusion, is an extremely fat Tahitian woman. She looks pasty as a pudding and has a temper like an earthquake beneath her faded straw hat. She is the one who sees to it that passengers and luggage are stowed properly. She's not a member of the firm. No, she is just one of those solid, sunny South Sea queens who likes managing people and things. She has a smile and a juicy joke for everyone, and loves nothing better than to shock those Westerners who appear a little too starched for her taste. She adores bombarding the tailor-made gentlemen on their yachts with frank invitations to come on board and help themselves to her wares. And when the gentlemen ask what wares, she screams with laughter, pointing to the brown girls instead of the mangoes and bananas. "Admission free!" she calls across the harbor. "No waiting line. Come and get it!"

The Polynesians on their own boat roll with laughter as they watch the faces of the proper foreign gentlemen. For it is clear from the expression on the yachtsman's surprised face that it has never really occurred to him before what the words "pleasure cruise" might mean. And his wife, witnessing the performance dressed in Bergdorf's best cruise-wear, shows in her slightly sour smile that she too has just understood the phrase, and is beginning to wish the idea of a South Sea cruise had never come up.

The wonderful drama of the harbor made me forget my disappointment with Papeete. That night, as I lay falling asleep in my cabin aboard the *Lalona*, I heard the strains of a familiar song which I now understood. "*Papeete, Papeete . . . ,*" the whispered words came softly through the night, wafted from a nearby beach where those who knew the wonder of the island sang of it with love.

Papeete made rather a different entrance into my cabin the next morning. I was awakened by the sound of distinctly female voices, which I thought at first must surely be coming from another of the cabins. But on opening my eyes I saw that I was wrong. There were, indeed, female voices in my cabin. They belonged to a band of giggling Tahitian girls who were standing around my bed, studying me with great interest. They had been taking a tour around the boat, and were now enjoying the unusual attraction of watching a foreigner asleep. I had no idea how long they had been there. My only thought for the moment was a grateful one that I had worn my pajamas for a change.

My waking up didn't disturb the girls in the least. They simply laughed even harder, and made themselves at home. Two of them sat down on my bed and began chattering at me in a language I could not understand. Another one smilingly tried on my hat, while a fourth held up my toothbrush, apparently asking whether she might use it. The party began to get dangerous, however, when one of them began prowling under my sheet. I suppose she just wanted to see if the bottoms of my pajamas matched the top. South Sea girls, as you may have guessed, are very curious.

I clutched my sheet around me desperately, and in the middle of the ensuing roar of laughter a huge figure appeared suddenly in the doorway. There was an abrupt silence, and I looked up, grateful to whomever my savior had been. It, or rather she, turned out to be an even more stupendously proportioned Polynesian woman than any I had seen so far. With a scowl and a stream of angry words, she chased the girls quickly out of my cabin and followed them, still screaming, down the hall. I enjoyed only a brief moment of respite, however, for the lady of authority was soon back at my bedside. She dived in through the door and sat down heavily on the only folding chair in the cabin.

"Those damned brats," she said, wiping the sweat from her face with an economy-size handkerchief. "Wait till I get my hands on them. I've told them to keep out of the cabins. They know they're only allowed on board if they behave. If anything disappears now they'll get the blame. Yet they're not thieving girls, Monsieur, they're really not. Though God knows this new generation has grown long fingers. In the old days you never heard of anything being stolen. But now . . . now they want cash for lipsticks and movies and motorcycles. That's why they've become light-fingered. And we can't lock the doors here, there aren't any doors. That's why we keep the lights on all night the way superstitious people used to do in the old days to keep away the ghosts. But the ghosts at least were only after your soul, while these modern ghosts will steal anything they can lay their hands on. They'll even steal the bed right from under you while you sleep, so that you land, flop, on the floor, right on your bottom!" With a crackling laugh she smacked herself on her own bottom, and wiped her sweaty face again.

She was without a doubt the most enormous woman I have ever seen. She was so large, in fact, that you could easily have hollowed her out and lived inside her. But at the same time she had that incredible charm with which giant Polynesian women are often gifted. Her name was Rubina, and she sat on my poor folding chair so crooked that morning that it never again regained its original shape. She sat there blithely talking to me, without ever once realizing that she had not been invited and that she had just told the escaping girls that it was not the thing to do to go pushing into strangers' cabins. She sat there perfectly unconcerned, and agreed, when I asked her, that she could do with a cup of coffee. When the French steward brought my tray, he stared at us with frank horror in his eyes. Rubina waited until he was out of sight, then, quivering with laughter, she cried, "Oh my God, he thought I'd been sleeping with you!"

Rubina was a flower woman. "Haven't you seen me down at the harbor?" she asked, surprised. "I saw you there yesterday. Couldn't possibly miss you. That checked hat can be seen a mile away. I took one look at it and knew you were an American. What? You're not an American? With that hat? Good God, what are you then? Oh, a Dane. Oh yes, I've met a Dane. I remember we had one years ago, always tottering around down by the harbor. Plastered from morning till night. We called him 'The Delayed Sunrise,' both because he snored all day long and didn't show his face until sunset, and because the old guy's romantic feelings had come so absurdly late. He was still looking for his one true love. I suppose that's what he came here for."

Rubina sighed, but not long enough for me to interrupt. "This Dane I was telling you about," she continued, "was still looking for his great love when he died of drink. But he could be quite wonderful to listen to. Sometimes late at night when he was really drunk, he would start talking about women and love—not drunken nonsense, but the most incredibly beautiful things you've ever heard—and I used to cry for the beauty of it. I'll never forget one time when 'The Delayed Sunrise' sat on a bollard and held the hand of 'The Mother of the Night.' Her name was Pomona and we called her 'Mama Po.' That means 'Mother of the Night,' though it would have been more appropriate to call her the Grandmother of the Night. She's dead now too. But she used to be one of the regulars up at Quinn's, the night club up the street. You've been there I suppose? Well if you haven't, then you'd better hurry up and go. You'll learn a lot there.

"Now, what was I saying? Oh yes, Mama Po. She moved later to the Moulin Rouge. There were more drunken sailors there than at Quinn's. She was such an old scarecrow by then, you'd think she'd have laid off long ago. But no, not Mama Po. She was much too romantic. Wouldn't give up. There was something delayed about her too. She loved nothing better than to get hold of a handsome young sailor who was so drunk by closing time that he thought all girls were pretty. You know the type, don't you? Well, it made Mama Po so happy to hear something like that, she looked like a young girl who'd just gotten engaged. She'd get all sentimental and make it all love and no money, even though, God knows, she could have used the cash. That woman had no sense, no sense at all. Oh well. But as I was saying, these two—The Delayed Sunrise and Mama Po—they sat holding hands on a bollard and looking at each other and I tell you, it was enough to make a person weep, the beautiful things they said to each other. Imagine, an old drunk and a worn-out whore. . . ."

Rubina emptied the coffee cup and stared thoughtfully down into the grounds with fortune-teller's eyes, as though she could read in the dregs of her coffee a strange fairy tale of two shipwrecked destinies clinging to each other in the last shining rays of hope.

With a puzzled smile she fetched her thoughts back out of the cup, and put it down with a thud. "Well," she laughed, *"aita peapea.* That means 'never mind.' It's our philosophy here on Tahiti, and it's something you foreigners should learn. You take things too seriously. If you can just learn to say *aita peapea,* and mean it, then you won't have come here in vain."

Rubina rose heavily from the folding chair and started toward the door. "I've got to get back to work," she announced. "There are tourists all over the place, and high prices in the offing. Which reminds me: let me give you a bit of good advice. If you want to buy souvenirs, for God's sake keep away from the sharks who try to drag you into their shops. The thing to do is wait until just before the boat is about to leave. Then they all come running down to the harbor and practically give their junk away. You can save a lot of money if you're careful, remember that. And thanks for the coffee. Come see me at the harbor, I'm always there."

In the doorway she turned with an intimate little laugh. "Oh, by the way," she said, "if ever you want a girl friend, ask me first. I know all the *vahines* of the harbor, and I can give you damn good advice. Some of them you must stay away from. Love's gone downhill on Tahiti. In the old days there was at least some feeling in it, even when there was cash involved. You should have seen my friend Erana. When her sailor left she cried so much there was high tide in the lagoon. She walked about like a widow, and refused to lift the mourner's veil from her eyes until the next ship came in. And then the whole thing started all over again. With Erana, every love was a great love. She must have set the world's record in wedding nights. But things have changed." Rubina sighed and shifted her massive weight from one sturdy leg to the other. "No, nowadays it's gotten all very muddy. The French like to think their ideas on sex are very liberal, but actually they're as naïve as babies. Try as they might, they can't figure out a way to tell the professionals apart from the rest. So they insist that all girls who have no regular employment or who don't live with their families must register in the profession and go for checkups with their *carte de sanitation*. It's stupid, that's what it is, but otherwise they couldn't cope with the situation. That's why so many decent girls must submit to being classed with those who are nothing but dirty bitches. Of course, there were no dirty bitches in the old days either. But what can you do. Anyway, as I was saying, ask me before you get mixed up in anything. I can give you plenty of good advice, and it's free."

I took Rubina up on her offer, and for the rest of my stay on Tahiti I remained under her protection. One of the best pieces of free advice she gave me was to postpone my planned trip around the island so that I could join a tour she and her friends were arranging for that Sunday. I took this advice, for I had plenty of time. The *Lalona*, it turned out, had had a minor heart attack on the long trip across the Pacific. Her engines were to be stethoscoped and that would allow us at least another week's time in Papeete.

A drive around the island is a firm tourist ritual on Tahiti. There is no way out of it unless you plan to spend your entire visit on the dock and it is the only way you will ever see Tahiti. The drive is simple, for Tahiti has only one road. It is eighty miles long and it circles the island, turning back in on itself when it has covered all the coast. It's an odd sensation to ride Tahiti's one road, for you realize as you speed along past the beaches that this is an island that has been settled like a doughnut. There is nothing in the middle. Everyone lives on the coast, where the fishing and fruit-picking is easy, and where a normal existence requires almost no effort at all. There are many fertile valleys in Tahiti's center, but none of them are cultivated; farm work is much too exhausting to attract any interest. Besides, the islanders ask, why bother? There's enough food provided, free of charge, to satisfy everyone. And so the valleys and mountainsides on Tahiti are left untouched, allowed to retain the rugged beauty with which they were created. And for this I'm sure all visitors are grateful, for the view presented is one of the most magnificent in the world.

The trip around the island is usually taken in a hired car, with a tip-happy Polynesian acting as combined driver and guide. But thanks to Rubina's splendid invitation, I set out instead in a ramshackle coach with my flower lady and her friends as guides. Packed in beside us was all the equipment for a wonderful picnic lunch: masses of good humor, food, and cheap French wine. The nicest thing about a Polynesian picnic is the consistently good spirit that's maintained throughout. There's no fuss and annoyance over minor accidents or delays. If your car is forced to stop because of a palm tree lying across the road, nobody frets. It just means having a new passenger along on the trip. A Polynesian would not dream of standing by the roadside to wait for a bus or car. If he needs to get anywhere, he simply blocks the road with a substantial tree and then goes home to make himself comfortable while waiting for someone to come along. When he hears the sudden screech of brakes, he knows the time has come. He ambles back to the road, helps the driver remove the tree, and climbs aboard for his ride. None of the original passengers will feel the least bit annoyed, for on Tahiti nobody ever hurries. A delay means extra time to enjoy the scenery, and what else could possibly be more pleasant?

Our picnic was held on a palm beach, and afterward we danced a hula on the sand. Dancing is good for the digestion, Rubina told me, and I promised her I would pass the advice along.

Since it was a very hot day, we soon trundled off in our coach to find a place suitable for swimming. To my surprise, we passed right by the temptingly crystal-clear water of a lagoon. The reason, I found out, was that Polynesians consider salt-water swimming unhealthy, and restrict their bathing pleasures to the fresh water of the rivers. We rode on until coming to a river with a waterfall, and there we stopped to dive in and play under the cool cascades. It's hard to say which was more intoxicating—the wine, the water, or the overpowering scent of Tahiti's favorite flower, the potent *"Tiare Tahiti."* Tahiti drowns in flowers, and her flowers never go out of season. It's summer all year round there, and the temperature never drops below sixty-eight degrees. Even the most suffocatingly hot summer's day is cooled by the breeze from the sea. And the heat, which is so welcome during the day, always magically disappears by nightfall, to be replaced by the island's own private brand of air-conditioning, the *hupe* or mountain wind of the night. It's a climate so perfect that we northerners seem insane to go on braving the cold, damp weather of our homelands.

All of which is not to say that rain is an unknown word to those on Tahiti. In the rainy season there are torrents of water, pouring indiscriminately and unrelentingly over everything in sight. But the rainy season is brief, and it passes. And once it is gone, sunshine bursts onto the island again, exploding every conceivable kind of vegetation into bloom. The soil of Tahiti is so fertile that nearly anything dropped into it will sprout and grow. "Even a fountain pen," Rubina swore. "It'll shoot up leaves in no time, though heaven knows what kind of fruit it will bear."

"Rubina," I said, "I'll settle with you on Tahiti on one condition: promise me I can plant a word in my garden and after the rainy season dig up an entire book."

Rubina shook with laughter and said, "You can, provided that you start by planting the right word." And with that she whispered the "right word" in my ear. It was a perfectly fine, full-bodied word, but one that would really have been a bit awkward to handle. If that word ever grew into a book, I'd be washed up with my publishers for good.

As we rode back home to Papeete that evening, I leaned back to stare up at the restlessly dancing clouds overhead. The Polynesians call them *raireva*, the "restless ones," for they sail from island to island and then are gone with the wind. *Raireva*, too, is the name given those strangers who come to the island, restlessly seeking a paradise on earth.

They say that it's the paradise hunters themselves who destroyed the paradise that was Tahiti. I'm not so sure though. In many ways Tahiti has not been destroyed. Civilization has done some damage, yes, but it has also provided some good—like the road which enabled us to see the inland wilderness of the island. For Tahiti is still a scenic paradise. No foreign invasion has yet been able to touch its primeval beauty. There are no artificial ripples in the calm waters of its lagoons, and there are no hot-dog stands or gas stations lining its one lonely road. Perhaps there will be someday; I hope not. But in the meantime, Tahiti is still Tahiti, and a must for any wanderer in the South Seas.

As for Papeete itself—well, it's only a small part of the island, disillusioning perhaps, but still unique. For Papeete, no matter what else you might say about it, is like no other city in the entire world. Where else would you find a metropolis of seventeen thousand inhabitants, of whom eight thousand are, according to the public registration office, "without profession"? And where else can you find a town so small and sad-looking equipped with three internationally famous night clubs? Those night clubs, by the way, are quite a refreshing experience. They offer nothing in the way of comfort and elegance, but they are the gayest spots I've ever seen. They're also the most democratic clubs in the world. The manager dances with his cook, while the baroness waltzes with a dockhand. Color makes absolutely no difference. When people take a night off in Papeete, they put aside all reminders of their humdrum lives. Great loves are found and forgotten in the course of an evening, and no one is at all the worse for wear. That's Papeete. Other capitals are centers of culture and business; Papeete reigns supreme as a capita of *joie de vivre*.

And then there are the famous Tahitian views of love. A foreigner arrives and falls in love with a beautiful Tahitian girl he's met in a night club. The night's adventure ends, he thinks, with a farewell kiss at sunrise. But that kiss is no farewell, not by a long shot. For the next day our foreigner will hear a knock at his door, and there, to his wondering eyes, will be the girl and all her belongings. She moves into his room with love, duster, and saucepan, and she stays there for as long as he stays on Tahiti. She darns his socks and washes his clothes, cooks his food and sleeps in his bed. And when at last he leaves, she waves him off with a smile. Tears may come later, perhaps, but they are gone quickly. After a couple of days she will dry her eyes and move with love, duster, and saucepan on to a new friend and a new house. The Tahitian girl may be sad, and sometimes she may be jealous. But her sadness is short-lived and her jealousy restrained. She knows that the best cure for the sadness of parting lies in the sweetness of starting anew.

In the old days it was always like that. But now it has all grown a bit muddy, as Rubina said. Still, it has no connection whatever with what we call immorality and wantonness. Our morality, the Tahitians think, is madness, for it goes against all the laws of nature. When Tahitian parents see new emotions awakening in their youngsters, they don't try to harness them. On the contrary, they encourage the children to be together and to express their new-found desires. Polynesians are convinced that a normal love life for a child can do no harm, and that in fact it is necessary if the children are to grow into healthy, happy adults.

So Tahiti has no old maids. Tahitian women smile when they hear that Western women have acquired equal rights with men. In their eyes Western women have acquired no rights at all, for they still must play second-fiddle in the game of love. The European or American woman is never allowed to take the initiative. If she wants to win a man, she must do so indirectly, with clothes and tricks and all the coquettish little devices that have been passed down from centuries back. The Tahitian woman will have none of that. She can quite openly take matters into her own hands and set out to conquer the man of her heart as energetically, and as frankly, as she wishes. She pursues her man without shame or fear, and when she conquers, there are no promises. For the Tahitian woman knows that even the greatest loves do not last. She has seen life, and she knows what it's like. Love is ephemeral, and she accepts it for what it is.

And that was why Madame Flaubert hated Tahiti. She had no cause to be jealous of her husband, as Madame Bijou would have led me to think. No, Monsiuer Flaubert was not deceiving his wife with Tahitian girls. He was still as gaunt and proper, and as prudishly French, as any businessman in Paris. But why then was Madame so bitter? I asked Rubina, and as usual she provided the one well-chosen word: *"Elle est éclipsée,"* she said, "and so are all the other French *mesdames* out here."

Madame Flaubert and all the other foreign ladies were "eclipsed," and that was the trouble. Even when they trusted their husbands, they could not trust the Tahitian girls. Each of the foreign ladies had erected a prison out of her marriage, and each one lived in terror that someday stronger and less respectful arms than hers would break the bars. Tahiti's foreign wives live in perpetual fear that they may become martyrs of the island of sun. And they form the best proof that Westerners and Polynesians cannot fit into the same pattern, for even on Tahiti they are worlds apart.

The word *eclipsed* can be applied to a lot of things on modern Tahiti. The island has, in a way, been eclipsed by foreigners, for alcoholism, VD, and cold-blooded prostitution are among the contributions we have made to what once was a land of cloudless skies.

Tahiti of today is partly clouded over. I will try to forget the tin roofs and the girls chewing gum and riding motorcycles. But

I shall never forget the road that circles the island. The road that Madame Flaubert refused to travel because she was afraid of the Tahitian girls who, on an island with only one road, also know only one road to love.

The direct road is, for them, the road that leads straight to heaven.

A lost Wednesday
and other magic

When I stepped off the *Lalona* on the Fiji Islands, I found I had lost two things: my toothbrush and a Wednesday.

I bought a new toothbrush in one of the many well-stocked shops of Suva, but I was never able to replace my Wednesday. I simply couldn't afford it. The toothbrush cost me twenty-nine cents. A new Wednesday would have come to about $1400, for I would have had to travel all the way around the world to get it back. Nothing less than another trip, you see, could have restored to me the day I lost while crossing the international date line between Tahiti and Fiji.

Mrs. Jollyheart, my lady of the absinthe and dolphins, was baffled by this mysterious disappearance. She had been looking forward to a week's stay in Suva, but the visit was completely ruined for her by the Wednesday riddle. She could think of nothing else but the missing day. When I met her on the streets in Suva, she would abruptly launch into a vague discourse on the possible whereabouts of our Wednesday, and it was only because I was up to date on her worries that I had the faintest idea what she was talking about.

"I think I've figured it out now," she said to me one day with a sly gleam of hope in her eyes. "Last week there simply *was* no Wednesday, anywhere. Or at least they didn't have one here in Suva, did they?"

I was forced to admit to Mrs. Jollyheart that there had indeed been a Wednesday in Suva that week. A perfectly ordinary Wednesday at that. "Oh," said Mrs. Jollyheart sadly, and went wandering off again.

We were able to solve the Wednesday question for one of the *Lalona*'s passengers by giving him both Tuesday and Thursday in exchange. This was for little Pierre, who had come aboard with his parents at Tahiti. We were usually very cold to newcomers, treating them like strangers trying to crash a private club. But Pierre was an exception. He was an irresistably charming child, and immediately became the pet of the entire ship. His fifth birthday was due to arrive on the following Wednesday, and little Pierre could scarcely wait for the big day. How could we possibly have told him the truth, that there would *be* no Wednesday on ship that week? Rather than dash all his hopes, we shrewdly offered him two birthdays instead of one, and celebrated on both Tuesday and Thursday. Two cakes and double the number of presents helped Pierre to get through this trying period without contracting the date-line complex that set Mrs. Jollyheart back for life.

The number of people who have had difficulty understanding the date line is enormous. Even Phileas Fogg forgot it in his calculations. When you travel east across the line, you gain a day; turn around and go west, as we were doing, and you lose one. Simple, but perplexing. It's like playing a game of tag with time.

This imaginary line, which was established by international

treaty, actually hits land at only a few places. In the north it runs through the Aleutians, and in the south it cuts through the Fiji Islands. For practical reasons, the line has been bent a bit in order to keep the Crown Colony intact; if not for this minor fraud, Fiji would have been split into two halves, observing simultaneous Wednesdays and Thursdays. The mixup would have delighted Mrs. Jollyheart, but apart from that it would have been impractical.

Actually, it was not until 1879 that the British decided to put a curve into the date line. Numerous complications in the lives of the double-dated islanders finally forced the authorities to make the change. But some of the complications were quite delightful.

In those days the missionaries kept a strict regime on the Fiji Islands. Naturally, they forbade shopkeepers to keep open on Sundays. But one wily grocer on the island of Taveuni used the date line to cheat the missionaries—and to keep within the law. He maintained—and he was probably right—that his house stood right on the date line. Therefore it was quite legal for him to keep his front door open from Monday to Saturday, and his back door open on Sunday. Since the back door was on the other side of the line, it was theoretically Monday there while the rest of the island was having Sunday.

Another story tells of the missionary and the drunkard who both lived on a small island near the date line. Nearby was another, smaller island, situated on the other side of the line. The missionary, who was a very industrious chap, conducted services on his own island every Sunday, and then sailed over to the other island where he conducted the same services again on the next day. Thus he was probably the only minister in the world who preached on 104 Sundays a year. But the drunkard was equally industrious. He got drunk on his own island six days of the week, and on Sunday sailed over to the other island where, it still being Saturday, he could keep on his merry routine. The drunkard had not seen a Sunday in years. His life was a row of wet weekdays, and no one could bother him for that. The missionary could not even reproach him for not coming to church. After all, Sunday is the day for church, and Sundays did not exist in the life of this drunkard.

People who live near the date line must still put up with problems of this sort. It's the penalty they pay in order that logic may be brought into the reckoning of time on the globe. The date line would be superfluous if people always stayed where they were and kept their own time. But since they don't, some form of order is necessary. The solution, confusing though it is to many, is to label the 180th degree of longitude the "date line" and to pretend that it is on this line that the sun rises each day. Of course, no one really *believes* this, but it is nice all the same and it does simplify matters for every one. Or nearly everyone. The rules of the game are not very hard: when it is twelve noon on the date line, it's midnight the previous day in Greenwich. Whether you gain or lose a day in crossing depends simply on which direction you're traveling. Since we on the *Lalona* had been going west, we had been forced to hand over a day on the date line.

The whole thing is so simple that it's very difficult to grasp. Mrs. Jollyheart never grasped it at all. She consoled herself by thinking she would get the lost Wednesday back on her voyage home. But since she was sailing from New Zealand back to England the other way, through the Suez Canal, she would still be going west, and so would never recapture her lost day. I tried to explain to her that the day was gone for good, and that she'd never see it again. She was grief-stricken. I don't think she will ever recover from the loss.

Altogether, Mrs. Jollyheart did not have a jolly time on Fiji at all. When she was not trying to trace her lost Wednesday, she worried instead about the Fijians still being cannibals. She knew perfectly well the practice of people-eating had been abolished, but somehow she could not quite fully believe it. She clung to me as we crossed the streets, and murmured nervously, "I do think they look a bit sinister."

And sinister in a way they did look, for the first Fijians we saw were native policemen, enormous dark-skinned strapping fellows dressed in full uniform with kilts. They were as tall as flag poles, and had feet the size of an Alaskan bear. And on top of their heads—making them look even more ominous—were huge quantities of coal-black hair, piled high in a fashion somewhat similar to the beehive. Only these beehives looked more like haystacks, for their owners took special care to keep them as wild and bristly as possible.

Ordinary civilian Fijian gentlemen wear modern shirts and tailor-made kilts with side pockets. If seeing everyone in skirts and piled-up hair confuses you, you can always tell the ladies apart by their flowered nightgowns. The missionaries' wives of bygone days couldn't bear the sight of all that native nakedness, and so they basted together for their charges batches and batches of the most dismal-looking floor-length flowered sacks. Many of the missionaries are gone now, but for some odd reason Fijian women still cling to these garments. Wandering the streets in their drab cotton nightgowns, they form a fitting tribute to the late but unlamented missionary movement in the South Seas.

Not satisfied with simply covering them all up, the missionaries also tried—in the name of God—to lop off their haystacks. Now, when Samson loses his hair, he also loses a great deal of his dignity. And if, on top of that, Samson's hair is neatly parted and flattened down, he's a lost man. You can always be sure, on Fiji, that a native with close-cropped, neatly parted hair is just an overcivilized oaf, not worth your interest. But those natives who wisely remain more Fijian than European are all, without exception, polite, dignified people with wide smiles and honest pride in their souls.

Tukua was like that. She was a primitive Fijian girl from the Lau Islands, with owl's eyes and teeth like a tropical piano with crooked keys. Her hair looked like the battleground of seventeen warring tribes, and her feet were about the size of a gorilla's. In other words, she looked ghastly. And I, of course, lost my heart to her. Her charm shone through all the unfortunate spare parts and enhanced—if not improved—the over-all impression.

One day, by way of experiment, I told her that I loved her. She didn't blush. Black girls are spared that awkwardness. But her face darkened with pleasure and she smiled happily at me, for she understood what I meant by my teasing. She knew I had given her a vote of confidence, and that I did not mean for her to take off her blouse. On her island, taking off one's blouse was a girl's answer to her suitor. The young man makes his declaration, and the young lady tells him with her blouse whether or not she's interested. Putting such delicate matters into words would be considered most improper on Fiji. No, the lady says it with her blouse. If she keeps it on, it's "no go, buddy, move along." If she takes it off—well, I leave the rest to your imagination.

It was Queen Salote's fault that I met Tukua. I had no intention of staying on Fiji, for if you remember, I was planning to use Suva simply as a stop-off point, as part of my journey toward Nuku'alofa in the Kingdom of Tonga. I was all ready to hop on the next plane for Tonga when I happened to read in the local paper that Queen Salote was off to New Zealand. According to the news report, she would be gone for about four months. As there was no point in my visiting Tonga when the queen wasn't home, I was forced to change my plans.

I sat around on the loggia of the Hotel Garrick for a couple of days, trying to decide what to do with myself until the queen would return. I pored over my map—while the rain poured over me—and finally I came up with the bright idea of staying right where I was.

The rain kept pouring even after I had made my decision. In Suva it always rains, regardless of the season. Everywhere else on the Fiji Islands, the climate is arranged with some sense of order. Rain one season, sun the next, so at least you know what to expect. Not so in Suva. I suspect the British like it that way, and for that reason placed their island capital right smack in the middle of the wettest rain belt this side of the Pacific. But perhaps it reminds them of home.

I sat on my watertight loggia and watched Suva's varied population parade by. Had I not known where I was, it would have been hard to guess, for the Fijians look more like Africans than South Sea natives. Their islands lie between golden-brown Polynesia and black Melanesia, and probably they represent a mixture of the two. Unquestionably, though, there are other ingredients in the recipe. African, Mongolian, Indian, Chinese, and even Egyptian blood have been added to a dish that naturally contains—as all the island mixtures do—a good sampling of seagoing European stock. The majority of the population in Suva, however, is Indian. Proud Hindus in flowing robes and turbans flock through the streets, making the town look for all the world like a primitive New Delhi transplanted whole across the sea. The British brought them over from India in the last century to work on the sugar plantations; hence the term "sugar Indians," which you will still hear used in Suva. They worked so industriously on the plantations that Fiji became the richest Crown Colony in the Pacific, and the Indians themselves became the mainstay of economic life on the islands, taking over from the British the role of rich independent businessmen in the colony.

The view of Suva's population was the only good thing the Hotel Garrick had to offer. My room looked as though it had been decorated by either a pupil of Einstein's or a secondhand dealer. So many cupboards and chests of drawers were crammed into its narrow space that it was nearly impossible to get from one end of the room to another without climbing on top of things. All that was needed to make the room look like a junk shop were price tags on the plush furniture, the knickknacks, and the romantic oil paintings. There it all was, looking as though we were expecting customers in the shop. Not that the shop was ever empty. Far from it. Customers flocked in and out all the time, but they never stopped to buy. They just looked.

I was treated to a constant stream of curious visitors, thanks to the two doors—one opening onto the corridor, the other onto the communal loggia—leading from my room. Neither of these doors could be locked. Even if I shut them carefully before going out, they were always wide open again when I returned. In Suva, a hotel door is something that stays open. Waiters and guests who wanted to go from the corridor to the loggia simply walked through the nearest room (usually mine), regardless of whether or not the guest was in. Nobody ever knocked. That would have been pointless when the door was already open and needed only to be pushed a bit for someone to get through. My room was as busy as a platform at Grand Central Station. And the rush hour lasted all day. Dressing and undressing had to take place in front of an open door, and there were always interested spectators to watch the proceedings. One fat Indian even insisted on sleeping in my doorway. Each evening he planted his camp bed firmly on my threshold, creaked slowly into bed dressed in voluminous white robes, and deposited his teeth in a brown laced shoe. I must say, though, that he slept well. His snores sounded like a vacuum cleaner being run through my dreams.

The Hotel Garrick was my first introduction to the complete lack of privacy on the South Sea Islands. At first it's a bit difficult to get used to, but you do adjust. And it's a good cure for the prudery with which we Westerners cloak our private lives. It took me only a few days to learn to discard my shorts without going into a circus contortionist's act. With a bit of practice, you too can learn to drop your pants and keep your head held high, no matter how large an audience of giggling chambermaids is present. I also realized, with adjustment, that the hotel porter must have thought me insane that first day when I asked about the keys for my two doors. "There are no keys," he said with a puzzled frown. "We don't lock doors here." And so they don't.

Why all the doors are, nonetheless, equipped with keyholes is another problem. However, it's not for me to question why. Perhaps the keyholes are provided for peeping through. Or ventilation. I don't know.

My first impression of Suva was a pleasant one. It's a nicer, cleaner, better built town than Tahiti's Papeete. But it was not long before I began to miss Papeete's shabby gaiety. Suva, though well-scrubbed, is one of the dullest places in the world. Of course it's rude to accuse a town of being boring; there must be some more elegant way of putting it. I tried very hard to think of one as I sat one evening having dinner with a group of English officers in the Fiji Club. The British have two clubs in Suva, one the Fiji Club, which, because it is the most exclusive, is called "The House of Lords," and the other the Defence Club, looked on as slightly second-rate and therefore known locally as "The House of Commons." Both houses are equally boring. The British use them as a means of pretending, while they are in the tropics, that they are really not there at all. This means cultivating the art of boredom to a degree unsurpassed anywhere else in the world, except, perhaps, in London. Naturally, the clubs have strong segregation policies, and so you can be sure that the one thing you won't find in the Fiji Club is anyone with an ounce of Fijian blood. Each race has its own clubs in Suva. If members of two different races wish to drink together, they must go to a public bar. The Fijian, however, must first produce a Government license—stating what and how much he may drink—before he will be served. I've no idea how the British authorities decide how much a Fijian can hold and whether he qualifies for a promotion from beer to scotch. But I do know that it irritates the Fijian no end to have a red-nosed and bleary-eyed British civil servant deciding whether or not a native "can hold his liquor." I met many an unlicensed Englishman who certainly couldn't hold his own.

Unfortunately, segregation is applied to a great many other institutions in Suva aside from drinking. It was not until just recently that Suva's municipal swimming pool was opened to Fijians and Indians. Formerly, admission to the pool, which was supported by the taxpayers' money, was limited only to "whites."

And that's the way it goes. I thought, when I set out for the South Seas, that I would be finding a wider world than the one I had known. But I was mistaken. For Suva is as narrow a world as any you'll find in the West.

I landed in an even narrower world—or at least a more cramped one—when I moved into a boarding house. The Hotel Garrick was bearable while I was just a tourist. But when I set up my typewriter between the two doors, I became a public attraction, drawing as enthusiastic an audience as someone in a side show. I needed more than ever to get my foot behind my own door. And I managed to do just that when my good friend Polly succeeded in getting me a room in a guest house called the Blue Lagoon. There was a long waiting list, but Polly knew the proprietress, a Mrs. Hungerleider, and so it was settled. In Suva it's very important to know someone who knows someone.

I hadn't seen much of Polly Thompson since disembarking from the *Lalona*. She had abducted Rudy to her moldering sixteen room villa, and there she had taken care of him until he was shipped to Samoa with introductions to the proper "some-ones" who could arrange to get him on to the Tokelau Islands. But now we would soon be getting together again, for once I was moved in with Mrs. Hungerleider, we would be neighbors.

Mrs. Hungerleider was a socially withered lady who had become a boarding-house keeper because her husband died an untimely death, leaving her nothing but a lot of empty whisky bottles and a large, overfurnished villa. This Victorian tropical palace had apparently been named "The Blue Lagoon" because the blue roof was the only thing in the house that wasn't brown. Mrs. Hungerleider, poor soul, had believed she was going to be a rich widow, and she assured me that she had been struck dumb— dumb, I tell you—when she discovered that there was not a penny left in the bank. This was undoubtedly the only occasion in her life when Mrs. Hungerleider lost her oratorical gifts. Ordinarily she was so eloquent that trying to get a word in edgewise was as hopeless as trying to stop Niagara by throwing a glass of water against the current. Her topics were very wayward. One day I thought in bewilderment that she was talking about how Queen Victoria had caught fleas, when in fact she had long since started to talk about a tame monkey she once had.

Her overwhelming communicativeness made it unnecessary for me to waste time looking up information about Fiji in books. The Japanese who recently invented "the talking book" must have used Mrs. Hungerleider as a model. She would also have been useful as a scarecrow. When she talked herself out into the garden with her bristly wisps of hair and her bared yellow fangs, all the birds fled in flight over to the neighbors' yards.

The garden at Mrs. Hungerleider's was actually a jungle in miniature. There were palms, bamboo and hibiscus bushes, frangipanis, flamboyants, and flowering African tulip trees. And far down at the end of the garden was a small slope with what is called, on Fiji, "sensitive grass"—tiny mimosa leaves that curl up when touched by a human hand. It was Tukua who introduced me to the "sensitive grass," and it was she who informed me that the sensitive leaves would not curl away if touched by an unsullied virgin. When I asked her to demonstrate this, she giggled with delight—and saved herself by ignoring my question and telling me, instead, that the leaves would curl up in a special fright if a girl came near them just after a slip.

Tukua also told me of a bird of prey on the Fiji Islands so sensitive that it dies of shame if it loses its prey while out hunting. She assured me that this was true and not just a legend. And she didn't smile when I said that God ought to have given all people so great a sense of dignity. For she herself was a child of nature who would have been capable of languishing away if she were ashamed of herself.

What American housewife can imagine a maid grieving to death if she feels she's not doing her duty? Yet Tukua was just like that. Together with a younger Fijian girl whom she had brought with her from her island, Tukua managed the whole boarding house to perfection. Mrs. Hungerleider was always fussing around, busily giving out orders in an attempt to convince herself that she had too much to do. She worked so hard to spoil everything that Tukua's efficiency was all the more impressive.

Tukua woke me up every morning at six with the Englishman's traditional early-morning tea. How she managed to wake me I never understood. Never before has anyone knocked so cautiously on my door so early in the morning. She let her knuckles whisper against the wood, but she did it so urgently, almost pleadingly, that this faint suspicion of a sound always woke me up at once. I also discovered why she knocked this way. Tukua had brought all the traditions of the Lau village with her when she came to the big town. And in her village, it was considered improper to disturb a chief or a white man in his sleep. But since it had to be done at the *Blue Lagoon*, Tukua had compromised, and tried to do it as softly and as apologetically as possible.

Mrs. Hungerleider constantly complained that it was hopeless to try to civilize Tukua. The plain and simple answer, though, was that Tukua did not want to be civilized. She had no respect whatever for what she called V*aka Piritania*—"British habits and customs." She approved of only one of the rules the English had introduced. Formerly the tribal law had segregated the men and women of the village at night. The English had by statute ordered them to sleep together. Tukua thought this was a fine law.

Tukua's best friend was called "Karisito," and she went to visit Him in church each Sunday. She thought He looked very lonely on His cross, and she worried about how He felt all the six days when nobody came to sing to Him. She was not especially well versed in Scripture, but she knew enough about the Bible to tell that there were some important parts of it missing. For example, in Genesis they had left out the fact that when God came down to earth to create man, He found the Fijians there already. They had been created by the snake god, Dengei, you see—you know, Dengei, the god with seven heads who lives in the rock cave at Nakauvandra.

Now it happened one day (Tukua explained to me) that Dengei came across two eggs lying on the ground. The eggs were so beautiful that Dengei decided to take them home and hatch them himself. Which he did. And when the eggs finally cracked open, a handsome boy and a beautiful girl stepped out of the shells. The proud god planted a tree which grew halfway up to the sky, and he put the children on either side of the thick wall of leaves and left them there with the strict injunction that they were both to stay where they were. But these Fijian children were very smart. One day when they knew that Dengei was listening, they said, extra loudly, to each other, "Isn't it a pity that the great god Dengei doesn't realize what an honor it would be to him if we were to populate the islands with others as beautiful as we? Think how all the other gods would envy him!" The snake god was so delighted with the idea that he immediately ripped away the tree and let the children embrace each other. For a wedding present he gave them pretty flowers and edible herbs. He also invented fire for them, and promised them immortality if they would obey him. But of course they didn't, and so he threw them out of their island Eden and punished them with diseases and death.

This was the story of creation that Tukua brought without a qualm to church, where she piously each Sunday sang her hymns and prayed her prayers.

She was also very superstitious. She refused to eat bananas because an old chief in her village had prophesied on his deathbed that he would be reincarnated as a banana. A sudden burst of wind, to her, was the giant bird *Manumanu*, flying past on wings so large they cast a shadow over the sun. A sudden sneeze was the warning of troubles to come. And a sneeze in a graveyard was even worse, for it meant a death in the family would soon occur.

But worst of all were the witch doctors. Tukua knew that they held the reins of both life and death, and woe to anyone on whom they had cast their terrible spell. For the powers of sorcery were limitless. With magic, you could do anything, anything at all. And sometimes this could prove quite handy. If you wanted to take revenge on an enemy, all you needed to do was step right up to your local sorcerer and purchase a pound or two of his help. Of course it could also be very frightening, for there was nothing to prevent an enemy from going off and sicking a witch doctor's magic on *you*. Naturally, this made for a great deal of insecurity on the islands.

"Can white men also be bewitched?" I asked, beginning to feel a bit insecure myself.

"No," Tukua shook her head sadly, "they're not susceptible." She looked terribly unhappy about this, and I strongly suspected that she would have liked it the other way. I certainly couldn't have blamed her for wanting to set a sorcerer on Mrs. Hungerleider.

Black magic and witchcraft are still widely practiced in the Pacific, both on the South Sea Islands and among the Australian bushmen. I witnessed an interesting black-magic struggle in Australia between the doctors of the Atomic Age and the sorcerers of the Stone Age. It was hard to tell for a long while which side would win.

An Australian bushman of the Guba-Wingu tribe was admitted to a hospital in Darwin. The doctors immediately established that nineteen-year-old Lya Wulumu was dying. But of what he was dying no one could tell. Every examination showed Lya Wulumu to be in perfect health. There was not a single thing wrong with him, yet his entire body was wracked with pain. He could not swallow, and had so much difficulty in breathing that he was hastily put in an iron lung.

Every conceivable treatment was tried, but nothing worked. For the dying bushman was a victim of black magic, and the white medicine men were powerless against its spell. Lya Wulumu's mother-in-law—who in this case must literally have been a witch —had "sung him to death." She had sung "The Song of the Weird Snake" to get rid of a son-in-law she didn't like. And now an invisible snake was twisting itself around the bewitched young man, slowly strangling him to death.

Lya Wulumu lived far out in the Australian bush country. He had been flown 260 miles to the hospital in Darwin, and was one of the few victims of black magic to reach a hospital alive. But it looked to the Australian doctors as though the long trip had been useless. Lya Wulumu's condition grew more critical with each day.

A bushman can be sung to death in three different ways. The spell is cast by pointing at the victim with a human bone while singing the magic song. If the witch sings "The Song of the Dream Shark," then death to the bewitched one will come by an invisible shark, tearing at his entrails and causing him to die within the course of a day. "The Barramundi Song," or "The Song of the Weird Snake," leads to a slow and agonizing death by strangulation. But the worst black magic of all is "The Song of the Great Devil-Devil." Under this technique, the bewitched one goes mad and wanders around in a nightmare of ghastly visions before he dies.

It sounds fantastic that such things should take place in our day and age, but they still do. Witchcraft is the last remnant of the ritual practices that were abolished when the white man came to the tribes. In the old days the Fijians settled their disputes with outright bloodshed and torture. But they found they could not do anything so obvious once the white man was around. For the white man regarded killing as a crime, and punished the offender by locking him up in a cage. So the tribesmen turned instead to witchcraft; it was just as effective, but safer, for the white man couldn't lock you up for casting a spell.

Many modern doctors have given up the struggle against witchcraft. Without being able to help, they have watched sound, healthy people die just because they were convinced that they were bewitched. They died of fear, and nothing within the realm of modern medical practice could have saved them. There is only one cure for black magic, and that is black magic itself. To treat a victim of witchcraft requires the greatest acting skill in the world, for the white doctor must convince his cynical patient that his magic is even greater than that of the tribal sorcerer.

Lya Wulumu was saved because he believed that the white witch doctor had power enough to break the curse of the weird snake. He believed the doctor was a better witch than his mother-in-law, and therefore the doctor's hex could cancel out the original one. It took many days of "magic" feats by the hospital's staff, however, before Lya Wulumu was convinced.

Tukua told me that the curse can be broken if a greater sorcerer intervenes and throws the curse back on its originator. The sorcerer called upon for this purpose is known as the "antagonist," and if he knows his business as well as he's supposed to, his magic will not only save the intended victim but will bring death to both the enemy and the original sorcerer.

On the Fiji Islands, being a sorcerer has its risks too. Aside from the danger of having the curse thrown back on him, the witch doctor must also beware of the dead victim's taking revenge. To protect himself against the angry ghost, the witch doctor must sneak up and thrust a knife into the dead body, or after the funeral pierce the grave with a spear.

Civilization has brought a few new techniques to the business of black magic. A well-known sorcerer on Fiji, who has since died a natural death, was a highly successful "antagonist" who cured his bewitched patients by prescribing a tablespoonful of whisky and reading a fragment from the New Testament. The charge for his services was the rest of the bottle of whisky, which the witch doctor himself then drank in order to soothe his own fears of the evil spirits.

Black magic is a curious mixture of quackery and superstition, but it does prove the theory that man can die from lack of the will to live. Investigators who have penetrated the mystery of black magic go so far as to say that the tricks practiced by the medicine men are highly beneficial to the tribal community. The witch doctors, they maintain, have for generations had a significant, useful influence over the tribal life. They were the highest authorities in the community, replacing both judges and police. They protected the tribe against criminal elements, not through a display of force, but through fear of the unknown. It was the medicine men's collusion with superhuman powers that made the tribe a solid community and not just a group of people who happened to live in the same small place.

There was a lot of black magic in Tukua's Christianity. She saw damnation as the worst of all curses; being sent to hell seemed, to her, even more horrible than being sung to death by "The Song of the Great Devil-Devil." And Christ himself she saw as the greatest of all Sorcerers, for His magic—witness the curing of the lepers and the raising of the dead—was far greater than any that had been known on the island of Lau.

When I told a local missionary about Tukua's beliefs, he became very deeply offended. His Fijians were pious Christians who had turned their backs on everything pagan, he said. He was so angry, though, that he sent for Tukua and questioned her, then assured me afterward that I had been completely wrong. Tukua never mentioned the incident to me, but I knew pretty well what had happened. She had lied most convincingly to the priest in order to spare his feelings. Tukua could lie magnificently when she wished.

Mrs. Hungerleider knew about Tukua's lying, and she had warned me of it long before. "Tukua's got her good points," she said, "but you can't trust her a yard. She is one of the most dishonest people I've ever met. But then," she added with a sigh of resignation, "they're all like that. You can't trust a one of them. They don't know the difference between what's true and what's not, and you just can't teach them a thing."

But Tukua did know the difference between truth and falsehood. She knew very well when she was lying, and she also knew very clearly why she was lying. She did not lie to get out of a jam. Even Mrs. Hungerleider was willing to admit that. No, Tukua lied because she had been brought up to believe that sometimes the truth is not very nice. Among the Fijians, common courtesy demands a lie whenever the truth is apt to hurt. It's simple good manners, and Tukua was a very well-mannered girl.

Tukua never discarded the strict rules of etiquette that she had been taught in her village. When I first moved in to Mrs. Hungerleider's, I used to wonder what the poor girl was mumbling every time she passed by me. I found out later that she was almost inaudibly whispering *Au se vosaleva*—"I am discourteous, sir." This was the polite formula used in the village whenever a Fijian passed someone entitled, because of higher rank, to an utterance of respect. To have passed a white man or a chief without murmuring "I am discourteous" would have been terribly rude. Tukua showed this respect to everyone in the house. Some of the boarders were clearly on her blacklist, but even they received the mask of courtesy from her. Tukua had been trained never to show her feelings when she was annoyed. She passed off minor everyday irritations with silence or a smiling white lie. Watching her, I felt amused at how much the so-called civilized world could afford to learn about civilized behavior from a primitive Fijian girl.

Tukua's so-called lies were delivered out of both good manners and basic human kindness. When she felt sorry for someone, she would try to reassure him with flattery. She knew that it is often the compliments that are least deserved that are the most pleasant to hear. Tukua was, for example, probably the only tenant of the Blue Lagoon ever to admire Miss Hammock's clothes. She felt sorry for an old girl dressing herself up so youthfully, and knew that there was nothing the old girl would have liked more than to hear that she did, indeed, look youthful and seductive. Of course Tukua knew as well as we did that no matter what Miss Hammock wore, she looked neither youthful nor seductive. As a matter of fact, she looked absolutely ridiculous.

Miss Hammock, as you may have guessed, was one of the more erotically inclined (though frustrated) lady boarders of the Blue Lagoon. She claimed to be a writer, but did not have a typewriter. She was only collecting material, she said. She was also trying to collect friends. But in this she was rather unsuccessful; her stock technique for attracting gentlemen friends seemed, somehow or other, never to achieve the desired result. The routine never varied. A new guest (male) would arrive at the boarding house. Miss Hammock would suddenly find that she was overcome by the heat. (This always struck me as rather unlikely, since the temperature remains the same all year round in Fiji.) "Oh dear," she would groan, "I just can't stand this heat today. I think I'll get these hot clothes off and go float on my nice cool bed." With that, she would go lumbering off to her room where, true to her word, she would lie floating on her bed without a stitch of clothes on. On these occasions it always happened—due to the heat of course—that her door would be left invitingly open. The technique was ingenious, but alas, it never worked. Try as she might, Miss Hammock was always left to float on her bed alone.

Miss Hammock's shape and her preference for the horizontal position naturally gave us material for many mean anti-Hammock jokes. But Tukua took quite the opposite tack. She used kindness and flattery in place of laughter, and the result was that, when Tukua was around, Miss Hammock behaved in a pleasant, normal, sensible manner. Tukua's primitive tact was far more effective than our Western-educated sneers, and I must say we all felt properly ashamed of ourselves.

Life in the Blue Lagoon was so much like that in a London boarding house that I often forgot I was off in the tropics. Not too often, however, for there were many pleasant—and unexpected—reminders penetrating even the brown façade of the Blue Lagoon. For example, on Sundays we were always awakened by the sound of cannibal drums. The drums were used instead of church bells, in order to call the people to their respective Sunday services. The paradoxical combination of pagan tom-toms and pious prayer-meetings is one of the many ironies that has resulted from the conversion of the cannibals who once roamed freely through the Fiji Islands.

The Fijians were, in fact, the fiercest cannibals the world has ever known. They were an incredibly bloodthirsty crew, as cruel as they were hungry. Tribes were constantly at war with one another. Peace was a state to be dreaded, and progress was measured in bodies. Widows were strangled at their husbands' funerals, and unwanted children were killed as casually as though they were kittens. Arguments were settled by one Fijian smashing another over the head with a club. "Senior citizens" were disposed of by being buried alive. At the dedication of a chief's new canoe, it was considered festive to wash the boat in a flood of fresh human blood. And when a cannibal king built himself a new palm palace, the posts were not rammed home until living men had been placed in the bottom of the excavation with raised arms tied to the posts. The Fijians knew no respect for human life, and they had no fear of pain or torture. Without a blink of an eye, a man would cut off his own little finger as a suitable expression of some grief.

Their diet consisted primarily of prisoners taken from enemy tribes. These prisoners were kept in cages and fattened up, prior to being slaughtered and roasted. A gourmet of a cannibal chief would make the victims line up on parade the day before a feast so that he could personally pick out the most tempting dishes. Choosing the menu required great care. Sometimes the chief would have arms cut off various prisoners and roasted on the spot so that he might taste the different samples. One chief made a show of his hospitality by erecting a stone for every victim served at his banquets. A missionary once counted them, and stopped when he reached nine hundred. Another missionary has described a feast where several hundred men, women, and children were massacred and served up at a sumptuous banquet. But usually the meals were more simple: a prisoner or two, nicely seasoned and roasted, was typical. Of course, there were occasionally not enough prisoners to go around. In that case the chief would be obliged to help himself from the members of his own tribe. Women and children, naturally, were chosen first. Not only were they more expendable than the men, but their meat (so the Fijians say) was far more tender and juicy. The greatest delicacy at a Fijian feast would be barbecued baby, usually served, because of its small portions, as an appetizer prior to the main course.

However cruel and inhuman it sounds, it has been suggested that cannibalism might have been a practical necessity rather than simply a taste for blood. Before the arrival of Europeans, there were no edible mammals on the islands. If you wanted a steak on the table, human flesh was the only possibility. A well-known nutrition expert has said that possibly the cannibals ate one another simply to get extra protein into their diets. This would be a logical explanation, were it not for the fact that cannibalism continued on the islands even after the cow and pig had been introduced. The Fijians reacted to these new meats simply by giving human flesh a new name: "long pig"—apparently meaning that we taste pretty much like roast pork, only longer.

The missionaries, of course, worked hard and long to try to cure the cannibals of their eating habits. They were up against some pretty stubborn reasoning though, as witnessed in a remark one old cannibal is said to have made to a pleading missionary. "Tell me that it's not right, but don't tell me that it's not good."

A tragicomic story from New Caledonia, where the natives were also cannibals, shows how little they understood our view of the problem.

A cannibal chief who very much wanted to be baptized was disappointed when the French missionary refused him because he had two wives. He reappeared a few months later with the same request, and the French missionary again pointed out that polygamy was not allowed. The cannibal smiled happily. "I know," he said piously, "but now I am a good Christian. Now I have only one wife."

"What happened to the other one?" the missionary asked distrustfully.

The cannibal chief smiled even more happily than before. "I have eaten her," he replied rapturously, in complete confidence that he had thereby done his Christian duty.

An end was put to cannibalism long ago, of course, though they say that there was just one case a few years ago on the Fiji Islands. Some natives on one of the islands killed a newly arrived stranger and ate him. But in this case it was both understandable and pardonable. The victim, you see, was said to have been a tax collector.

On the little island of Mbau, there reigned in cannibal days a notorious king called Thakombau. Or at any rate "Thakombau" is the way his name is pronounced; the spelling is "Cacobau." The Fijian language is a funny, soft, oompa-oompa language with very few words and almost no grammar. It would be very easy to learn were not the spelling so completely without rhyme or reason. The village Nggonggo is writen *Qoqo*, and if you want to send a letter to Ngglethombi you must write Quelecobi on the envelope. This absurd spelling was composed by the authorized missionary book-printer, Johann Sebastian Bach, who was responsible with a few other missionaries for compiling a written Fijian language. Now Mr. Johann Sebastian Bach, who was both a relative of the composer and a very practical man, suffered from acute shortage of type. The problem would have grown serious, had not Mr. Bach discovered, to his immense relief and delight, that he could do without the characters c and *q*, which have no corresponding Fijian sounds. He annexed these two letters and, without any fussy consideration for linguistics, used *c* instead of *th* and *q* instead of the Fijian *nng* sound. Since he was always short of *m*'s, he wrote the frequently occurring *mb* sound as *b*. The spelling is strange, but even stranger—to me—is the fact that this incomprehensible Bach alphabet-fugue is still played on Fiji's modern typesetting machines today.

All of which means that the island Bau is called Mbau, and the cannibal king Cacobau, who lived on that island long ago, was called Thakombau. When we took a trip to the island, we had to carry both our food and the missing letters.

Mbau is one of the world's smallest islands—so small that it could easily be plunked right down into the middle of Manhattan where it would take up only a few square blocks. It's about as big as a small city park. But Mbau in its heyday was more than an island playground. From his plate-sized domain, Thakombau ruled over the entire Fiji group. His aim was to become King of Fiji, and he succeeded by gaining the support of the newly arrived English merchants and missionaries. He won their friendship simply by becoming a Christian and allowing himself to be baptized without delay. In addition, he adopted drastic measures and forcibly Christianized all his subjects just as energetically as the newly converted Chinese general who once baptized his soldiers with a fire hose. Thakombau didn't use a fire hose, but the result was exactly the same. If Paris was worth a mass, then, thought Thakombau, Fiji was certainly worth a bath. Any Fijians who protested had their skulls crushed against the executioner's stone in the middle of the island. The stone, by the way, is still in existence. It now stands in the church, where it is used as a baptismal font.

Thakombau had himself crowned, though with less splendor than when British monarchs are crowned in Westminster Abbey. The crown was made of gilded zinc, with fake stones taken from old English penny brooches. And these crown jewels were symbolic of the economy of the Christian cannibal king. He was up to his ears in debt because the Americans were demanding a large sum of money in reparation for various assaults made on their citizens. If Thakombau did not pay, the Americans threatened to do something drastic, like sending a warship to Fiji and carrying the poor king away. To avoid this catastrophe, His Majesty had to raise money, and he had to do it fast. The only asset he had for sale, though, was the Fiji Islands, and even that, strictly speaking, did not belong to him. But disregarding such technicalities, Thakombau set out to try to sell his islands. Unfortunately, nobody seemed to want them. Twice he tried approaching the British, offering his islands at a bargain price. No dice. Then he tried his sales technique on the Americans, but Washington simply ignored the offer. Even colony-hungry Bismarck said "thanks, but no thanks" on behalf of Germany. Not until 1874, when Thakombau had all but given up and was nearly resigned to spending the rest of his royal life as king of a United States penitentiary, did England finally decide it could use a few more islands. The delighted cannibal king signed the contract immediately and thereupon stepped down from his palm-leaf throne.

Although his royal power thus ceased to function, Thakombau was not the least bit sorry. By selling his islands he had acquired enough money to pay his United States debt and still have enough left over to lead an even more kingly life than he had before. The ex-King of Fiji became a luxury tourist and gladdened his subjects by bringing home many strange souvenirs from foreign lands. In 1878 he returned from Australia bringing measles, which thrived so well on Fiji that more than 40,000 people fell victim to the epidemic.

In the meantime Christianity had spread as epidemically as the measles. The only remnants of Fiji's pagan days are now to be found in the museum in Suva, where they are all—except for the cannibal drums—displayed neatly behind glass. The cannibal drums, of course, have wound up in the churches as a substitute for chimes. Even the organ in Suva's Anglican Church has built-in cannibal drums which can be played by keys and air pressure. The organ with that cannibal touch is a gift from a wealthy New Zealander who apparently thought that if the Canary Islands could have organs with built-in chirping, then Fiji ought to have an organ with built-in drum beats.

An organ is, incidentally, almost superfluous in a Fijian church. The Fijians like singing hymns, and when they sing, they sing with conviction. And loudly. You don't have to enter a church in Suva in order to hear the choir. Their voices ring out in a thundering chorus that resounds each Sunday from one end of town to the other.

The descendants of the cannibal king have become so modern that permission to visit the chief on the island of Mbau is granted only on paying the admission price of a bottle of whisky. For a fifth of rye, left politely at the door, you may step right in and inspect the chief as closely as you wish.

Since there were so many of us Blue Lagooners coming to visit the current chief, we thought it best to bring two quart bottles of Suva's finest. We were received with large, grateful smiles, and in return were treated to tea and freshly picked coconuts. The whisky was put discreetly behind a screen, where it was being reserved for use at one of the chief's own private parties.

Our outing to the cannibal island was rather tame, but that didn't stop the ladies from fluttering with anxiety. Tukua must have been amused by these spoiled modern white women who regarded a twenty-minute row in a flat-bottomed boat as one of life's most hazardous experiences. Matters got even worse when, on the way back, we were trapped by the low tide and had to walk back to the mainland. Tukua had to escort the nervous Mrs. Hungerleider, who was convinced that all sorts of dangerous beasts were lurking under the mud. Miss Hammock hung around my neck like an amorous porch swing, both horrified by this grim ordeal and delighted by the opportunity to cling close to a man. Mr. Rose, of course, carried his delicate little child-wife all the way, but that was nothing new. He was bent on carrying her through life, for that was his idea of the role of the considerate husband. Mr. Rose was a recently appointed colonial civil servant, and the young couple had arrived in Suva as newlyweds. They moved in with Mrs. Hungerleider while waiting for their new house and their first baby. The waiting time in both cases was estimated at nine months. In their armorous excitement over the mystery of propagation, they regarded Mrs. Rose's pregnancy as a matter of world interest. There were news bulletins every day, reporting on the course of this earth-shaking event. Little Mrs. Rose was being cared for like some rare hothouse flower. There was great anxiety when it was found that she needed gentle massage, for masseuses don't grow on bushes out in Suva. But they searched diligently, and finally came across a fat old Fiji woman who seemed to be a master at her trade. Oh, those fine old natural methods, both Roses informed us with enthusiasm, nothing like them, no sir, they can't be beat.

When we got back from Mbau, we all retired early. It had been an exhausting day, and none of us, thank God, were up to the usual rounds of bridge. Little Mrs. Rose was, of course, immediately tucked away into her hothouse, while Miss Hammock, who'd had enough floating, went to bed behind a closed door. It was deathly still in the boarding house when, late at night, there came a gentle knocking at my door. I recognized Tukua's whispering knuckles and opened the door at once.

She stood outside, her eyes full of shining mystery, and asked me in a murmur if I would like to come to a party her friends had arranged down by the lagoon. "They say that maybe the paloloes come tonight," she whispered eagerly.

As it turned out, the paloloes did not arrive until dawn, but the waiting time didn't seem very long. Tukua's friends entertained with songs and dances on the moonlit shore. The "sitting" dances of the Fijis are strange and beautiful. The dancers sit with their legs crossed and dance only with their hands, singing their own accompaniment as they weave intricate patterns through the wind. Not all the dances were so calm, though. When the men rose to perform an ancient Fijian war dance, the spirit of cannibalism rose from its grave and danced with them.

In the intervals between dances, we refreshed ourselves with Fiji's national drink, kava. It's a very strange drink, with peculiar effects. Kava, or *yanggona*, as it is also called on Fiji, is made from a pulverized jungle root. The powder is put into a fruit-straining bag, and onto it is poured water as clean (comparatively) as you can get it. Then you force the water to drip into a large wooden bowl by washing your hands in the bag. If your hands are not clean when you start, they will be when you finish. The strained liquid is then drunk to the clapping of hands and ceremonial chants. It tastes pretty much like the way it was made.

The *yanggona* root is a sort of pepper plant containing certain narcotic ingredients. You become intoxicated by the kava, but not drunk in the ordinary way. Your eyes become heavy and sleepy, while your mind grows clearer and clearer. You feel enormously energetic until you try to stand up. Then you flop back again, and decide to remedy the situation by drinking more kava. Expressed scientifically, kava contains a narcotic that simultaneously develops fatigue while stimulating the mental faculties. In practice this means that all kava parties end up in the same festive way. Everyone sits around half asleep, and no one has the energy to utter a word. This is the grand climax of the party.

That night on the beach we restrained ourselves and drank only enough kava to get mildly high. We had to stay awake and lively until the paloloes arrived.

The palolo mystery is one of the strangest phenomena of the South Seas. The paloloes are small coral worms living under water with their heads wedged into the porous cavities of the reef. Like all living creatures, they must propagate. But they do so in a highly peculiar way. Or rather it seems peculiar to us. I'm sure that so far as the paloloes are concerned, the entire process is quite natural.

Once a year the body of the palolo breaks off from the head and rises to the surface of the sea. The heads stay under water (where they subsequently grow new bodies), while the headless bodies indulge in an unrestrained mating orgy on top of the sea. It's the strangest wedding in the world. All the participants go off on a promiscuous mass honeymoon and leave their heads at home. This grand event takes place every year in October or November, approximately eight days after a full moon. What determines the timing is not known. But scientists think the worms have a sort of built-in thermostat in their tails which is affected both by the temperature and by the phases of the moon. When the thermostat hits the right level, some sort of alarm goes off and sets this headless love affair in motion.

No matter how it actually happens, the mating of the paloloes was an unforgettable spectacle to watch. The rising sun stuck its blood-red fingers into the sea of desire and passion, and it looked for all the world as though the sun itself had risen from the stormy arena of propagation. "Look," the sun seemed to say, as it pointed its fingers toward the seething mass of life begetting life. "Look and learn, for we are all like this. Life is like this, no matter how much you try to hide its truth behind your cloak of sophistication. This is how the obscure forces of life play their perilous games with you. This is how the primitive force of creation drives you into one another's arms in the headless embrace of the senses. For your heads are as far removed from your bodies as any of these left behind in the reef. Look, and learn."

Our party finished that morning with a breakfast consisting of freshly caught fried coral worms. If you want to know what they tasted like, I'll have to admit, frankly, that I've tasted better. Much better. Unfortunately, as guest of honor I was obliged to eat more than any of the others. I managed it. But it is not easy to clench your teeth when you have to clench them through fried coral worms.

"Good God, do you mean you really swallowed those things?" cried Polly Thompson when I finally arrived at her place the following evening. "How could you! Ugh, those cannibals. It's like eating somebody's miscarriage, that's what it is."

Polly, I should explain, had telephoned me that morning and announced that she now felt fine again. So fine that she would even invite me over to dinner. "No, no excuses, I absolutely insist, you must come!" Well, that was morning. Then came noontime. "I do hate to cancel things like this, but really, I'm just not myself, awfully run down, how about tea?" Three o'clock: "Look here, I've just made up my mind, *don't* come for tea, it's dinner instead, no no, it's not any trouble, this time I'm sure, see you at six-fifteen." Five-thirty: "Look, do you suppose we could just skip dinner and make it for drinks at about nine? That is, if this migraine doesn't start in again. But it won't, it can't, I refuse to let it, this is definite now, all right?" So all right, I said.

At eight o'clock I had stopped thinking of nine, for at seven Polly had called again to cancel everything. "It's this migraine you know, horrible thing, I feel as though my head's falling off, in fact I wish it *would* fall off, but anyway let's just make it for another night, all right?" All right, I said, and let myself be roped into a game of three-handed bridge with Mrs. Hungerleider and Mr. Rose, who could not hold hands with his flower because the flower was being massaged. But in the middle of Mrs. Hungerleider's four hearts, the telephone rang again. Polly. She suddenly couldn't bear not seeing me. The migraine? Still there, but I could keep it company. "Look, do come, please," she urged. "I've been in bed all day and look a frightful mess, but I do promise to tidy myself up a bit. All right?" All right, I said. And went.

To say that Polly had tidied herself up a bit would be the understatement of the century. She was dressed in a rustling kimono of rainbow-colored silk, and had put her hair up in a Chinese pagoda held together by strings of pearls. Around her neck she had looped an entire coral reef of conch shells. Her feet were tucked—tidily, I'll admit—into a pair of golden Indian sandals with small tinkling bells. And—to add a more formal touch to this array—at the last moment she had grabbed six yards of flaming-red Chinese silk and wound it around her hips like a low-fitting Greek toga with a bridal train. An enormous Cleopatra-style fan completed the effect, and she sailed in flapping it wildly, looking as colorful and sounding as noisy as a flock of peacocks on display.

Bottles and glasses were already set out on a table, and I had no doubt that Polly had warmed up in advance. She was in an even more rollicking mood than usual, and at once turned on the phonograph to its highest pitch. The record changer was fed with a handful of assorted platters, and the party began. We started with a whisky and "Indian Love Call." Next came an Argentine tango, which Polly danced solo. "Silent Night, Holy Night" was played to the accompaniment of Polly's yodeled coloratura chorus. The bottles were tipped again as we wiped a tear away over "I Wonder Who's Kissing Her Now." "I wonder who's kissing *him?*" Polly sighed.

"Who?"

"Rudy. My sweet, adorable, lovable, wonderful, Rudy."

"Oh," said I, and drank a toast to sweet, adorable, lovable, wonderful, Rudy.

"Do you think he misses me . . . ?"

The evening would have gone along splendidly if I had had the sense to restrict my conversation to Rudy, love songs, and paloloes. But unfortunately I went too far. I made the mistake of mentioning Mrs. Rose's massages. Polly was pumping me about what went on at the Blue Lagoon, and I stupidly saw no harm in mentioning this among other things.

"My God," she interrupted, "you mean that poor thing is in there being rubbed? Get out," she shrieked. "Out, out into the car, hurry, at once! If we don't get there in time, there may be a murder!"

Like a bullfighter, she tore the six yards of silk from her hips. She flung the drapery around her shoulders and went bounding out to her chariot—a Morris so small that she filled it up to the last inch when she sat at the wheel. How she got in or out of the car I never understood. And how we both managed to fit in it is something beyond my imagination. On three wheels and a prayer (mine) Polly cursed her way to the Blue Lagoon where she swept every living thing aside as she stormed her way into Mrs. Rose's room. With an iron fist she lifted the terrified masseuse off the floor and abused her with a torrent of Fijian invective before throwing her down the garden steps and out onto the mimosa grass.

There was wild panic in the Blue Lagoon. Little Mrs. Rose was sobbing hysterically. Mrs. Hungerleider, who had all the cards for a small slam, dropped them and collapsed. Miss Hammock sank into her horizontal position and the distraught father-to-be cried that Polly would be responsible if his wife gave birth prematurely from shock.

But Polly settled herself into an armchair as calmly as a volcano after an eruption well done.

"Young man," she said blandly, "you'll have me to thank if your wife gives birth at all. I don't know how you got hold of that hag. But I do know you made a mistake. That woman's specialty, you idiot, is rubbing babies *out* of expectant mothers. *Out*, do you understand, so that the woman has a miscarriage. It's no damned wonder your wife enjoyed it. The baby may be half dead already. My God," she shook her head angrily, "why the hell didn't you ask somebody? This rubbing technique is what the Fiji women use for abortions. The old hag probably thought that was what you wanted. Though why, I don't know. It's usually done only when a woman feels too old to have any more. And she could see your wife is still a kid. The old bitch. Now do you see why I threw her out?"

"Oh well, it's all right now," she ended. "But don't just sit there. Why doesn't someone get out a bottle of whisky so we can all toast the health of this unborn child!"

Hell moves into paradise

Polly flew off the handle again when I told her of my latest plans.

"Are you out of your mind?" she cried. "You must be insane, utterly insane. It's those coral worms you ate, I knew it, I warned you what they would do. Now you've got worms on the brain. Well, I forbid you to go. It's sheer suicide. You can't. I won't let you. And if you do go, you needn't bother ever visiting me again. I'll not let you set foot inside this house, I promise, and what's more . . ."

Even Tukua, who felt quite at home with sorcery and magic, looked at me with a gloomy warning in her eyes, as though I had told her I was going to visit the devil himself.

Shudders would undoubtedly have trickled down her spine had I told her that the eyes of a dead woman were making me go. Or perhaps it's more correct to say that I was going because the dead eyes would not leave me alone, that they haunted me, day in and day out, until my thoughts were filled with them to the exclusion of all else. Tukua would have said I was going to hell. And hell, in a way, is the only name for the island to which I was going.

Tukua's whispering knuckles knocked on my door like the ominous hands of a ghost that morning when she called me an hour earlier than usual. I had to get up at five in order to be at the harbor at six. There at the quay the motor schooner *Makogai* was waiting for her passengers.

It was just before sunrise when I arrived. The Pacific shone like silver, reflecting the light of the setting moon, while the mountains beyond were rimmed with the sun's first gold. There were only a few of us on board when the schooner weighed anchor. We sailed out into the pink waters of the dawn, skimming through a scene as peaceful and idyllic as a tourist's dream. Our departure was like a clipping from a travel brochure.

But we were not tourists. True, we were on our way to one of the Pacific paradise islands, an island so small that it is marked only as a pinhead on the map. Makogai is its name. You will not find it mentioned in the travel brochures, but its name is known to every human being in the Pacific. They know it as one of the most wonderful islands in the South Seas. And yet, no one ever dreams of visiting this fairy-tale island. People hope instead that they will never see it. They dread it as they would hell itself, for they know what Makogai is.

Makogai is the island of lepers. It is a paradise island to which only the doomed are condemned.

So we were not tourists. Our pockets were not full of good advice about exciting excursions and attractive beaches. We had no lists of important sights to see. Our lists, such as they were, contained only instructions about the things we would have to do and the things we would have to be very careful not to do: Don't shake hands with anybody. Don't put anything on the ground. Wear special clothing and special shoes. Take a bath every evening when leaving the camp. Wash the clothes. Disinfect the shoes. Take care. In the days to come, we were going to live among eight hundred infectious lepers. There was no need to be nervous, but we would have to be careful all day long.

The list of regulations was a strange prelude to a sailing trip so beautiful that I could not help feeling like a carefree tourist after all. The mild morning breeze played pitch and toss with the golden pennies of the sun. And the sea itself shone in every shade of sky blue and sea green as we carefully navigated our way through the archipelago with its riot of tiny islands. The skipper had no idea how many Fiji Islands there were. "I don't think they've ever been counted," he said. "If you include all the tiny little islets with just room enough for a summer bungalow, you'd have at least three hundred." He pointed a calloused finger toward a small island with toy hills and doll's palms. "That one's for sale," he shouted, "want to buy it?" Yes, I said, I think I'd like to. For then I could have a kingdom of my own and a princess to live with for the rest of my days. The captain laughed. "The price is $112,000; pay that, and the kingdom is yours." I shook my head sadly. "I can't afford to pay that much for happiness," I said. "You could if you could find a rich princess," smiled the young doctor standing beside me.

The doctor was on his way to Makogai to learn more about leprosy. "I want to make it my specialty," he said. From all he told me about the dread disease, he obviously knew a great deal about it already. But he wanted to know more. "Only recently has science discovered how to cure these unfortunates," he explained. "The miracle in which doctors refused to believe has now happened. But the work must go on." He smiled, happy in his chosen field, where he too might become instrumental in bringing miracles into the lives of those who would once have been lost.

Leprosy has been known since ancient times, and it has always been thought of as the worst of all possible diseases. Traces of leprosy have been found on skeletons from earliest antiquity and on mummies from excavations in Peru. The "unclean" of the Bible were lepers. In the Middle Ages, leprosy was widespread all over Europe. No cure for the disease was known. Lepers were simply isolated and ostracized. Death was all they had to look forward to. They died in a hell of solitude and putrefaction, and could not even seek one another's company to find comfort in common misery. There was a ban on any two lepers marrying, and even leprous members of the same family were kept strictly apart. They were declared "officially dead," and made to drag on in life as living corpses.

And a dreadful thing is this living death. The body putrefies and is covered by supperating cysts and sores. The arms and legs wither. Toes and fingers drop off. Hands and feet become deformed lumps of flesh. The disease eats its way into the nose and ears. The face is transformed into a grotesque death mask. And it is all a slow and painful process, for the bacteria like to take their time. They don't release a victim until they have turned the poor wretch from man into monster. Then, and only then, is the dead allowed to die.

Not until the beginning of this century did scientists discover that a vegetable oil, Chaulmoogra oil, contained substances which appeared to attack the bacteria which by then were known to cause the disease. The oil was taken in the form of medicine, and could only alleviate the disease, not cure it. Chaulmoogra oil caused such violent choking sensations in the patient that strong doses of it were impossible.

Primitive people had their own remedies for the disease. A missionary on one of the islands last century reported that some native tribes claimed to cure their lepers by hanging them head down over a smoking fire. They maintained that the smoke from burning a poisonous jungle tree was an infallible cure. On the Fiji Islands they had a more effective treatment. Anyone suspected of having leprosy was bashed over the head with a club. It was brutal, but kind. The victim was spared many years of inhuman misery, and the danger of infection was reduced. When the English came to Fiji and banned "the club method," the disease gathered speed again.

What has made it so difficult to stamp out leprosy in civilized

A Tongan girl sings her praise to life in the South Pacific; her song and her joyous smile reflect the spirit of the South Sea Islands.

(Above) The Samoans live without windows, walls, or doors. The author lived in a palm hut similar to this one. (Below) Plantation workers load up their wagons for the weekly trip to market. Copra is the chief source of income for those who live in the South Seas.

(Left) This half-Chinese Samoan woman's husband is half-Danish, half-Australian. Her blonde-haired, blue-eyed daughter, therefore, is one part each Samoan, Chinese, Danish, and Australian. The islands have produced many mixtures as beautiful as these. (Below) These sarong-clad Samoan maidens are seated beside one of the many "happy" lagoons in the South Pacific.

(Above) Coca-Cola has conquered the ex-cannibals of the South Seas. This smiling little boy is a descendant of the once bloodthirsty Fiji Islanders. (Below) A young Tongan dressed for his role in a ritual dance.

(Above) *The main street of Nuku'alofa ("Love's Place"), capital of the Tongan Islands.*
(Below) *Tonga's miniature white palace, from which the king-sized Queen rules over her tiny kingdom.*

The Queen of Tonga. Salote loved and revered by all h subjects.

(Below left) The Queen's grandson, Prince Uluvalu ("Prince Eight Heads"), playing with the two hundred-year-old tortoise, "Tui Malila" ("The Prince of Malila"). The giant tortoise was a gift from Tonga's first tourist, Captain Cook. (Below right) Queen Salote's two sons, Crown Prince Tungi (left) and Prince Tu'ipelehake (right).

(Above) The Tongan Army, shown here in full force, is the smallest in the world. (Below) Two Tongan girls enjoy a football game from the privacy of their homemade "box."

The author with two Tongan matrons.

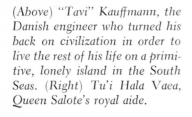

(Above) "Tavi" Kauffmann, the Danish engineer who turned his back on civilization in order to live the rest of his life on a primitive, lonely island in the South Seas. (Right) Tu'i Hala Vaea, Queen Salote's royal aide.

areas has been the awareness, on the part of the victim, of his fate if anyone discovered he were leprous. Lepers were deported to a remote island and left to rot away by themselves. Sometimes they would be entirely forgotten by the world outside. Occasional supplies would be tossed ashore, but often there was not even that slight bit of assistance. The lepers would be isolated forever from all other human life. Little wonder they did nothing about it when they knew they were already sentenced to death; all they wanted was to hold on to what was left to them of life. Witness this tale that has circulated throughout the South Seas.

A young man on a Pacific island once found an irritating rash all over his body. He was immediately declared leprous, and was shipped off to a desert island and thrown into a hut with a leprous old man who was already more than half gone. There the young man lived for many years on the barest subsistence, cut off from all human contact but that of his slowly decaying friend. When the old man died, he had to dig a grave with his bare hands in order to hide the stinking corpse. The young man continued his life in miserable solitude until a foreign doctor one day happened to come across him. The doctor was traveling through the islands, investigating what life might yet be left on each of the remotely settled leper prisons. When he examined the young man, he established that the boy had never even had the disease. The rash had been just a rash, one that had long since disappeared. And by some miracle, he had not even been infected by his long contact with the old man.

With such horrible stories fresh in their memories, the leprous and their relatives did all they could to hide the disease. And the result was that it spread at epidemic rate. The natives were not afraid of living with leprous relatives. They were convinced that a leper might infect an enemy, but never a relative or a friend.

Strangely enough, there is some truth in the idea that one can —like the young man on the island—live in close contact with a leper for many years without being infected. The two diseases to which leprosy is most closely related, tuberculosis and syphilis, are far more contagious. Doctors still don't know for sure how leprosy is transmitted. The generally accepted theory is that the bacteria are caught at an early age, but that the disease does not actually break out until many years later, and then only if there are favorable conditions for its development. What these favorable conditions are is still unknown.

When the English came to Fiji, they founded a colony for the internment and treatment of lepers on the little island of Beqa. For various reasons the place proved unsuitable, and in 1911 the forty lepers on the island were transferred to Makogai.

Makogai is a small volcanic island situated so far away from everything else that it has never had more than a handful of inhabitants. Low hills divide the island into two parts, making it easy to divide the land into a "clean" half and an "unclean" half. The inhabitants were allowed to remain on the "clean" half of the island, while the other half was reserved for the lepers. Most of the inhabitants decided to stay because they found they could make a good, easy living working for the leper colony.

The idea behind moving the patients was to establish a headquarters for all lepers in the Pacific, not only from the Fiji Islands but from all the other groups as well—the Gilbert and Ellice Islands to the north, the Samoan, Tongan, and Cook Islands to the west. Even New Zealand was included, for there, too, you will find a few isolated cases of leprosy. At the same time, Makogai was intended to create a colony for the lepers that would no longer remind them of a prison or prison camp. No more barbed wire and fences, no more filthy hovels and abandonment to the elements. The founders of the colony knew that the disease would never vanish so long as its victims were treated like criminals: Give them good, decent conditions, and they will no longer hide. They will come forward of their own accord, and those who can be cured will be cured. Those who cannot be saved will at least live out their last years under the best possible conditions. They will be cared for, and loved, instead of being tossed like monstrous straws into the wind.

From a distance, Makogai looked sinister. It appeared out of the sea like a blue shadow late in the afternoon, as small and as depressingly lonely as an outcast island tossed far away from all other life. But as we drew closer, we saw from the deck that the rumors of Makogai's beauty had not been exaggerated. The coral reef directed our small ship through the Sea King's foam-fenced waterways, beyond which we could see wet mermaid streets whose cobblestones reflected the pastel glints of sea and sun.

There was no bowing hotel porter waiting for us at the dock. Our reception committee consisted of white nuns in sun helmets, and a civilian medical superintendent. They were smiling and happy to see us. No tragic cloud hung over our arrival.

"No, our island is not a cemetery," smiled Dr. MacDonald as he led us up the cobblestone path. "You'd better get rid of any such morbid notions quickly. I'll admit there is sadness on Makogai, but it's nowhere near as bitter and hopeless as it once was. And you'll see a great many happy faces here, now that there is hope for some of them."

He pointed toward a slope standing a little way inland, where many wooden crosses were planted like flowers of death amid the luxuriance of life.

"That's our only cemetery," he said, "and I'd like to have it moved to a less conspicuous place. But in a way," he smiled, "the sight of it performs a service. Those crosses are a cheerful reminder of how much this place has changed. In the old days, a new cross was put up every day. Now there are no more than a dozen new ones each year."

Dr. MacDonald was the medical superintendent on Makogai, and we would be staying with him for the duration of our visit. There are no hotels on Makogai, and guests are rare and few. Relatives and friends cannot visit the patients as they do in other hospitals. Visiting hours are not daily, but twice a year, when a boat with visitors for the patients is sent from Suva to Makogai. Anyone else may visit the island only on a special permit, and those are seldom given. Leprosy is not considered as contagious as it once was, but nonetheless every possible precaution is taken in order to keep the disease from spreading.

We would live, of course, on the "clean" side of the island. It seemed hard to understand that on this little island, without any traffic, we could not start the car before telephoning the "traffic controller" and obtaining his permission to drive across to the other side. Why, we asked. Are there so many cars? "No," Dr. MacDonald laughed, "as a matter of fact, there are only two—my own car and the camp truck. But there's only one road, with steep slopes on both sides, and so narrow that you can't pass. Therefore we have a traffic controller at each end, and no one is allowed to set out on the fifteen-minute drive until we've made sure the road is clear." Imagine—traffic problems on a pint-sized island, with only one road and two cars!

The superintendent's villa stood on a ridge with a view for miles over the play of color in the coral reefs. "But the view is the only entertainment we can offer you," said Mrs. MacDonald when we had been introduced to what would be our home for the entire time of our visit. The superintendent's wife was like a breath of Paris—admirable in a woman who had gone from a secluded life on the Solomon Islands to an utterly remote one with the lepers. "Still, here at least I can get a few new dresses sent from Suva," she said. "You should have seen us after our years of isolation during the war. We didn't think we looked too bad, until we got on a huge tourist liner going to Australia. Compared to the other women on board, I looked like an antique in a museum."

The MacDonalds had a little boy of four, and with the self-assurance of an only child he promptly promoted me to uncle. Unfortunately, I did not make a very exciting uncle. I tried all the little tricks that had always made me a hit with four-year-olds. Elephants, tigers, snakes, monkeys—I've performed these numbers so many times that I know how to pick the hits. But the lonely boy on the island of lepers wouldn't bite. He had never been to a zoo. He knew nothing of the great wide world, and it meant nothing to him. The elephant Abdulla in Bombay that hit me on top of the head, the tiger Lakshman that liked to chew my fingers affectionately, these his brain registered only with an unsmiling "I see." For he didn't see at all. These were pictures from an unknown world, and his imagination could not reproduce any of them. Not until we got around to sharks was contact established. And then it was the four-year-old who told *me*.

The first thing I saw in Mother Mary Valentine's office at the hospital was the photograph that had brought me to Makogai. On the prioress's wall hung the picture of the old nun whose face had impressed me so deeply when I came by chance across the photograph in Suva. It was a face filled with serenity. The eyes were both stern and mild, and they held an expression of shining faith and renunciation. I had asked at once who it was. "Don't you know?" came the shocked answer. "That's Mother Mary Agnes, the saint of Makogai." And Makogai? I had asked. "The island of the lepers. Hasn't anyone told you about it?" No, no one had, for no one talks about it.

And that was how I came to know of Makogai, the island everyone in the South Pacific knows about, but that no one ever mentions. Looking at the eyes in that faded photograph, I knew I would never rest until I had seen, with my own eyes, what she had seen and believed in with hers.

Mother Mary Agnes died on Makogai in 1954, shortly after her eighty-fifth birthday. She came to the Fiji Islands in 1889, and became the friend and protectress of the lepers. When they were herded together to be sent to Makogai, Mother Mary Agnes of course went with them. She was a very tiny woman with a heart of gold and a cheerful smile. But she was also very strict. She demanded order and discipline from everyone, and she got it. She used to say that she could make them all obey simply by raising her bushy eyebrows. She retired when she was eighty, and could have returned to her French native land, which she had not seen since she was very young. But she preferred to stay with her lepers. There, a year before her death, she was given the award of the Legion of Honor as a tribute to her heroic and devoted work.

In her will she asked to be buried among the lepers, and she could not have given *them* a greater tribute. All of Makogai wept on the day Mother Mary Agnes was carried to her grave. And the carrying took a long time, for each of the lepers insisted on helping to carry their beloved benefactress, just for a couple of steps, before another "unclean" and tortured hand took over the light burden which weighed so heavily on them. They loved their sainted lady, and knew that with her fearless love she would not have regarded these hands as unclean. Makogai will never forget Mother Mary Agnes. Her grave is decorated each day with a profusion of fresh flowers, and her photograph hangs on the wall of nearly every hut on the island.

Mother Mary Agnes and Makogai's other brave angels in starched headgear deserve every bit of the tribute they receive. Few people anywhere have matched the courage displayed by these anonymous heroines who spend their lives in exile in order to help the poorest and sickest of all. Thanks to the new methods of treatment and the reduced danger of infection, the nuns are not confined as closely as they used to be. But in the old days they knew, when they came, that they had sentenced themselves into a lifelong exile from which they would never be released. When they walked ashore on Makogai, they knew there was no turning back.

"It was dreadful then," said old Sister Mary Clement, who had been on Makogai for forty-four years. "Not only was there no chance of cure, but we could scarcely even treat them. The wards were worst of all. The patients—well," she smiled apologetically, "there's no other way to put it—they stank."

She described to me how she had often spent several hours dressing a single running sore. Some of the patients were hidden in bandages from top to toe, leaving only the eyes and nose free. That is, if there were still a nose. Many of the patients had only a stinking, putrefied breathing-hole left. All the wards were poisoned with the stench of living corpses. One newly-arrived young nun was forced, in the beginning to leave her work every half hour to go outside and be sick. She lost sixty pounds in six months, and had to enter the hospital herself to gain back her strength.

It seems something of a miracle that none of Makogai's nuns have ever been infected. But leprosy's paths are unpredictable. Just how unpredictable is shown by a sad case from the Gilbert Islands. A Gilbertian and his five children had to leave their home and go the tragic way to Makogai. First came two small boys. Then the father and two other sons. And at last an infant girl on her own. They were severe cases, and all six died on the island. But the mother, who had lived with them for so many years and who had nursed all five of the children, never caught the disease. She was the only one who had been saved, and that, in a way, was her tragedy.

There are two types of leprosy. One form results in hideous sores. The victims get rashes and running cysts all over the body and on the face. When the dead are given a post-mortem, it is nearly always shown that the intestines were also infected. The other form of leprosy attacks the nervous system. The skin dies and becomes insensible. The limbs begin to drop off. A patient on Makogai who was sitting with his back to an open fire was severely burned when his clothes caught fire without his even noticing. His skin was so dead that even when he was being carried to the hospital, dying of first-degree burns, he could not feel the slightest pain.

Ernest Wolfgram, one of the heroic figures of Makogai, had the disease in this form. In the end his skin was completely dead, but under that dead skin he suffered the most violent pain together with an excruciating itch that nothing could soothe. One of the old nuns told me how Ernest would sometimes run shrieking along the beach in order to give vent to his suffering. "The itching is worse than the pain," he had said. "I simply can't describe it. It's beyond words, and more horrible than anything else I have ever known."

Wolfgram was of half-European descent, born of a well-to-do family on Tonga. He was a handsome, promising young man who had been sent to New Zealand to study. It was there that doctors discovered he was leprous. It is often difficult for doctors to diagnose the disease. For many years an Indian photographer in Suva suffered from what he thought was eczema; he tried many cures without success, never guessing what the trouble might be. One day a foreign doctor who was a specialist in leprosy came to Suva as a tourist and happened to stop in at the photographer's shop to have some film developed. He noticed the photographer's hands and asked what the trouble was. "Eczema," the photographer replied. "Can you suggest something that will help?" The doctor was able to suggest something all right, but it was not the kind of suggestion the Indian had hoped for. The doctor went directly to the health authorities and informed them that this man, who in his shop came into daily contact with hundreds of people, was a leper and probably highly infectious. The photographer was sent to Makogai, where he died some years later.

Ernest Wolfgram, too, died on the island of lepers; but before his death he accomplished much toward making the island a happier place than it was. In spite of his crippling disease, Wolfgram never lost his energy and determination to make a bad lot a better one for those condemned to it. The workshops and boatbuilding yards on Makogai are his work. He opened the first technical school for patients, and taught there himself for as long as he was able. He started sports clubs and organized games. He founded the Makogai Boy Scouts Association. All this and more—yet he was only forty years old when he died.

There were never very many Europeans on Makogai, possibly because the disease doesn't thrive under well-ordered hygienic conditions. Altogether the island has had only a dozen European patients.

George was one of them.

George was popular in Suva. He was young, handsome, and charming. The girls flocked around him and vied with each other for his attention. It came as quite a shock to those who had known him, when George was one day packed up and sent to Makogai as a leper. He stayed there for almost twenty years. But he came back. And the girl friend of his youth had waited for him all that while. She was a telephone operator, and had faithfully said her line was busy all those years.

George's story is one of the few with a truly Cinderella-like happy ending. For unlike George, most of those who come to Makogai never go back. And unlike George again, most who come to Makogai are not remembered by those they leave behind.

George lived in his own house on Makogai. Fortunately for him, his case was mild enough to permit him to live in almost complete freedom. The most severely infected patients are treated in the large hospital buildings on Dalice Bay. But the rest of the settlement is pleasantly free of any sort of hospital atmosphere. Most of the lepers live in small villages along the coast. They have their own houses, which they have built themselves. The Samoans live in a Samoan village with airy thatched-roof huts on posts. The Fijians have set their cool palm huts in an opening under the palm trees. And the Tongans have established their own little private kingdom. It is all just as though they were at home—and that is the most important thing about modern-day Makogai. The lepers cannot leave the island, but aside from that there is no hint of prison walls. They manage their own housekeeping and get ample weekly rations from the hospital if they're unable to do their own farming. Those who can raise their own produce receive cash instead of rations, plus extra money for whatever crops they sell to the settlement. They have schools, workshops, recreation grounds, and tennis courts. They have boatbuilder's yards where they can build their own canoes. They can sail in the lagoon, they can fish, they can swim. They have complete freedom, with only one exception. Men and women must live apart. The nuns claim that this separation creates no problems, but it may be that the nuns view the matter too lightly. For to many of the younger men and women on the island, this enforced celibacy is painful to bear. The fat, happy nun who looked after the only shop on the island knew a lot more about it than her pious sisters. She told me how at Christmastime the young lepers came to her to buy little gifts which were certainly not for themselves. The young man does not use perfume, and the young girl does not smoke a pipe. But they were sold what they wanted without any indiscreet questions. The nun knew that the gift was a cautious declaration of love from an unhappy heart. Christmas is both a sad and a joyful celebration on Makogai.

The strange atmosphere of joy and sadness is something you find all year round on the island. As you walk about, you see smiles that are bitter and tears full of joy. And no wonder: for consider the paradox of this island world. People here are cared for as they are nowhere else in the world. Every material need is provided. Yet at the same time, more than half of them face nothing but slow and uncertain death, and all of them have been cut off forever from those who once were close.

It's a strange world, and stranger still is its pain. Nowhere else will you find such a concentration of despair, and nowhere else will you find such blind, persistent hope. The hopeful faces are not so common as you would like, though. Those with something to believe in are far outnumbered by the countless others to whom hope is a forgotten word.

I walked through the hospital wards where those who came too late (as some still do) are cared for until they die. I walked past row upon row of withered arms, deformed hands, half-eaten faces, and decaying legs.

I stopped at one bed to talk to an adolescent brown-skinned boy, all skin and bones but with a handsome face. He sat up in bed, restlessly rubbing his legs, which were so thin they looked as though they were only bones covered by a thinly stretched layer of skin. His large childish eyes were clouded with despair. He was very ill, and knew he was going to die. To make things worse, a short time before, his only friend had been allowed out in a canoe; the canoe had capsized, and the friend had drowned in the lagoon. With his only friend dead, life seemed totally empty and useless. His family and friends had long since abandoned him to the nuns. There was nothing left but pain and more pain and then death. I hated standing by this child's bed, trying to give him my useless smile of encouragement. For what could I have possibly said to him that would have made it any better than it was? I could not even shake his hand or put a comforting arm around his pitifully thin shoulders. The regulations would not allow it. Perhaps it would have relieved his desperate loneliness if he could have cried on my shoulder. My shoulder was ready, and my arms were open to comfort him. But we both knew that even the slightest human touch was impossible. The disease had built an invisible wall between us, and neither of us was permitted to surmount it.

So I moved on down the ward, and tried to forget. But forgetting isn't easy on Makogai. For so long as you are on the island, you will be surrounded by tragedy in its many painful forms.

As I walked on through the hospital corridors, I came across another, seemingly tragic, case. Or at least that's the way it looked. A nun came wheeling an old man in a wheel chair. He looked as badly ravaged as any I had seen; both legs were gone, and he had only one tooth left in his grotesquely grinning mouth. I would not have imagined that the nun would tell me something about him that would make me smile. But smile I did, for old Wanikai, I found, was the happiest of all Makogai's sick inhabitants. He hadn't the faintest idea how old he was; all he knew was that he had been born in Queen Victoria's time. He was sent to Makogai from his own island after being declared leprous; and, indeed, I thought, he certainly looked it. But he was not leprous at all! The specialists on Makogai had quickly established that it was all a mistake. Wanikai was in pretty bad shape, but so far as leprosy was concerned, he was as healthy as a horse. They were going to send him back to his island, but he begged to be allowed to stay on Makogai. The authorities relented, and let him remain in the colony. When I met him, Wanikai had lived for many years among the lepers without catching the disease. He probably never will be infected. He was given a wheel chair so smart that he wouldn't have traded it for a Cadillac. And so old Wanikai, the only patient on Makogai who is not leprous, is the happiest of them all on the island of lepers.

Makogai is full of strange experiences. One afternoon I went down to the beach with a nun to watch the Girl Guides train. One of the girls was dazzlingly beautiful. I could not take my eyes off that wonderful brown face, radiant with seventeen-year-old freedom from care. But when at last I did pull my eyes from her face, I let myself in for a shock. Her hands were withered beyond recognition. There was scarcely anything left to show that once they too had clapped and waved as wildly as the hands of any child.

And there are children on Makogai. One of them, the pet of the island, was a two-year-old named Kusmawati. She came toddling along down to the beach, running on small, fat legs and laughing at some private two-year-old joke. Kusmawati didn't look leprous, but my nun told me that she was. Her mother had been expecting her when she was first sent to Makogai. Strangely enough, it is rare for a leprous mother to give birth to a leprous child. The infant is usually taken away from its mother immediately after birth, and then sent back to the mainland where it can be cared for by relatives or friends. The mother is not allowed to touch her child, and is permitted to see the infant only from a distance. And so it was with the Indian woman who had given birth to Kusmawati. The disease had taken her brutally from her home, and the child she had been looking forward to and had borne in pain was not even allowed near her. Leprosy makes a strange demand on maternal love; it asks that a mother be happy when her child is taken away. In this case, maternal love had been put to an exceptionally severe case. Before Kusmawati was sent to Suva, she was discovered to have a mild form of the disease. I am sure that no mother has ever wavered more between joy and sorrow than when this woman was told the dreadful news that she would have her child to keep on the island of lepers.

Later in the day, I paid a visit to Tony from Tonga. Tony was a handsome young Polynesian who did not look the least bit ill. He was as robust and athletic as any young man of his age, yet in spite of his healthy appearance, Tony was a leper. The rash on his back and the blood tests proved that he still had the disease, although his was one of the mild cases that was on its way to being cured.

Tony smilingly showed us around his house, but the smile existed only on his lips. He wore his cheerfulness like a mask, trying to hide the sorrow that bled from his eyes. When we parted, there was a repetition of the usual sad little scene: the hand that automatically reaches out for an encouraging handshake, then drops to one's side like a useless prop. My hands grew strangely restless and homeless on Makogai.

As we left Tony's house, the nun beamed at me with pride. "Now do you see how happy our patients are? Why, Tony's having just as much fun here as he would at home." I smiled sadly at the nun. Her naïveté was as much a protection for her as my unshaken hands were for me.

Tony was unhappy in his exile, but at least he knew that it would someday be ended. Ended because he was lucky enough to have been born in an era when medicine could cure him. Tony will be cured: the doctors have no doubt of that. It is only a question of time, and so Tony must be patient. Ten years before, Tony would have looked into the mirror and seen a ghastly half-eaten-away face. Tony could have learned a lot from Rami, a boy whose face was horribly ravaged. Yet Rami's eyes held no sorrow; he was exuberantly happy, for he believed that he had become one of the nicest-looking boys in the world.

Rami was seventeen years old, and he had lived on the island of lepers since he was six. By the time he was eleven, the disease had spread so violently that his face had swollen into a distorted mask of death. The bacteria had made the young boy look like an old man, with the bloated face of a horribly syphilitic drunkard. But six years later, Rami was a changed man. He would look in the mirror and smile with joy, then point to a photograph of himself taken when he was younger and ask if anyone could believe that he had once looked like that. Rami's new face was still scarred. He had not become handsome as we think of it. Yet he himself thought he had turned into something beautiful to see. And watching his face lit up with radiant joy, I thought that Rami had indeed become one of the world's most beautiful sights.

Rami was happy, and he could have taught the rest of us a very valuable lesson in living. Rami lived, as we all do, in an atomic age. But Rami saw and appreciated the good it had brought him. The rest of us, on the other hand, are fond of wandering around complaining that we live in the most evil era in the history of man. We light our pipes, lean back, and assure one another that we're living in a sick world which in the name of progress is concentrating on bombs and missiles. We complain that the secrets science is wresting from nature are being put into the service of death. But Rami didn't share this dark view. He was jubilantly happy that he had been born in an atomic age, and he was convinced that humanity could never have known a happier time. For Rami knew that he had only modern science to thank for the fact that he was not only alive, but had been transformed from a grotesque monster into a nice, smiling young man.

Few of us appreciate the miracles of modern medicine. It takes seeing a Rami to remind us of how much progress to *save* mankind has been made in this era we live in. For years doctors throughout the world worked to find new remedies for the horrible living death of leprosy. The first revolution came when American doctors found an improved version of Chaulmoogra oil which was given in the form of injections, and produced considerably better results. Over the years the new remedy was improved, but it still had no effect on leprosy in its more advanced stages.

The disease continued in its decaying path until modern science, at long last, found that certain of the new sulfa drugs could be used to treat the leper. In the beginning, these were used only through injections. But now the treatment of patients with sulfa tablets is becoming more and more common. The effects of these new preparations are all but miraculous. Even the doctors have been amazed by the fantastic results.

The new treatments began as late as 1948, and fortunately old Mother Mary Agnes lived to see the miracle of which she had dreamed for so long a part of her life. The reverend mother, who had become the boy Rami's substitute for a real mother, had grieved over the child's fate. She had nothing to give him but the solace of the Bible and the comfort of her own motherly embrace. Both helped, but not enough. For all the love and faith in the world could not erase the bestial features of the leprous child's face. But Mother Mary Agnes was able to see the boy Rami smile again when a modern medical wonder gave him back a human face. And it may be that, as in the Bible, she clasped her hands in prayer and told her God that He might now let her leave in peace.

On the island of the lepers, whole batteries of unused Chaulmoogra oil stand wasting on the shelves. But no one minds the waste. For now all the patients need is to make sure they take their sulfa tablets regularly. The little white pills mean that someday soon the isolation of lepers will be ended. Many doctors are now convinced that new cases, caught before they've had time to advance, can be cured quickly. A few weeks in the hospital, and the disease should be no longer contagious. The patient will be able to return home to continue his cure under the care of his own family, without risk of infecting anyone. Dr. MacDonald, my authority on these matters, assured me that he himself would rather be infected with leprosy than with tuberculosis. The leper today has a far better chance of a complete cure.

The miracle that has taken place in leprosy can be seen in the statistics kept on Makogai. Not only are there fewer deaths each year, but the number of discharged patients—a fate that was never before even dreamed of—goes up with each passing year. Oddly enough, the influx of new patients is also rising. But that is because those who would formerly have concealed the disease now come forward voluntarily because they know they can be cured. Now they are just as eager to come to the island of lepers as they once were afraid of being sent there.

However, nobody is discharged as "cured." The doctor's certificate always states that "the disease is arrested." After discharge, patients must report regularly for medical inspection. They must also—perhaps for the rest of their lives—continue to take the sulfa tablets. But that is a small price to pay, they feel, for the chance to return to life from a living death.

"It's just unbelievable," Dr. MacDonald said during our last breakfast before my departure. "You realize where this will all end, don't you. *I'll* be out of work!"

I was serious and perhaps a bit uneasy when I sailed to Makogai. But I left the island with sense of joy and hope. Miracles are being done. A new era has reached the island of the lepers.

Makogai has become so modern that even the nuns have begun to ride motorscooters. The fat nun from the shop came puffing down to the quay in veil and sun helmet on her motorcycle to say good-by. She drove slowly and carefully, in spite of the fact that she would have to hurry back to her work. She had good reason for driving carefully. A few months before she had lost control of her motorcycle and had steered smack into one of the huts and driven halfway up to the roof. As she was well padded by nature, she escaped reasonably unhurt from the accident. But several patients who had been getting well in the hut suffered severe relapses from the shock.

These modern times set everything topsy-turvy. One of the nuns who was in charge of Makogai's new movie house was forced to develop her own unique methods for combating the forces of modern life. The movies shown to the lepers came twice weekly from New Zealand, where they were not carefully chosen by a group of pious nuns. As a result, the movie nun felt it her duty to be the guardian of public morality by viewing the films herself before showing them in public. The trouble was that she was not equipped to be a censor. The movies were always rented, and so she was not free to cut or splice them in order to remove the objectionable parts. But she came up with an ingenious solution to the problem. During the performances she would sit beside the projector, and whenever there were signs of a scene she didn't think proper for the patients, she would put her hand in front of the lens and keep it there until the too-intimate kiss was over. She managed these moral eclipses with great skill, and I don't think it ever occurred to her that by catching the scene of seduction in the palm of her hand she was getting "unclean" hands in a way very different from the lepers.

When I returned to Suva, I tried to explain to Polly over the telephone that I had not gotten unclean hands from my visit to the island of lepers. But she refused to listen. "I warned you before you left. I'll not have anything more to do with you, do you hear? I don't want to see you near me! Or at any rate, not until you're sure you haven't been infected. What's that . . . ? The incubation period's five years . . . ? I see." There was a brief pause over the wire, then, "All right, then I'll see you in five years. Be good. Good-by!"

She slammed the receiver down so hard that the sound could be heard clear across the parlor of the Blue Lagoon. I suppose she was afraid that even a telephone conversation with me might prove infectious. I resigned myself to not seeing Polly for the next five years, but in vain. Next morning she was on the telephone again.

"Come at once," she said breathlessly, "there's no time to spare, you've got to come immediately. I don't care what I said yesterday. Yes, yes, bring all your bacteria with you, leprosy couldn't make me any more wretched than I am now. But hurry, you must come at once. I'm completely beside myself. Something terrible has happened . . . !"

The tragedy of the sea
and the comedy of love

Polly looked pale as a ghost. "You'd better have a drink," she said. She quickly filled two glasses, then announced, in a doom-filled voice, *"There's been a tragedy in our lives."*

As I looked around, I could see that it was going to be a tragedy all right. The stage was set for something like *Mourning Becomes Electra*, with Polly playing all the roles. All the props were in order. Whisky bottle standing ready for action. A stack of newspapers piled ominously on the floor. And a picture postcard lying face down in solitary splendor on top of the twelve-foot-long mahogany table.

"Is that the corpse?" I asked cheerfully, pointing to the postcard on the table.

Polly stared at me in horror. "You know! You know all about it!"

"Naturally," I said. "I'm the one who did it."

She shook her head in annoyance. "No, I can see you don't know anything about it. You wouldn't joke if you knew."

"Oh yes I would," I replied. "You forget that I have a very morbid sense of humor. Have some leprosy," I added, extending a reasonably clean hand.

The Tragic Muse turned her usual shade of red and looked as though she might burst into a volcanic frenzy. But no, that would have spoiled the act. The play must go on, no matter how stupidly the audience behaves. Polly turned her back to me, and continued the performance. "It's just too horrible for me to tell you. You'll have to read it for yourself. Here," she said, handing me the postcard, "read this, and then you'll understand."

I turned over the postcard and examined its brief message. *"Thanks for the introductions,"* it said. *"Hope to sail for Tokelau Islands on Joyita at beginning of October. Everything under control. Best wishes. Rudy."*

I read the postcard twice again before I gave up. "I don't get it. What am I supposed to understand?"

Polly downed another shot of whisky, then moaned, "Wait, you'll understand soon enough. You'll soon see what a terrible, terrible, terrible thing has happened!" With that she cleared her throat, wiped away a tear, and picked up the top newspaper from the pile. "Listen," she said, and then began to recite:

"The Joyita has disappeared on her way to the Tokelau Islands. Extensive searches have so far proved fruitless. It is feared that all on board have been lost. . . ."

The newspaper fluttered to the floor while Polly collapsed into a conveniently ready chair. Her groans joined those of the chair as both settled into a spell of gloom.

The scene changed to Ibsen's *Ghosts*.

"I loved Rudy as I would have loved my own son. I wanted things to go well for him. That's why I sent him to my friends in Apia. That's why I arranged for him to get on the *Joyita*. How could I have known I was sending him to his death? I only wanted to help him. And instead"—here her voice faltered, then dropped to a dreadful hush—"instead, *I have murdered him.*"

A sudden stillness filled the room. Dark clouds seemed to hover over the dining-room table. I put out my cigarette and started to suggest that perhaps Rudy hadn't been on the *Joyita* after all. But her eyes stopped me in mid-speech. Polly Thompson was clearly enjoying her drama, and she wanted no comforting words to spoil the scene.

"Read on," she commanded.

I reached for a pile of papers, and read on.

It had all happened during the past week, while I was cut off from news on the leper island. The *Joyita* story had made front-page headlines in all the papers. It was the biggest sensation in years, and the newspaper owners were playing it for all it was worth. They had dug out their boldest type faces (most of them hidden away since the end of the war), and suggested with an air of mysterious vagueness that the incident might develop into an international conflict.

This is what had happened . . .

The seventy-ton motor ship *Joyita* left Apia on October 3 on her way to the Tokelau Islands with twenty-five people aboard. Normally the trip should have taken forty hours. But by evening of October 5, the *Joyita* had not arrived. Fakaofa, the Tokelau island toward which the ship had been headed, telegraphed Apia to say that the ship must have turned back in mid-voyage. But the *Joyita* did not return to its home port. The authorities in Apia grew anxious, and an extensive search was begun. Seaplanes of the New Zealand forces stationed on Fiji searched the waters where the ship should have disappeared. All ships in the vicinity were asked to keep a lookout, and the Pan American and TEAL airlines took part in the search by rerouting their planes and making wide detours. But so far every effort had been in vain. No disabled ships had been reported. Neither wreckage nor survivors had been found.

The *Joyita* seemed to have vanished off the face of the earth. The sea had been calm as a lake on the day of her departure, and the weather had remained clear for several days afterward. Yet there was not a single trace of the missing ship. It was one of the strangest mysteries that had come along in years.

The *Joyita*'s disappearance seemed to be only the last chapter in an exciting and colorful history. For the *Joyita* was a lady with a past.

She had started out in life as a pleasure yacht for the movie star Mary Pickford. The ship had been built in 1931 in Los Angeles, and had traveled a golden path from Hollywood to Honolulu and Pearl Harbor, carrying some of Hollywood's most shining stars on her deck. Champagne flowed and ukuleles strummed while the luxury vessel cruised from one pleasure port to another. But those golden days disintegrated when the Japanese bombed Pearl Harbor. The *Joyita* was drafted into military service, and stripped of her civilian clothes. She was stripped so well, in fact, that by the time the war was over she was fit for nothing better than toting freight. Instead of screen stars on her deck, she had frozen fish in her holds. Her downfall seemed complete.

Yet romance was not dead on the *Joyita*. Not by a long shot. The ship was bought in 1952 by Dr. Katherine Luomola, an anthropologist living in Honolulu. And through Dr. Luomola, the *Joyita* once again played a leading role in a typically Hollywood drama. For Katherine Luomola had fallen in love with an English skipper named Dusty Miller, and Dusty Miller had long ago fallen in love with ships. Now, Captain Miller was at this time about forty, and there was nothing in the world he wanted more than to own his own boat. Needless to say, he saw more in Katherine Luomola than mere charm. One look at her and he knew his ship had come in. Katherine handed over the *Joyita*, and Dusty Miller in return handed over half his heart. The other half stayed on deck with the *Joyita*. For Captain Miller loved his ship beyond all else in the world. Everyone who knew him at the time has remarked on his tender feelings for the boat.

Unfortunately, Captain Miller's love for the *Joyita* far exceeded his talent as a businessman. He was a first-class skipper, but he knew nothing whatever about handling money. The *Joyita* was still being used to carry frozen fish from Canton and Christmas Island to Honolulu, but her finances were in bad shape. Captain Miller ran into debt and was asked, none too politely, never to show his face on the islands again. He sailed off to the Samoan Islands, and there the same story was repeated. Again, both ship and master were exiled. Their next—and last—try was at the port of Apia in the New Zealand sector of Samoa. But business there was just as bad. The ship had been laid up for more than five months after a single trip to the Tokelau Islands.

There was no doubt that the *Joyita* was a fine little vessel. Her refrigerated holds were so solidly lined with cork that the ship was considered virtually unsinkable. Unfortunately, Captain Miller did not inspire the same confidence. His never-ending debts had earned him a reputation in every port throughout the South Seas. In addition, rumors were circulating around the harbor to the effect that the ship was no longer in topnotch condition. Without cash, Captain Miller had been unable to provide adequate maintenance for the *Joyita*. He loved her with all his heart, but love alone can't keep rust off the bottom of a boat.

Katherine had suggested that Dusty sell the *Joyita*. The New Zealand Government was interested, but their interest soon faded when they heard the price: $70,000, and not a penny less. Katherine Luomola had paid only $17,000, but that affected Dusty Miller not the slightest. He loved his boat, and would accept nothing less than a king's ransom for it. The fact of the matter, quite obviously, was that Captain Miller did not want to sell his boat at all. He remained convinced that with just a bit of luck he could make a go of his ship.

And lo and behold, after six months of near-hopeless waiting Captain Miller was given his bit of luck. The Apia firm of E. A. Coxon & Company was interested in trying to establish a regular export of copra from the Tokelau Islands. They needed a good little ship, and, wonder of all wonders, they were willing to take a chance on the Miller-*Joyita* team. To say that Coxon's offer was generous would be a masterpiece of understatement. They offered not only to finance the entire venture, but to provide oil, food, and all necessary repairs as well. Dusty's "bit of luck" sounded like the chance of a lifetime. If the trip went well—and its success was all but guaranteed—Dusty and *Joyita* would be back in business for life.

The voyage was important to others too. Two members of the Coxon firm would be going along and bringing £1000 in cash ($2800) to pay for the copra. The New Zealand Government also had an interest in the trip; two of its officials would be sailing over to look into a few serious problems that had recently arisen on the islands, among them a grave shortage of drug supplies. Mr. Hodgkinson, the New Zealand Health Inspector, and Dr. Parsons, a government surgeon, were being sent with a large supply of drugs and the responsibility of investigating the matter once they arrived. Dr. Parsons would also be performing a serious operation while on the island; a case had arisen demanding the attention of a specialist, and the patient was considered too badly hurt to be moved.

Altogether there were twenty-five people on board the *Joyita* when she set sail from the port of Apia. Most of the other passengers were Polynesians heading home to the Tokelau Islands. There actually wasn't room for that many people, but ships are rare between the outlying islands and travelers are willing to undergo any kind of discomfort whenever the chance for transportation arises. Included on the passenger list was a woman with two small children returning home after a festive visit. And there was also a young radio operator named Joseph Pereira who had moved heaven and earth to get a place on the ship. His name had been inadvertently left off the passenger list, and Captain Miller had told him there was no way of rectifying the mistake. It looked as though fate itself had tried to keep Pereira safely on shore. But the young man had defied fate and had mobilized all his connections in order to get his name back on the list again.

Now eight days had passed without the slightest sign of life from the *Joyita*. There was a radio set on board, but Captain Miller was notorious for never keeping contact with stations on shore. Moreover, just before his departure the chief of Apia Radio had specifically ordered Miller to make radio contact every day between 10:00 A.M. and 4:00 P.M., out of consideration for the officials on board. Captain Miller was also told that the 2182 frequency, reserved for small vessels in distress, would be tuned in at all hours. But not a sound had been heard from the *Joyita* since its departure from the harbor.

Radio stations on every island flashed call signals across the sea. "Calling *Joyita* . . . calling *Joyita*. Give your position . . . give your position. Calling *Joyita* . . . calling *Joyita*. Over to you . . . come in . . . we are listening for you." Silence was the only reply.

Hundreds of reports came in from amateur operators who claimed they had received signals from the *Joyita*. But none of them were worth taking seriously. So many runaway rumors flew through the islands that I would not have been at all surprised if some old lady reported receiving a radio message from the *Joyita* on her knitting needles. The sensation seekers had their rumor aerials out, and the clamor was on.

The press, of course, took this opportunity to revive every similar story they could find in their files.

In September 1952 the motor vessel *Awahou* had disappeared on a journey between Sydney and Lord Howe Island. The ship and the eighteen men on board were never found. But in the *Awahou*'s case, at least there was an explanation for the disappearance. The ship had run into a typhoon and had sent out distress signals. When the radio was silenced, everyone knew what had happened.

More mysterious was the catastrophe of a ship off New Caledonia in July 1953. The motor ship *Monique* was on her way from the Loyalty Islands to Noumea, a journey of less than seventy-seven nautical miles. The ship had been in contact with Noumea during the evening and had reported all was well. But next morning, when Noumea tried to call the *Monique*, there was no reply. In dead calm weather the *Monique* disappeared without a trace, taking with her a total of 120 passengers of whom twenty were Europeans. Not even a piece of wreckage was left to tell the tale. There were many rumors, but no answers. The mystery of the disappearance of the *Monique* remains unsolved.

One of the more imaginative theories in connection with the *Monique* was that the ship had been sunk by flying saucers and that spacemen had carried the 120 vanished passengers off to a distant planet. The air was now thick with similar rumors about the *Joyita*.

This was just the thing for Polly. She immediately became as interested in spacemen as she was in men in general. She literally bombarded me with flying saucers that evening when we discussed Rudy and the *Joyita*, after I had plowed my way through the stack of newspapers. In a flash Rudy was snatched off to Mars, where he stood blinking signals at her. We stood on her veranda inspecting the heavens, and Polly pointed to the largest and most conspicuous planet: nothing less would do for Rudy. As it happened, the planet she chose was Venus. But I decided to let the distinction pass; if Venus was Mars to Polly, then Venus might just as well be Mars, and nobody would be the least bit bothered by it.

One of the newspapers revived a rumor about mysterious submarines in the Pacific. This paper revealed that when the *Joyita* arrived a bit late in Fakaofu on her first journey to the Tokelau Islands, the natives had come paddling out in canoes and said how anxious they had been over the delay. They had heard rumors of a Russian submarine sinking an American fishing vessel and carrying off the whole crew. The attack was supposed to have taken place near where the Japanese fishing fleets operate. The Russian motive, supposedly, was to throw suspicion on the Japanese and thus create friction between the United States and Japan. An angry Japan would be more amenable to negotiations with the Communist bloc.

"May we ask where this rumor hails from?" the newspaper demanded. "The natives on the Tokelau Islands have never seen a submarine. They know nothing about power politics. They are not even able to tell a Russian from a Japanese. Wouldn't it be a good idea to search for the origin of this fantastic rumor? Perhaps it would throw light on some of the recent 'mysterious' incidents in the Pacific."

Polly put down the editorial and moaned, "Oh, no, my poor Rudy! You *know* how he's always dreaded the idea of getting into a submarine. And now they're going to plunge him down to the bottom of this horrible ocean, and God knows what will happen. Maybe they'll send him to a slave-labor camp in Siberia. Yes, that's just what they'll do, I'm sure of it, those Russians are just . . ."

"Polly," I interrupted, trying to speak as calmly and as firmly as I could, "don't you think it's about time we gave both flying saucers and Russian submarines a rest?—at least until we know for sure whether Rudy was actually on board?"

Polly's lips curved down in disgust. "Your optimism amounts almost to a disease," she said. "I'm convinced Rudy was on board. I can sense it."

And she kept on sensing it until the next postcard arrived. Rudy's message was, as usual, succinct:

"Brother not in Tokelau Islands, now on New Hebrides. Found this out from English yachtsmen on cruise, who offered to take me there with them. Am on New Hebrides now. Heard about Joyita. Hope you weren't worried.   Best. RUDY."

"He hoped . . . He hoped I wasn't worried!" gasped Polly. "Why, the nerve. When I think of all I've done for him. You'd think he might at least have sent a telegram. But no, not him, I suppose it never even occurred to him that I might be sitting here thinking he'd been eaten by sharks or was working himself to death in a Russian slave camp. Have you ever heard of anything so inconsiderate in your life?"

"Well . . ." I began.

"That's what I thought," she answered. "Now don't just sit there staring at that bottle. Pour us a couple of drinks. The least we can do is toast Rudy's narrow escape."

With Rudy safe and sound somewhere on the New Hebrides, Polly completely forgot that there'd ever been a ship named *Joyita*. But while Polly put the disappearance out of her mind, the newspapers and the experts did not. Their chatter continued, and opinions multiplied faster than rabbits. Each expert had his own theory, and each disagreed with all the others.

The only expert I met who had anything sensible to offer was an old sailor whom I'd run into down at the harbor. He considered himself no expert at all, for he was willing to admit the truth—that he knew nothing whatever about what had become of the ship. Nobody else knew anything either, but that didn't prevent them from tossing theory after theory into the air with the fervent conviction of those who think that a guess is as good as a proof.

When I asked the old man what he thought had happened to the *Joyita*, he simply smiled and said, "Let me tell you instead about some of the things *I've* seen on this great and terrible ocean. I've sailed this sea all my life," he added, "and I know full well all the fearful things that can happen."

He sipped his beer and began telling me some of his tales. He told me of the dreaded Pacific typhoons that the natives call "the murdering wind." He told me of the terrifying Pacific thunder, a blaze of flaming lightning accompanied by a howling, hellish storm that can drive both ships and captains mad. He told me of the submarine volcanoes that on an innocently blue, dead-calm day can suddenly shake a ship to pieces with an insidious attack from the underworld of the Pacific. And he told me of the grim game of the waterspouts, the sky devils, who with long black tentacles whip the water up into a hissing witches' cauldron and dance a fiendish dance around the ship before attacking.

The old man finished his monologue by emptying his beer glass and wiping the front off his beard with a skilled backhand stroke.

"So you see," he explained, "there are many things that could have happened to the *Joyita*. I won't guess because I don't know. Nobody knows but the men who sailed on that ship. And nobody's going to know unless we find one of those men. There may be survivors. And they may not be found for a long time. Sometimes it takes years before we stumble across people shipwrecked on a desert island. But if there are survivors, they'll live. There's plenty of food, fruit and fish, to keep a man alive. And coconut milk is as good as water for curing a thirst. No, they'll live, and they'll be safe. No cannibals nowadays, and the only dangerous animals are the sharks. Well," he said as we stood up to leave, "all we can do is wait. And pray." He smiled and thanked me for the beer, then turned and disappeared into the crowds filling the harbor.

On my way back to the Blue Lagoon, I decided to stop in at the local newspaper office to pick up my afternoon ration of rumors. Even at a distance I could see that something was up. Hundreds of people were mobbed in front of the building, all clamoring for the chance to buy a paper. I managed to get one myself just before the edition was all sold out.

One glance at the front page and I could see why all the excitement. There were only two words, printed in the largest, heaviest type in the memory of man.

J OYITA F OUND

I could scarcely wait to read the rest of the story. Clutching my paper tightly, I hurried home to find out what had actually happened. Think of it, the *Joyita* found after a disappearance of thirty-four days—nearly five weeks!

But the new development had provided no answer. Just the

opposite. The mystery was now even deeper than ever before.

On the morning of November 10, the *Tuvalu* sighted a heavily listing ship drifting approximately ninety miles from Udu Point on the island of Vanua Levu. On drawing nearer they discovered that the ship was the *Joyita*. The missing boat had turned up in exactly those waters that had been most extensively searched. The vessel was listing heavily to port, but was not sinking. It was a simple matter to tow the ship in to shore.

But finding the *Joyita* didn't solve the riddle. For what had become of the twenty-five people who had been on board? A collision was out of the question, since neither bow nor hull had been damaged. It couldn't have been a waterspout, typhoon, or underground earthquake, for any kind of natural catastrophe would have destroyed the entire ship. No, something had happened, and the something was even more mysterious than the ship's original disappearance. A large part of the superstructure had been broken off, including the deck cabin. The passengers' property lay strewn in wild confusion across the deck. In the middle of the debris was found the ship's clock, which had stopped at ten minutes of twelve. There were vague traces of a fire or an explosion. Large parts of the cargo had disappeared, including all the sacks of sugar and rice which were known to have been on board. Many clues indicated some kind of plundering. People began talking about a pirate attack, especially since the £1000 belonging to the two English businessmen had also disappeared. Rumor hinted the biggest sensation in years. Pirates in the twentieth century! It made a fantastic story—a ship with a Hollywood past, a band of unscrupulous thieves, and murder on the high seas. But there was one rather odd hitch in the pirate theory. A tarpaulin had been temporarily rigged up on the quarter deck. It looked as though the people on board had sought shelter from the burning sun, thus protecting themselves from the worst enemy of those who are shipwrecked in the Pacific. But why then had they left the ship? It made no sense for twenty-five people to risk their lives on life rafts when their ship was still perfectly safe. Captain Miller, the businessmen, the health officials—everyone on board knew that the *Joyita* couldn't sink. Yet they had apparently fled the ship in a state of panic. Why? What could possibly have frightened them all away?

Nobody knew. And so the rumors began again.

Two pocket knives labeled "Made in Japan" were found on deck, and that started a new burst of international frenzy. The *Joyita* had sailed into a Japanese fishing fleet, and the men on deck had seen "something the Japanese didn't want them to see." So naturally the brutal Orientals had boarded the ship and murdered every human being on board. And naturally again, they had thrown all the bodies overboard in order to hide the evidence.

What is most amazing to me about rumors like this one is that people actually believe them. The Australian press immediately picked up the story and began broadcasting it from one end of the country to the other. The Fijian press went one better, and dug out of their files all the gruesome tales they could find of Japanese atrocities during the war. The authorities in Suva tried to counter the story by sending out a radio denial in what the Australian press referred to as "an ice-cold Oxford voice." The Sydney paper *Truth* announced that an aerial photograph of the *Joyita* surrounded by Japanese fishing boats, taken just before the ship had disappeared, was being kept in a safe in New Zealand military Headquarters on the Fiji Islands, where it was heavily guarded by armed soldiers. The Fiji English and the New Zealand press immediately replied that there was not a word of truth in the *Truth* editorial. The Japanese papers took the matter quite calmly. They simply printed a few lines about "wild rumors" and "how silly can people be," and for the most part ignored the entire furor.

But the wild rumors continued to grow. Angry men pointed out that since the *Joyita* belonged in Honolulu she was officially American. They inquired about the United States reaction with as much drama as though they expected, momentarily, to receive a declaration of war. The excited talk about "international complications" went on until a totally unexpected American reaction turned up—to Polly's enormous delight. The American turned out to be an expert on flying saucers, and he was convinced that the twenty-five passengers had been whisked off by spacemen. And there we were again. I decided to retire from active interest until this theory had gone the way of all its predecessors.

The saucer theory had been almost exhausted when the voice of America broke into the arena again. The voice came from a man named Budd Carew, who lived in Sierra Madre, California. And the answer this time was *mutiny*. "I knew both the crew of the *Joyita* and the conditions on board," said Mr. Carew. "There was a great deal of friction, and I'm not the least surprised by what happened."

Tukua had her own explanation for the disappearance. On the Fiji Islands there is an old custom that sailors must throw food into the sea to placate the anger of the sea gods. If there is a kava party on board, a cup of kava must be poured into the waves as a sacrifice to a thirsty god. But the foreigners on board the *Joyita* had had lots of whisky—foreign kava, Tukua explained—and they had not offered the gods a single drop of it. Therefore the inevitable had happened. Tukua shrugged. The sea gods had only taken their rightful revenge.

For some reason, the British authorities decided to surround the entire affair with the greatest secrecy. Naturally that stimulated the rumors even more. "It is indeed suspicious," thundered every editorial, and "It is clear that the answer to this mystery is being hidden by the authorities—we demand that the truth be exposed!" But if the British knew anything, they weren't saying. They only clamped down even harder on every security regulation. When the *Joyita* reached Suva, it was as difficult to get permission to go aboard as it would be to gain admission to a Russian munitions plant. But I was lucky, and one morning I climbed up onto the deck of the ill-fated *Joyita*.

It was a strange experience to stand on the ghost ship, surrounded by all the silent witnesses to the disaster. The sea had given back the *Joyita*, but the *Joyita* could not speak. Her masts, her deck, her planks had all witnessed a tragedy that had driven twenty-five people into terror and perhaps into death. But they had left no answer behind them on the ship.

Near me on the deck were some of those gentlemen who are known officially as experts. But the experts were no more talkative than the ship. The authorities had forbidden their breathing a word about what they might find. They tiptoed about, looking very expert indeed, and they all smiled as secretively as those anthropologists who, after reading the hieroglyphics, won't tell anybody whether the story is a clean one or a dirty one. Our lips are sealed, they smirked. And their lips would stay sealed until the maritime inquiry, which was scheduled for the following January in Apia.

Since Queen Salote was still in New Zealand, I had to find something new to fill in the waiting time. I decided to move to Samoa so that I could be on hand for the inquiry when it was held.

I managed to celebrate New Year's Eve in Suva before I left. The party took place at Polly's, and it was an unforgettable event. So unforgettable that my head still aches from the thought of it. The champagne flowed and Polly flowed boisterously with it. She drank herself into oblivion in order to forget the lengthening shadow of time. Polly knew, as we all do, that a year is only a fiction, an arbitrary fragment of time that is meaningless in itself. It's an illusion we've invented to stem our fear of infinity. We twist time into a circle, and fool ourselves into thinking it starts all over again every year. And Polly was trying desperately to fool herself.

As a matter of fact, we must all have been trying pretty desperately to fool ourselves. Or at least that's the only explanation I can give for the somewhat insane game with which we wound up the festive night. Champagne does odd things to people. It not only makes them happy, it makes them brave. The most dangerous experience of my life, including the Korean War, was when I squeezed into Polly's little Morris along with an incredibly large number of other happy guests and, with Polly at the wheel, went flying on two wheels along a narrow mountain road up to a rich man's villa high up on a cliff hanging over the sea. How we managed to get there alive I shall never know. Perhaps we accidentally spilled some champagne into the sea, and so won—without knowing it—the protection of those angry unknown gods whose vengeance had wrecked the *Joyita*.

The party at the villa reached its gay climax when a group of strong, handsome young men with whom Polly had been flirting outrageously, finally picked her up and tossed her head over heels into the swimming pool. It was a crude joke, but Polly knew how to take it. After she had been fished out of the pool she simply shook herself dry and laughed. "Thanks, boys! That was wonderfully refreshing, just what I needed." And with that she turned right around and plunged voluntarily back in. "Come on and join me," she shouted, as she floated in full array. There was no doubt about it; time may have taken its toll, but there was still good stuff in Polly Thompson.

When I woke up next morning, I had one of the worst hangovers in history. I lay back in bed and groaned bitterly over the stupidity of starting a new year with both a bang and a whimper. Here I had been about to make all sorts of high-minded resolutions—to correct this, to stop that, to do more of the good things and, all in all, to try to make myself into a Nobler Man. And how were these fine resolutions to be put into effect? With a drinking orgy and a king-sized hangover. I hid my face under the pillow and groaned again.

To make matters even worse, Tukua insisted on waking me as usual at 6:00 A.M. I was furious. Time after time I had tried to explain to her that there were mornings when I liked to sleep late. But it was no use. She understood what I wanted all right, but the girl was dead set against any kind of change. If it was to be 6:00 A.M. some days, then it would have to be 6:00 A.M. *all* days, and nothing I could say would make her change the routine. Now here she was again, with her sweet, careful knocking, yanking me awake after no more than an hour or so of sleep. I cursed furiously under my breath and tried to ignore both her and my tea.

But it was a damned good thing she did wake me up, for otherwise I would never have caught my plane. In my dissipated state I had completely forgotten my intention of flying to Samoa on New Year's Day. I leaped out of bed and cheerfully greeted the new day. The fact that Tukua had thoughtfully laid a few aspirins out on my tray helped matters enormously. With headache gone and Samoa before me I relished the thought that time, for once, was at my service. I could go back and redo what had already been badly done.

It was a beautiful moment. I looked happily out at Mrs. Hungerleider's jungle and contemplated the noble ways in which I would usher in the New Year again.

Had I lost my mind? No, not at all. Don't forget the date line. By flying from Fiji to Samoa I would cross the line and so gain a whole new day. When I arrived in Samoa it would still be December 31, and I would be able to celebrate New Year's Eve all over again, this time, I hoped, in a more suitably solemn manner.

I left Suva on a January morning and arrived in Samoa on a December afternoon of the previous year. I had planned to be smug as a sorcerer when, for the first time in my life, I would have managed to conquer time. But my plans were forgotten and my smugness lost when I saw where the date line had brought me. The seaplane landed on the glass-like water of an intensely blue lagoon, and as I stepped out onto the sands of an incomparably idyllic palm beach, I turned traitor and renounced every bit of love I'd declared for all other islands. Samoa is Paradise. There is no other name for it. With eyes wide open and propellers whirring, I had flown into the Garden of Eden.

Like Paradise, Samoa is hard to get into. Angels with flaming swords, transformed into drawn blue fountain pens, stood guarding the entrance, carefully choosing the Elect.

Luckily I had all the necessary credentials. The authorities on Paradise are very strict. Tourists must prove they can fly away again by handing over a paid-for return ticket to the angels in charge. The archangels of Samoa want no free-wheeling paradise seekers cluttering up their peaceful island; they had enough of that during the last century.

But once you do manage to get past the passport-control officials, you will find yourself heartily welcomed to Samoa. They don't like to let you in, but once you're there, they embrace you happily and say that they're glad you've come. Of course, they insist on your announcing, at regular intervals, that Samoa is the most wonderful place on earth. And you oblige, with pleasure. The only trouble is trying to find the right words to describe just how wonderful it really is.

There are the same palmy beaches and the same balmy flowers that you'll find on the other paradise islands. But between the palms grow cocoa trees which, with their colorful cone-shaped fruits in every stage of ripeness, look like newly trimmed Christmas trees all year round. The hibiscus bushes bloom like multicolored birthday cakes; they're so festive-looking that the Samoans love using them for decorations. They snip off the flowers, fix them like butterflies onto needle-thin palm strands, and build artistic flower pagodas in front of their houses. The pagodas are set out like welcome mats, bidding every stranger a "good day" and "do step in." And step in you do, because there is nothing in the world as open as a Samoan house.

Stepping into a Samoan house, by the way, is a lot easier than entering a house anywhere else. For there are no walls. A Samoan hut consists of an open-air dance floor covered by a thatched roof held up by poles. In case of rain there are blinds that can be rolled down on the windward side. Walking the dark roads of Samoa at night is like entering another world. Miniature palm hills rise on columns lit by oil lamps, and the light shines down upon each group of singing children. The tropical night is filled with a thousand melodies, all softly sung to the gentle accompaniment of ukuleles and guitars. The darkness itself seems to sing, and the handsome brown people, shaped like gods, dance and laugh.

But trying to describe Samoa is impossible. It can't be done in words. If I could hire a "talking chief," then the problem would be solved. He would say everything that needed saying. But Samoa's "talking chiefs" don't speak English, and that's a shame, for they are the most gifted orators in the world.

In America, when you go to pay a birthday visit to your old grandfather, all you bring is yourself and a suitable present. You shake hands, say "best wishes," and that's that. Try that on Samoa and you'd be disgraced for life. Grandpa would never talk to you again. On Samoa you hire yourself a "talking chief" and bring him along to make your speech. He's paid to open the floodgates of his eloquence in your behalf, and his words flow like cascades in a fountain. No paltry comments like "best wishes" or "happy birthday" from our "talking chief." No, what he says will go something like this:

"We pay tribute to you and greet you on this day—you, the pride and ornament of our family. In our ignorance and humility we turn to you to draw light from your wisdom as the flower turns to the sun. We are the children, you the father whose magnanimous support and wise guidance is the compass of our life and the helm of our souls. We know that you love us, and we reciprocate your love a thousandfold. . . ."

And so on. The talking chief can carry on like that for hours, and it sounds so beautiful and convincing that it's rather sad to have to admit that the inspired speaker simply gets intoxicated by words and by tomorrow will have forgotten every one of his beautiful clichés. But no matter. He will think up new ones when next he is commissioned, and so his problems are nil.

The best commission a talking chief can receive is a request for a tribute to Samoa itself. His love for the island is so great that he will deliver the speech free of charge. And the speech will be no ordinary one, such as those he is hired to perform. No, for tributes to his island he has a special reserve of the most poetic phrases he knows, and he will pile them lavishly, one on top of the other, when he sings his praises to Samoa. For the Samoan knows, even better than any tourist, that Samoa is indeed a paradise on earth.

So there I was. Back in the old year, and smack in the middle of Paradise.

Are there hotels in Paradise? Yes, there are. No less than four of them by my last count. It was off season, so I had no trouble finding a room. That is, if you could call it a room. It had only three walls. It was a good thing I had already got used to the lack of privacy in Suva, although by comparison Suva's hotel rooms were practically secluded. At least there I had doors. Open doors, but still doors. On Samoa there are not only no doors, there are no walls in which to put the doors that aren't there. But I must say the hotel service on Samoa is excellent. For a very modest payment I received not only a facsimile of a room, but a chambermaid to sleep with me in it. Samoans take the word "chambermaid" quite literally. The lady is expected, for her pay, both to make the bed and to be made in it. I'm afraid I offended my young lady by not accepting her offer. But how can you tell so generous a creature that if her face were a bit prettier and her feet a lot cleaner, then perhaps . . . ?

Besides, this was to be my second New Year's Eve, and I had sworn solemnly to celebrate it in a dignified and ennobling manner. This excuse, however, I kept to myself. I gave up in advance any idea of trying to explain to the chambermaid that I had traveled back to the old year in order to say Happy New Year to my better self. My chambermaid wasn't interested in my better self. It was the other one she wanted, the one I had left behind, I hoped, in Fiji.

Since I was the only guest in the hotel, it looked as though I'd have the place pretty much to myself. But solitude wasn't quite what I'd had in mind. It would be solemn all right, but not exactly ennobling. Besides, it would feel too much like any other night of the year. My problem was solved, however, when the hotel manageress, on hearing that I was from Denmark, immediately told me about an old Danish skipper who lived on the outskirts of town. I decided to surprise my fellow Dane with a New Year's visit. That, I thought, sounded suitably noble and fine.

Although distances in Apia are small, it took a long time for me to reach his house. There was so much to see along the way that I immediately fell into the wonderfully slow pace of the island. Nobody hurries on Samoa. There's all the time in the world to spend, and nowhere else to spend it. Even my watch seemed to slow down to a dreamy stroll.

I ambled along the coast-line road and admired the ranks of flowering Christmas trees. The Samoans, too, were flowering in the streets. They're not afraid of color in what they wear. Or perhaps I should say in what they don't wear. Two yards of flowered cotton around the waist and a flower behind the ear are all the well-dressed Samoan needs to feel properly arrayed. The remaining elegance, from shoulders to hips, is tailored only by God. There's no need for shoulder pads or other shaping tricks, for people here come equipped with the virtues we others have to buy by the yard. The brassière industry would go broke on Samoa. Young Polynesian girls need neither hoisting nor padding beneath their thin blouses or veils.

The missionaries who won their prudish battle on Fiji lost it on Samoa. The Samoan ladies cheated the missionaries at their own game. Not until the ravages of time decree that there are no more tempting sights to hide do the Samoan women hop into their high-necked, winsome little nightgowns. A Samoan lady dressed in missionary style is announcing that the time has come for her to retire from public life.

With their high-necked dresses, the missionaries also brought Christianity and churches. And if there's a scarcity of Western dresses on Samoa, it's more than made up for by the number of churches on Apia's main street. There are so many churches that Apia probably holds the world's record. With 3,500 souls and twelve churches, Samoa's capital outdoes the Eternal City itself.

"In other parts of the world our biggest problem is to get the natives to build churches," a Catholic priest told me. "But here we have to ask the Samoans for God's sake *not* to build any more churches."

And with the churches came the religion that has caused so much trouble in other parts of the world. For elsewhere the missionaries tried to bring in a Western God who not only demanded a new faith but who also insisted on new customs and morals as well. Many natives on other islands have been convinced that Our Father was a German factory owner with a villa and a car, a pompous gentleman who would admit no one to Heaven who was not properly dressed in collar, tie, and well-pressed trousers. And then there were the many tragedies to which the new moral concepts led. A typical story is that of the devout Polynesian who, having lived all his life in respectable bigamy, was told that his soul would be doomed to perdition. It was difficult for him to grasp that he could expect the forgiveness of this Western God only by brutally putting all his wives but one out into the street.

But on Samoa the clash between Christianity and the old way died in its tracks. The Samoans shuffled the cards, and they dealt themselves the winning hand. The result was that the Samoans wound up a lot happier than the missionaries. I once discussed the problem with an old Catholic priest. I met him quite by accident, and once more wondered at how strangely fate weaves its threads in and out our lives.

"I know they're all Christians," I said to him. "But are they good Christians?"

"My friend," he smiled, "ask me anything else, but not that. However," and here he looked innocently away, "if you *force* me to answer, I suppose I'd have to say, in all honesty, that even though the Samoans are not, from a strictly dogmatic point of

view, Our Father's best children, they are certainly His happiest.
And I daresay He'll probably find room for these happy children
in the Paradise up above."

The old priest gave me an arch glance. "This is just between
you and me, of course. I'd rather you didn't mention my saying
anything, ah, to that effect. I might be accused of heresy, you
know, and that's such a nuisance. Although I'd probably know
how to defend myself." The expression that suddenly crossed his
face looked very familiar to me, and I had an idea where I'd seen
it before.

"Do you by any chance know Father Cicero from Tukutuku?"
I asked.

The old priest looked at me in pleased surprise. "Indeed I do.
How do you happen to know him? Tukutuku is pretty far away.
It's not very easy to visit Father Cicero's island. Have you ever
been there?"

"No," I answered, "I met him on the ship coming over."

"Oh . . . and what did you think of him?"

I laughed. "That he was the happiest man I'd ever met in my
life."

"No wonder! You met him right after he'd been acquitted."

"Acquitted?"

"Yes. Didn't you know he'd been called to the Vatican to
defend himself against some charges made by a visiting bishop?"

"No. What were the charges?" I was frankly puzzled by the
whole affair. It had never occurred to me that Father Cicero's
secret might have involved a trial in the religious courts.

The old priest looked down and thoughtfully fingered his cross.
"The exact wording of the main charge was that he 'tolerated the
natives' indulgence in sinful practices.' "

"You mean free love?" I asked.

"Well," he answered, "not really. At any rate, the Church is
pretty much forced to close its eyes on that point. No, the real
problem was that they held dance parties."

"Dance parties!" I echoed. "Is that forbidden?"

"Yes . . . but you see it's their only entertainment. And then," he paused and smiled, "there was the little matter of wine. They brewed it themselves. And drank it."

"I know, Father Cicero told me about it. He said their home-made wine was delicious."

"He told you that? Well, it's true. He drank their orange wine. But the cardinals drink both red and white wine."

"And was that the line of defense he took at the trial?"

"No, he didn't put up any defense at all."

"And yet he was acquitted?"

"Yes. Because a pure heart is the best defense of all. Besides, he also had a defense counsel speaking in his behalf. But that's something he didn't know. And, in fact, he must never know about it. He's got to believe that pure faith and goodness can win."

"Well, who was the defending counsel?"

The old priest pointed modestly to himself.

"You?" I cried. "But how? Were you in Rome?"

"No, I didn't have to make a formal appearance. You see," he explained, "I was Father Cicero's predecessor on Tukutuku. He was my curate for a year or so before I left. That's why I was able to write to the Vatican and explain that after a long life on that island, I could guarantee that there were only two possibilities: either the Church must adapt itself to the people, or the people will turn their backs on the Church. I had taught Father Cicero that myself. And therefore I wrote to the Vatican that if anyone had to be punished for Tukutuku's being what it is, it ought to be I, and not Father Cicero. That's what I wrote. I'm an old man, and I'm sure God will forgive me my sin."

"What sin?" I asked.

"The sin of telling an outright lie. For it wasn't I who taught Father Cicero at all. It was he who taught me. Before Father Cicero came, my island was one of the most wretched places on earth. I forced those people into a religion so strict that it made their faith into a punishment instead of a pleasure. They saw me as God's policeman, and they respected me simply because they were afraid. They hated me, and, in a way, hated my God. I was furious and jealous when I discovered that my young colleague didn't share their hatred. And when I found out how he had won their friendship, I grew even angrier. He would go off to a small village on the other side of the island. To hold prayer meetings, he said. I thought it was suspicious that he held so many meetings in just the village that was farthest away from me and my vicarage. So one evening I sneaked out there to spy. I realized what was going on even from a distance. I could hear gay music and shouting. And when I got close up, I could see Father Cicero sitting happily on the side lines, encouraging this riotous dance party simply by allowing it to go on.

"Well, as you can imagine, the gaiety stopped the minute I appeared. I broke up the party, and next day I explained to them that both they and Father Cicero had sinned, and that Father Cicero would be sent away on the next schooner to Papeete."

"And then he left?"

"No, he didn't leave. Something happened, something I shall never forget. The following evening I heard some noise outside my house. I went out to see what it was, and found that the entire population of the island—men, women, and children, young and old, the sick and the strong—all of them had gathered before my house. At their head stood the island's old chief, a beautiful man with a long gray beard and a deeply compassionate face. When I appeared at my door they all fell on their knees. They stretched clasped hands imploringly toward me, and I saw tears streaming down their cheeks. I have never—before or since—experienced anything like it. A whole island, an entire little world, crying at my feet. I was moved because I thought they had come to ask my forgiveness. But I was mistaken. They had come to ask something far different.

" 'Stern father,' the old chief said, 'we have all come to you, our hearts sorrow-stricken and our tears overflowing, because we fear for the life of our island itself. For many years Tukutuku has not been a happy island. We have come not to accuse you, but to open our hearts. We think you have meant us well, but you are not one of us. You are different, and you have tried to make us different too. You have taken away our fathers' customs, and now we have become like ships without rudders; we have drifted away from all that we once were and now we do not know what we are. We were our fathers' sons, but now we are as orphans. In our desperation we prayed to our old gods, but they did not hear us. And we became mindful of your telling us they were dead. We turned to your God then, and we prayed: O great white Father, give us back our happiness, we beg you. Grant us, your unhappy children, a smile that may lighten our darkness. And the miracle happened. God, who once gave His Son on the cross, had mercy on us, and sent us once more His son. For we know not what else Father Cicero can be. Like the Son of Our Father, he has brought us love and kindness. Stern Father, in our bewilderment our hearts had grown wicked and hard. Father Cicero redeemed us from our sin; he became our light in the darkness. If you send him away, the sun will set, never to return. Therefore we pray and beg you in the name of the all-powerful white God to let us keep him who has become the Saviour and Redeemer of Tukutuku.'

"The old chief fell silent, and I stood there, looking out over a sea of faces wet with tears. Tukutuku wept, and for the first time I understood the naïve faith that shone from all those dark eyes. I realized that without my having willed it, I had sinned against these, God's littlest children. I too was forced down on my knees by my God, and my face too became wet with tears. Only for me they were the tears not of sorrow but of penitence and guilt.

"I asked them to go their separate ways. 'Go in peace,' I said. 'Tonight I wish to be alone with God. Come back tomorrow, and come in your most festive dress. For I think I will have glad tidings for all this island.'

"I stayed awake all that night, and at sunrise I called Father Cicero to my side. 'I have had it out with God,' I said, 'and I've now made up my mind. I shall leave, and you will stay. Tukutuku is your happy island, and yours it must remain. But I will not leave for another six months, for I still have much to learn from you.'

"In the early morning they came back, and again I stood with an entire island at my feet. They were festively dressed, but their faces were solemn and anxious. I made my announcement, and suddenly their faces lit up as radiantly as did those of the shepherds long ago near Bethlehem. Again I was overcome by tears as they humbly came up one by one to cover my hands with kisses of joy and gratitude.

"And then they danced a dance the likes of which the world has never seen!" The old priest smiled as happily as though he were hearing the story of Tukutuku for the very first time.

"And since that day," he concluded, "Tukutuku has been Father Cicero's happy island. The natives were allowed to keep both their faith and their naïve happiness, because I lied when that happiness was endangered. May God forgive me."

I could not find it in my heart to tell the old priest that he was also lying to himself when he called the Samoan's happiness naïve. As the guardian of biblical morality, he needed—like the Church—to close his eyes to the facts. I often wondered how much the missionaries were aware that Christianity had actually helped make the free-love life of Samoa an even freer one. The old faith, with more devils than gods, had many strict rules. When those rules were violated, both devils and gods demanded fierce retribution. Every facet of pagan love life had been surrounded by the taboos of superstition; those who sinned against the taboos were resigned eternally to the torture chamber of the avenging devil.

But Christianity offered a white God whose love "passeth all understanding," a God who forgave and forgot so long as His broken rules were atoned for. The Samoans were quick to embrace Him as the patron of both heavenly and earthly love. They recomposed the solemn minuet of Christian morality into a hula-hula in which all steps were equally good. A Samoan goes to church several times each Sunday, and sings each time with such spirited piety that Our Father must rejoice in His heaven. In the intervals between performances, the Samoan walks back to his hut and just as piously (and as spiritedly) forgets those commandments concerning the flesh. As a result the Christian religion on Samoa has become the gospel of free love.

The Gospel was easy to see in the streets. Not free love itself—although that wouldn't have surprised me—but its fruits. The Samoans play fair with love. The so-called free love of the West is not free at all, for it cheats love by stopping halfway. Sexual freedom is exalted, but its consequences are not. Children are avoided at all cost. The Samoan girl, on the other hand, welcomes a child from her lover. She welcomes it so much that, as one noted anthropologist has told me, Samoa has set the world's record in breeding as a result. And I could see the truth of this on my very first day in town. The streets are filled with children; playing fair with love on Samoa has resulted in more than half the population being under eighteen years of age.

As I continued my stroll down Apia's main street, I stopped to stare at the twisted hulks of wrecked ships lying along the beach. Those ships are a grim reminder of the ways in which the gods have always protected Samoa.

Whenever a new paradise was discovered in the Pacific, the white men sent their missionaries there as the forerunners of the businessmen and warships. The islands were occupied and annexed in the name of religion, the flag, and civilization. The white men came to spread culture, or so they said. But they expected a few coconuts in exchange for the culture they brought. On most islands it worked fine. But not on Samoa. There the white men found to their indignation that the Samoan coconut was a lot harder to crack than they had expected.

Now usually this culture-spreading worked on a first-come, first-served basis. The first foreign power to arrive simply won the prey for its own. But in Samoa's case, the cultural attack was launched simultaneously by no less than three great powers—England, America, and Germany. This was in the good old days when international conflicts were discussed with guns, and all three proud nations sent fully armed ships to prove their honorable intentions.

These grim, fire-breathing vessels must have looked strangely ominous among the peaceful canoes of the blue lagoons, but the Samoans weren't the least bit upset. They loved every minute of it. The cheerful folk of the sunshine islands had always craved a bit of excitement in their humdrum everyday lives. They rallied to the cause, and became overnight the world's most energetic amateur politicians. The Samoans are born speakers, and they love nothing better than to wage a friendly war with their tongues. They were not the least bit disturbed by all the missionaries being in violent disagreement over the one true God. The Samoans chose the God they liked best—Catholic, Baptist, or Methodist— and in that way also got a heaven-sent chance to argue the matter with all their religious opponents. The warships and guns of the Christian world didn't bother them either. Formerly they had fought each other only with words; now they lined up behind one of the three powers and threatened each other with the guns of their choice. To the Samoans, it was all just a new game. And a very funny one at that.

The foreign would-be conquerors stood in the middle of the stage and roared at each other like the heroes they pretended to be, while the Samoans scurried back and forth in the wings. The backstage players switched so many cues that the white men up front lost their way and stood helpless in the impenetrable jungle of Samoan politics. The result was that this peaceful people, with their firm belief that all the good gods protect Samoa, nearly threw the three powers into all-out war. It was as upside-down and inside-out as could be. The Samoans, who were supposed to have been the pawns, instead became the players in this game of chess with the foreign powers. The situation came to a head in 1889, when the warships tossed more menacingly than ever on the happy lagoon at Apia. The guns were ready to fire for what was called in those days an "intolerable encroachment on national honor." The great political jukebox played its familiar song, and it looked as though only heaven itself could intercede to prevent the war.

And heaven itself did intercede. Not for the foreign powers, who had each been praying to their own avenging God, but for the Samoans. Moments before the first cannon were to be fired, a Pacific typhoon came thundering out of the blue and blasted down on the floating fortresses. It happened so suddenly that only the British battleship *Calliope* managed at the last minute to whip out of the lagoon and ride out the storm on the open sea. The Germans had their armored ships battered into scrap metal on the coral reef. Hundreds of lives were lost in the foaming surf, and the rusty skeleton of the German warship *Adler* still lies on the beach opposite Apia's main street as a perpetual warning to others.

The storm cooled the great powers off. With their battleships wrecked, they settled down to solve the problem by mediation. The English decided they were in enough colonial hot water elsewhere and withdrew, leaving Samoa to be shared between Germany and the United States. The Germans received Western Samoa's two rich islands of Upolu and Sawai'i, while the Americans took the Eastern Samoa island of Tutuila which, in the bay of Pago Pago, has the best natural harbor in the entire Pacific. As a consolation prize, the United States also received the toy islands of the Manua group. When war broke out in 1914 the New Zealanders landed in German Western Samoa and occupied it without resistance. The Germans surrendered by saluting stiffly, while the Samoans simply stood back and smiled at the foolishness of these new white men who had done what they called "liberating" Samoa. "What are you liberating us from?" they asked. The Germans. "Oh, well, they weren't so bad; you just had to get used to them." Will you co-operate with the New Zealanders? "Of course we will, why not?" And so ended another chapter in the stirring saga of Samoa. Western Samoa became a New Zealand mandate, first under the League of Nations, then under the

United Nations. But ask any Samoan who owns Samoa. He'll tell you the only right answer: "Why, we Samoans of course. Who else?"

And who else indeed. While all this uproar was going on, the Samoans sat back and had a wonderful time as happy, interested spectators. They talked and argued and made up new rules. They went along with the Germans because for the most part the Germans left the Samoans to themselves. They teased the New Zealanders because they took themselves so seriously. They accepted the United States for its cigarettes and chewing gum and they applauded the American cowboy. They went unconquered simply because they were indifferent to their conquerors. They ignored the foreigners and refused to let themselves be civilized. Like carefree chickens they scratched in an imported civilization and picked up a grain every now and then. But only the tastiest and most colorful grains would they touch. They were Samoans, and Samoans they intended to remain.

Considering the way a Samoan spends his week, it's impossible to blame them for wanting to remain as they are. On Friday they work a little in their gardens and plantations. On Saturday they prepare for Sunday. On Sunday they go to church several times, dressed to the teeth, and in the intervals fortify themselves with feasts and boisterous gatherings. Monday is used for recuperating from Sunday. On Tuesday they fish or go visiting to discuss politics and local news. They play cricket and football. Wednesday and Thursday are spent in the same pleasant way. And on Friday they start all over again.

The energetic gentlemen from abroad are excited and morally indignant about this on behalf of themselves and the profit principle. Everyone must work, they preach.

Why? ask the Samoans.

If you work you can make lots of money. You can have fine houses like ours with windows and walls. You can have tailor-made trousers, automobiles, and all the wonderful things hanging on the evergreen Christmas tree of civilization.

Now what would we do with all that? reply the Samoans, and go ambling on through their languid, peaceful days.

They live coolly and cheaply in the airy palm huts which they've built themselves for only a few cents. They need no cars because they're never in a hurry; they'd much rather walk. A Samoan wardrobe consists of two yards of colorful material, and jewelry is fished from the coral reef or plucked from trees. They live their lives in a bountiful garden without forbidden fruits. They know their island is a paradise, and they know why they were put in it. For God to them is a Samoan, and they manage His earthly branch.

Politics and free love are not Samoa's only forms of recreation. Far from it. For Apia has a splendid movie house, and there are four different shows a week. Each movie is shown to a packed house of enthusiastic Samoans, most of whom are younger than the films themselves. It takes at least five years for Hollywood's newer productions to travel to Samoa, and most of the pictures are a great deal older than that. Newsreels are saved from the year one, and thrown in helter-skelter regardless of their age. My biggest surprise in Apia came when, sitting in the theater watching a newsreel, I suddenly caught a glimpse of myself as a newly arrived war correspondent in Korea six years before. The most popular films, however, are the American Westerns. The Samoans find love and kisses boring; they can do plenty of that sort of thing themselves. What they like instead is to see lots of wild fighting and shooting, with galloping horses and trotting Indians to carry the gay scramble on. And they don't take their Westerns sitting down, either. They gallop, trot, fight, and shoot right along with the heroes on the screen, and enjoy it, I'm sure, even more than the actors themselves.

Near the movie house is Apia's only "dance establishment." One glance at its façade was enough to tell me what was going on within those walls. This unassuming temple of entertainment was called "The Moana," and from that I could guess the rest. With a thought of my Moana from Tahiti I marched resolutely on.

On the other hand, "Catholic Hall," an auditorium next door to the Catholic Cathedral, was really used for dancing. With admirable tolerance the Catholic fathers have made their hall available for wild Polynesian versions of the imported jitterbug. Alcoholic drinks are forbidden, but that makes no difference to the Samoan teenagers who are already so drunk on jazz and rhythm that even the reverend cathedral next door starts to rock and roll.

Catholic Hall had a very different atmosphere, however, when it was turned into a courtroom for the maritime inquiry on the *Joyita* disaster. The big event was long overdue, and the reason for the delay was quite obvious: the commission, together with its experts, had failed to solve the mystery. They had found out a little bit about what had happened on the night of the disaster. But they still had no inkling whatever of what had become of the twenty-five people on board.

While waiting for the inquiry I had picked up a new rumor which sent me off on a journey to Pago Pago in American Eastern Samoa. The new rumor had been whispered in my ear with the greatest secrecy: The *Joyita* mystery was a case of poisoning and opium smuggling, and what's more, Captain Miller had been seen on the streets of Shanghai just two weeks ago! It sounded fantastic, but my source seemed trustworthy. A man in Pago Pago had proof, he said. Aha! said I, and set off to track down that man.

The trip to Pago Pago as a deck passenger aboard the *Isabel Rose* was an ordeal. Our voyage took half a night, and the ocean tossed in sideways swells that made the ship roll around like a whale that had swallowed a distillery. I lay on deck pretending I was a sardine. It was not difficult, since I was tightly sandwiched in between a heavy, inflated matron and a talking chief who looked like a hippopotamus traveling incognito. The matron lay half fainting from seasickness, with her left breast cradled in my hat, which I had put between us in an attempt at self-protection. By a lucky stroke of fate, our hat and brassière sizes were respectively the same. When she had to go to the rail, I was left playing the castanets with her false teeth, which she trustingly deposited in my hand. The weather was so rough that the chief flanking me on the other side just managed to inform me that he was a talking chief before seasickness paralyzed his vocal chords completely. He said not another word until we arrived at Pago Pago's harbor. He was the only silent talking chief I've ever met.

Pago Pago became famous both for its American naval base and for its musical-comedy-style policemen. They used to march proudly through the streets in black shirts with bright-red hems, equally bright-red belts and turbans, and nothing else. They were called Fita-Fitas, and their enthusiasm for their jobs went with the name. At first the policemen on Pago Pago were equipped with traditional American-style buttoned-up uniforms. But the result of all this unaccustomed wrapping in the heat was that all the policemen caught colds. Not until the Americans designed the new chorus-girl uniforms did the Fita-Fitas stop sneezing.

And speaking of sneezing, I might mention that in spite of its perpetual summer Eastern Samoa's capital has the most cold-catching climate in the world. Pago Pago lies just below the mountain known appropriately as "Rainmaker." The mountain does exactly what its name implies; it snatches all the clouds it can find, chews them up, and transforms them into rivers of rain. It was this perpetually damp climate that inspired Somerset Maugham's famous short story *Rain*. The infamous Sadie Thompson Hotel is still to be found in Pago Pago, but it has had to endure the humiliation of being converted into a warehouse.

As a substitute for the old Sadie Thompson, the Americans have built the ultramodern, delightful Rainmaker Hotel, which is the only good hotel you'll find anywhere on the Samoan Islands. It's also the most expensive, and payment must be made in dollars. But hard currency at the Rainmaker buys a lot of Western-style soft comfort.

Pago—as the town is called by its own residents—is a small, tropical, idyllic bungalow-town with the most cozy prison in the world. The prison is set up right in the middle of the market place, so that the prisoners behind bars may follow everything that's going on in town. For seven years the Samoan Chief Napoleon sat behind those bars killing time by composing wistful jazz tunes. Many of his songs are now known throughout the Pacific.

Although Napoleon was sentenced for murder, he had a good reputation in the town. His murder had been one of the nice, pleasantly acceptable sort that nobody really minds. A hot-blooded Samoan had assaulted one of Napoleon's pretty daughters; like any angry father anywhere else in the world, Napoleon lost his temper. He hit the cad over the head with something hard, and accidentally killed him. The American judges figured the deed worth a ten-year sentence, but after seven years of good musical behavior, Napoleon was released. To compensate for his long prison term he was given a lucrative position in the American foreign service. Frankly, I find it incredible that Hollywood has never come out with a musical about the musical murderer, Chief Napoleon of Pago Pago.

And while I'm at it, let me ask why Walt Disney has never made a motion picture about the shark off the coast of Samoa who appears whenever you sing for him. The musical shark is an American subject, and I'm sure he'd be pleased to pose for the cameras. In addition, he has a friend who's a turtle and the turtle's as talented as he.

I learned about the shark and the turtle from the manageress of the Rainmaker Hotel. A few other guests and I had been standing around, asking her questions about the island. Naturally, we were pretty skeptical when she got to the musical shark. "Why don't you all go out and see for yourselves?" she asked. We were fairly sure she was pulling our legs, but obediently we prepared for the worst and followed all her instructions. We crammed our pockets with candy and lollipops. Was this for the shark or the turtle? No, for the children. What children? The children in the village where it took place. They sang when you gave them the candy. Oh, we saw. We saw the biggest practical joke of all time descending on our innocent shoulders. Should we also bring some salt to sprinkle on the shark's tail? No, that wouldn't be necessary.

And our skepticism wasn't necessary either. The instructions worked, and when we reached the village dozens of children appeared out of nowhere and lined up for their chocolates. They knew we would have the candy, and they knew what the price for it was. They would have to sing for the shark and the turtle. And this they did, after lining us up very neatly on a rock looking over the bay.

The bay was the circus ring, and both performers appeared exactly on schedule. After the children had sung for about ten minutes, a large turtle came poking its head out of the pale-green water. It swam around the ring a couple of times, then waved good-by with its flippers and disappeared. The juvenile chorus then changed to a song about the shark, and sure enough, after a suitably dramatic build-up, His Excellency himself came nose first out of the sea. With amiable condescension and the toothy smile of a prima donna he sailed on a triumphal tour around the small circus ring of the bay before waving good-by with his fins and shooting to the bottom with a tail shimmy as coy as that of a Disney mermaid.

"And now we want the explanation," announced a matter-of-fact American who'd come along on our trip. "What's the gimmick?"

But there was no gimmick, no trick, no explanation. The performance had been thoroughly checked. The village children did not secretly throw soft-centered chocolates out to the fish. The only explanation anyone can offer is that the two sea creatures simply feel like appearing whenever they hear music.

Pago Pago is nowhere near as picturesque now as it once was. The Fita-Fitas are gone, and the American sailors have gone with them. The musical comedy is not quite as gay as it once was, but Chief Napoleon's songs are still sung and the sharks and the turtles still listen.

Life was so cozy on Pago Pago that I nearly forgot the insidious purpose of my visit. In case you've forgotten too, I was there to track down the man with the clue to the *Joyita* mystery.

One day while I was ambling, as usual, down the street, I bumped into a man with a large bottle in his hands. One look at his face and I knew my search was over. I whispered the name of my source, showed him all my credentials, and together we sneaked off to a bar to discuss the matter.

"Do you have the proof?" I whispered urgently.

"Yes, here," he whispered back, offering me the large, nearly empty bottle he had been carrying in the street. "I've had it analyzed, in fact I've just come back from the laboratory, and now my worst suspicions have been confirmed. It's poison! One of the world's most deadly poisons! And this bottle," he paused and dropped his voice to an almost inaudible murmur, "belonged—to—Captain—Miller!"

I stared blankly.

"Surely you understand what this means?"

"No, tell me."

He leaned forward across the table and began his sinister tale. "During the Pacific war a precious load of opium was hidden on one of the remote South Sea islands. Captain Miller and his fellow conspirators managed to get hold of the map showing the position of the hidden treasure. But Miller didn't have the cash to finance a trip to the island. So—he waited for his big chance. When Coxon's made their contract with him, he knew he had the whole thing sewn up. Naturally they knew nothing about it. They paid for the trip, gave him free supplies and—here's the payoff—provided him with a thousand pounds in cash to live on until he could get rid of the opium! Only the doctor, the health inspector, and all those Polynesian passengers threatened to put a snag in his plot. So-o, there was only one thing for Miller to do."

I waited expectantly, my heartbeat hammering away so fast I could scarcely catch my breath. What *would* Miller have to do?

"Murder," he said softly. "Murder on the high seas."

"But how?"

"Oh, it was easy," my informant shrugged. "Miller faked some kind of engine disorder. Poisoned the crew. Then waited in the prearranged place for the opium-smuggling ship that was being manned by his mob. The passengers were all forced overboard at gunpoint. Miller and his men got rid of the evidence, then set off for the opium island on the other ship. Now he's in Shanghai."

"Wow," I said.

"That's right," he said. "And this bottle is the final proof. Now don't whisper a word of this to anyone. You know what'll happen if Miller and his men find out we're onto him."

I nodded solemnly and sneaked away.

I would never have whispered a word of this grim tale to anyone had I not discovered that I was apparently the last person in Pago Pago to whom the man with the bottle had confided his story. He had sworn to each of them that he would take poison himself if his tale were not the honest-to-God truth. Most people I met seemed to think he should have done so.

Back in Apia at the maritime inquiry I was ready to take poison myself over the fact that most of the witnesses were more concerned with saving their own skins than with helping to find out how twenty-five people aboard the *Joyita* had lost theirs. This was particularly true of the men who were called "the responsible authorities." Whatever their authority might have been, it had not been responsible.

The *Joyita* herself proved the best witness of all. The ship, for all its silence, was able to speak all too eloquently about some of the reasons for the disaster. And the ship was able to point a none too flattering finger toward those who bore the blame.

The experts had examined the ship from top to bottom, and bit by bit, like a jig-saw puzzle, they were able to piece the story together.

That the ship had been hit by some sort of catastrophe was fairly certain. When had it happened? At ten minutes to twelve, said the ship's clock. Day or night? The light switches testified all the lights had been turned on, so it must have been night.

How long after the *Joyita* had left Apia? The fuel supply on board could give the answer. The firm in Apia knew how much oil had been delivered. When what was left had been deducted and what had been used compared with the average oil consumption per nautical mile, it showed that the *Joyita* had covered about 243 miles before her engines had stopped. With the *Joyita's* normal speed in good weather, that would have placed the disaster at half past nine on the evening of October 4.

So something had happened on the night of October 4 between nine-thirty and ten minutes to midnight. But what?

Here the *Joyita* began to take over the case for the prosecution.

One of the *Joyita's* two diesel engines had been in hopelessly bad condition on the ship's departure. Old Mrs. MacCarthy could testify to that.

I got her evidence in advance, one evening when we were sitting in her garden and talking about Henry. Old Mrs. MacCarthy's only wealth was children. She had borne many herself, and when they had flown from the nest it was more a sorrow than a relief, in spite of the family's limited income. To the Polynesians, children are life's greatest pleasure, and Mrs. MacCarthy comforted herself by adopting new ones as the others grew up.

"We took Henry when he was quite small," she told me sadly. "He was always such a good boy. We watched him grow up, marry, and welcome his first son into the world. I felt uneasy when he took that job as an engineer on board the *Joyita*. I had heard so many rumors about that ship and Captain Miller. They were to have left on Saturday, but late that evening Henry came home and told me the departure had been postponed till Sunday. They had worked hard all day to repair one of the diesel engines, but it was still out of order. Sunday afternoon he came home again and said it was hopeless to get that diesel engine to function properly. But now they were probably going just the same. Captain Miller had said something to the effect that they could carry on with the repairs while they were traveling. I tried to persuade Henry not to go, but he said it was too late to jump ship. It was as if he had a foreboding that something would happen. 'Take good care of my wife and son if anything should happen to me,' he said before he left."

Mrs. MacCarthy spoke from her heart when she stood in the witness box. Hers was the voice of all the mothers and wives of those who had been on board the ship. But her evidence was dismissed as pure hearsay. What the commission wanted were facts.

And they got facts. Mr. Sutherland, who had previously been an engineer on the *Joyita*, appeared and corroborated Mrs. MacCarthy's story. He could assure them that in his time, too, they had had trouble with the diesel engines whenever the weather was bad. And engines rarely improved by being inactive so long without maintenance. No, Mr. Sutherland was quite sure those engines had been in bad shape when the *Joyita* left port.

Apia's harbor master was called to the stand. Why had he permitted the *Joyita* to leave the harbor when it was known that her engines were out of order?

Strangely enough, the harbor master had known nothing about it. No one had mentioned to him that the engines needed repair. And he had, incidentally, no authority to hold back a ship sailing under a foreign flag, even if he *had* known its engines were in bad shape. The *Joyita* was registered in Honolulu and was therefore an American vessel.

The court raised another question. Where was it written that foreign ships didn't have to comply with the harbor master's instructions? In some ordinance or other. Which one? The harbor master didn't know.

Had he noticed anything wrong with the diesel engines when he piloted the *Joyita* out of the harbor? No. There had been no piloting. Wasn't that a violation of harbor regulations? Well, yes, actually it was. But the regulation had not been strictly enforced in years.

Next the court climbed the social ladder up to tall, thin Mr.

Smith, who at the time in question had been New Zealand's Acting High Commissioner on Samoa.

Had the government representative no misgivings about sending two officials to the Tokelau Islands on a ship which according to everybody was not in a condition to go to sea?

The reply was startling. The Acting High Commissioner had not known that the two officials were going with the *Joyita*. Wasn't the Government supposed to approve their travel arrangements? Yes, but that would have been the health authorities' responsibility, not the High Commissioner's.

In Apia, where everybody always knew everything about everybody else, suddenly there was nobody who knew anything at all. It was very strange.

The experts held the floor again. There had been another fault in the *Joyita*. Some years ago the ship had had a new superstructure built. The work must have been carried out by an unqualified ship's carpenter, for it was badly put together and unsafe. The deck cabin was not properly secured, and the planks themselves were so rotten that a strong sea could easily wash the superstructure or a large part of it overboard. And that apparently was just what had happened.

The examination of the *Joyita* had also disclosed that some pipes below the deck were half-rusted, and leaked. These pipes pumped sea water to the engine-room cooling system, and it was quite certain that the men on board the *Joyita* had not discovered that they were leaking. It was impossible to get at the pipes without breaking up the deck, and the deck planks above the pipes had not been touched. The defective pipes hadn't been discovered until the *Joyita*, after being pumped dry on shore, still drew water. The sound of water seeping in had been reported by a night watchman on board. He could hear it only because of the deathly stillness on the ship.

The *Joyita* had now revealed so much herself that a reconstruction of the first act of the drama was now possible.

On the evening of October 4 the diesel engines had stopped. Either the cooling system had broken down or water from the leaking pipes had entered the engine room. An electric auxiliary pump in the middle of the deck showed that after the engines had stopped an attempt had been made to pump the ship dry. This pump on deck indicated that by then the engine room was already under water.

The next silent witness was the ship's radio, which was set on the 2182 frequency, the wave length reserved for small ships in distress. So they had tried to send out distress signals as the *Joyita* had drifted helplessly at the mercy of wind and waves, with water still rising in the engine room. The radio had probably been in order, but the batteries might have been weak or ruined by sea water. And a defect in the connecting lead to the aerial, apparently an old, undiscovered damage, would have made it impossible to send sufficiently strong signals even with good batteries.

So far everything seemed clear. But what had happened after that?

According to calculations, the *Joyita* had been in waters with plenty of islands. It would have been easy to let some strong men try to row ashore and summon assistance. Why hadn't that been tried?

This the representative of the Coxon firm could, unfortunately, explain. There had been no lifeboat on the *Joyita*.

But surely the ship had had a lifeboat?

Well, yes . . . yes, but it had been left in Apia.

Left in Apia?

Yes. Before the departure he had been out to discuss the final details with Captain Miller, and when he left the ship he had rowed back to shore in the lifeboat. His house was close to the beach and it was nearer than having to be sailed all the way to the harbor. But hadn't he sent the lifeboat back to the *Joyita*? No, Captain Miller had said he didn't need it. Didn't need it? No; on the Tokelau Islands they only used the native canoes, which could get across the coral reef more easily. And if a lifeboat were needed on the way? Captain Miller hadn't mentioned that. And had he, who had chartered the ship and had an interest in its being well equipped, not protested against the lifeboat being left behind? No again. When the captain said he didn't need it, he had thought no more about it.

And so the lifeboat had been used merely to get this man ashore and save him a small trip around the harbor? Well, yes, you might put it that way.

The *Joyita*'s only lifeboat had been lying safely on shore when the ship was in distress. Had there been life rafts and life belts on board? Yes, several rafts and plenty of life belts. Had the *Joyita* had sails which could have been hoisted if the engines failed? No. Could the *Joyita* have reached land if there had been sails? Yes. Were the life rafts equipped with oars? No. Could they be maneuvered, then, in any particular direction? No. You mean they would just have drifted with the current? Yes.

The *Joyita* had long ago delivered her own verdict of "guilty" for the men who shared the responsibility for the disaster.

But what had happened to the twenty-five on board? Well, there were some possible explanations.

It could have been that while the heavily listing vessel drifted it had been struck by a strong sea, which had washed part of the rotten deck cabin overboard. It was possible that some of those on board had been washed away with it and drowned. But it was unlikely that all the passengers would have been in the deck cabin. Could the life rafts and life belts also have been washed overboard? No, said the former engineer, Mr. Sutherland. The life-saving equipment was securely lashed to the deck. Even the strongest sea could not have torn it loose.

We were now in the realm of guesswork. If the disaster theory were right, and some of the people on board had lost their lives, could an understandable panic have led the survivors to assume that the ship would sink and that their only chance was to seek refuge on the life rafts? No. Captain Miller would never have allowed it. He knew the ship couldn't sink, and at the same time he was so attached to his *Joyita* that he would rather have gone down with his ship than abandon her. That he should have been one of the victims of the deck cabin was not likely either. In a crisis the captain's place is in the wheelhouse, and the wheelhouse was undamaged. But then, even supposing the captain and the other experienced sailors on board were dead, might it not be assumed that the passengers had left the ship in terror? No, not likely. These islanders who spend half their lives at sea know from past experience that so long as a vessel doesn't start to sink it's a far safer place than the rafts. If they had stayed on the ship they would have been saved. There was plenty of food and drink, including a supply of Samoa's famous illegal "jungle beer," which aroused the only laugh of the entire inquiry. It was announced that just before the bottles of home-brew were to have been examined, they had all mysteriously exploded!

Another riddle was that the planes taking part in the search had not seen the *Joyita*, although the area in which the ship was found had been searched with special care. There were varying explanations, said an air-force representative. Over a limited area— as, for instance, a lake—it's 100 per cent sure that the search will be effective. But in the open sea you can't count on being more than 50 or 60 per cent certain. They had searched for 215 hours, and the area had been extended as far as the New Hebrides and the Loyalty Islands. Because of the great public interest in having the *Joyita* mystery solved, they had gone beyond the limits of an effective search. The crews had been overworked. Normally a man cannot sit by a radar screen for more than forty-five minutes at a time. His eyes get tired and he starts seeing spots and stars. For a man searching with ordinary binoculars, six hours at a stretch is the absolute maximum. But the conditions had meant that these limits were not adhered to. At the same time the crews' effectiveness had been reduced by a psychological factor. On Samoa people had criticized the military authorities for not searching the right places. In Apia it was the general opinion that the current would send the *Joyita* or her life rafts in a northwesterly direction, while the official military charts of the Pacific currents indicated that a drift in a southwesterly direction was the only possibility. The vigorous criticism which both the press and gossip leveled against the search methods made some of the men regard their task as hopeless.

The fact that large parts of the cargo were missing did not necessarily mean a pirate attack. The first thing those on board would do when the vessel shipped water and started to list would be to lighten it by throwing some of the cargo overboard. And after the examination it could be stated categorically that there was no question of a collision with another vessel.

The commission emphasized this in a declaration that repudiated all the wild rumors about the *Joyita*. At the same time the experts' theories as to the cause of the catastrophe were accepted. But the maritime inquiry ended with an official statement that, on the basis of all information available, it was impossible to say what had happened to the missing twenty-five people.

The only one who thought he knew was an old Samoan-European who had watched the maritime inquiry and put his local knowledge and sound comments at my disposal throughout.

"Well, how are things?" I asked him one day when I thought he was looking a bit worried.

"Not so good," he replied. "I had a message this morning that I'm out of touch with the cosmos."

It was a little difficult for me to say with suitable conviction that that was just too bad. Fortunately his contact with the cosmos quickly returned. Among other things it told him that those who had disappeared from the *Joyita* were safe on a small island in the Santa Cruz group. That was where they could be found; but nobody would listen to his suggestion of sending a ship to relieve the shipwrecked.

Apart from the cosmic explanation, it was not all that unlikely.

This was proved by another of the baffling mysteries of the Pacific that took place and was solved, all while the *Joyita* affair was in the news.

A small motor ship, the *Arakarimoa* from the Gilbert Islands, sailed from Tarawa on December 28 together with another ship, the *Aratoba*, on the way to Maiana, carrying twelve and eight passengers respectively. The two ships lost touch with each other during the night. The *Aratoba* arrived on schedule in Maiana the following morning, having traveled the nineteen miles between the two islands. But the *Arakarimoa* seemed to have disappeared. The ship had been given up as lost when it suddenly reappeared at the Solomon Islands on February 28. The engine had broken down three hours after departure and the ship had drifted with the current for two months without radio and with small food supplies which quickly gave out. After that there was only raw fish and sea water. An old man died on board, and a woman had given birth to a baby which also died. She herself was drowned along with her five-year-old son when they had tried to struggle ashore after the ship had been grounded in a storm off Guadalcanal. Only eight of the original twelve managed to survive the horrible ordeal. And those eight lived simply by staying on board the ship. If the twenty-five on the *Joyita* had done the same, some of *them* would have been alive too. And my man of the cosmos thought that they were.

Naturally, the cosmos man was regarded in Apia as being a bit of a mental case, though he seemed to me to be just as sane as Theophile and Marcelle. If I had been a millionaire, I would have paid for an expedition to the island where, according to him, the survivors were to be found. One should not be too skeptical in the Pacific. The strangest things happen there.

I've often wondered why I met so many "cosmic" people on the Pacific Islands. It must be something in the air. The distant horizons bring people closer to heaven, said Father Cicero.

The old Danish skipper who lived in Apia had both feet firmly planted on the ground.

"They ought to talk less of flying saucers and a little more about the responsibilities of the skippers and the authorities," he said. "The Pacific's no duck pond for playing games. If both ships and radios were in order, and the authorities checked all the vessels, we wouldn't have so many of these so-called mysteries."

I did not find my fellow countryman at home that New Year's Eve when I went to visit him. With no other plans in mind, I walked back into town and passed one of Apia's clubs where the New Year was apparently being ushered in with as much rioting as at Polly's. Enthusiasm seemed to be running high, and I was pretty sure I could just walk in and join them without introductions. The temptation was strong, but I closed my ears and walked on. After all, I had come all the way back to the old year in order to welcome the new one in a more dignified fashion.

I walked through the town and out along the beach. It was New Year's Eve and I was alone, but that didn't bother me. "Do you know," I inquired of the palms, "that I'm walking in the middle of yesterday?" I sat down beneath a palm and felt so pleased at having cheated time that time wound up cheating me. I had come out as far as a small Samoan village when I realized that it was half past eleven. Yesterday's New Year was soon to be today's. I had to do something about it. Something solemn and dignified, of course. But what? I was the proud owner of four bottles of whisky. They were in my hotel room, and I had bought them for a special reason. The New Zealand authorities do not allow the sale of alcoholic beverages to Samoans. Only "whites" can have a certain number of "points" which permit them to buy liquor. Immediately after my arrival I had received forty-eight "points," which the hotel manageress quickly helped me to convert into four bottles of whisky. But my forty-eight bottled pints were in my so-called room at the hotel. Here under the palm tree I couldn't even toast myself with a glass of water. My New Year's Eve was beginning to feel too solemn and dignified to be bearable. I had nobody to wish a Happy New Year to but myself and the man in the moon.

But I found someone else soon enough. The paradise island took me in its arms and tricked me.

It began under a palm. Another palm, that is. There are so many of them that they all look very much alike. But the palm I was leaning against was rather special: it was round-shouldered. I chose this particular palm for two reasons. First, its sway-back trunk fitted my own. Second, it gave me an excellent balcony seat for a performance I had decided to watch by way of celebrating my second New Year's Eve.

From my seat in the darkness of the gallery I was able to have a full view of all the picturesque goings-on of a Samoan family gathering. It was better than any variety show. The performers wore costumes that were brief but colorful. They played the ukulele, they danced, they sang and passed around the bottles (probably filled with the forbidden home-brew) under the flickering light of the hut's oil lamps, while I watched and silently applauded from my invisible grandstand seat in the open-air theater.

In addition to all the other gala activities of the evening, my Samoans had fireworks too. I sat back delighted as the great colorful flashes roared through the sky and lit up every tree and bush in sight. The flaming rockets turned everything flaming red. Including me. For suddenly I realized that with the light from the blazing firecrackers, I too had been lit up and mercilessly exposed to my unknowing hosts.

Let's switch the situation to a private garden party in an American suburb. Suddenly a female voice shrills through the air. "My God, Edward, there's somebody out there prowling under that tree." Skeptical, irritated bass: "Oh, nonsense, Elizabeth, you're just imagining things." "No, Edward, I am *not* imagining things, look for yourself—see, there's somebody out there, look, I think he's trying to get away." "Where?—oh, *there*. I'll be damned, you're right, Elizabeth." Angry barking in the direction of the tree: "You'd better get out of there, you, before we call the police, do you hear me?" Indignant voice later identified as Mildred: "Really, don't people have any respect for private property any more, I don't know what's happening to this neighborhood, ever since those you-know-whats started moving in, why nice people just aren't safe any more." Slightly hysterical voice from the hostess again: "Edward, if I've told you once I've told you a thousand times, we've got to get a watchdog here. Think of the girls. Joseph, get your sisters into the house, quickly now, you never know what sort of fellow it might be. Mildred, I think we'd better go inside too."

And so on. You can provide the rest of the dialogue yourself. That, as you know, was a transmission from the suburbs. Now, ladies and gentlemen, we switch you to Samoa.

Many voices again, but none of them agitated. The entire gathering rushes toward the stranger and drags him into the center of the garden. General smiles and laughter. An old man, probably the grandfather, bows and makes a polite speech: "Foreign friend, why do you stand alone in the darkness while we are celebrating here? This is a special evening. Come, share our happiness with the New Year. We shall make you our honored guest, and offer you everything we have." New voices break in, urge the stranger to take a seat and cover him over with floral wreaths.

A different world, you say? Yes, it is. The Samoan village into which I had stumbled was as far afield from my Western suburbs as life on another planet. And what cheered me most was that, once all the formal welcomes were over, I stopped being a strange two-legged animal on which they had to gaze in open-mouthed wonder. Their mouths stayed open, all right, but not in amazement. After the formal overtures were over, I was simply another friend of the family. They treated me as though I were a long-awaited guest who had happened to arrive a bit late.

The party and the dancing continued, and the bottle of forbidden "jungle beer" danced right along with the crowd. They had no bottle opener, but none was needed. The young Samoans bit the caps off with their teeth. As I watched all the merriment around me, I suddenly had one of my brightest ideas in years. I put my bright idea into words, and one of the young Samoans was immediately sent to my hotel to get the four bottles of whisky. There was no need to give him a key. My room was, as I've said, about as easy to get into as a public square. The messenger, who looked like a milk-chocolate Hennes, came flying back on winged feet. My "points" were poured into glasses, and the gaiety rose ten degrees with every point. The old grandfather smiled and informed me that it was now my party. From a lonely stranger against a round-shouldered palm, I had suddenly been transformed into the upright host of a major gathering. Even Cinderella would have been jealous.

The old New Year had long ago sneaked over from Fiji and was hanging around in the dark and grinning at me. The old folks had retired to their huts, while the young ones kept going strong. They were in top form. They danced, both for me and for themselves, while I sat with a soft brown hand in mine and a just as soft brown arm around my back. Both hand and arm belonged to a girl named Luna. She was lovely looking, and not a day over sixteen. During one of the intermissions, Luna laughingly shouted something to the others, and a handsome young couple jumped out onto the nonexistent stage and began to perform. Luna explained with an enchanting smile that this was a special number being done in my honor.

If I were to import that dance number into a New York revue, it would be difficult to find the right title for it in the program.

"Samoan Invitation to the Dance" would be all wrong. It was an invitation, all right, but not to a dance. With a little courage and without fear of the censors, I might be able to call it "Erotic Dance Act from Samoa." No outline of the story would be necessary. That ballet spoke for itself. In spite of its disarming humor, it was strong stuff. Too strong, perhaps, for my Western-educated taste. To my European eyes, it was the most obscene dance I have ever seen.

When Miss Luna got up to dance, solo, one of the other girls took her place beside me. She, too, was delightful, but she didn't intertwine her fingers with mine, nor did she place a soft arm around my neck. Why she was whispering hot words of love in my ear I couldn't understand, until finally I realized that she was acting as middleman for Miss Luna. She came right to the point before Miss Luna returned. Her friend did not think I should go back to the hotel to sleep. She had a mattress and a mosquito net for two. Miss Luna's emissary pointed smilingly toward the palm hut where mama, papa, grandpa, and aunts were all snoring peacefully through the night. In there?

She looked surprised when this peculiar European shook his head and said, "No, no thank you." She couldn't hear how very loudly his built-in European morals were shouting behind that smile.

The girl stared at me in shock for a moment, then immediately silenced the entire party and told them all about it. And with this I contributed my share to the entertainment of the evening. Nobody has ever appreciated my humor the way those Samoans did. The joke went over as successfully as a firecracker, and everyone—excluding me—rolled helplessly on the grass with laughter.

When I finally returned to the hotel, I had a puzzling problem to work out. Before going to bed the second time for the first time in the new year, I tried to settle up my resolution account. I had promised myself that my extra New Year's Eve would be celebrated in a proper manner. Had I kept that promise?

It was impossible to say. Before sleep claimed me I decided that I had neither won nor lost my own challenge. It was a draw: I had celebrated the New Year with proper impropriety.

But in my dreams the old year laughed a mischievous Samoan laugh.

Sinners in the South Sea sunshine

More guests came to the hotel in Apia, and I moved into a room with a door. I'm not sure why I have this compulsion about doors, but have it I do. Sometimes I think maybe I should see a psychiatrist about it. My chambermaid clearly thought I was off my rocker when I morbidly insisted on having a room with walls and a door that could be closed. She would also have thought me a bit mad if I'd ever told her what I thought of Apia. For Apia, like Tahiti's Papeete, falls far short of the charms of its island.

This small capital, with its 3500 inhabitants, is the Samoan's version of New York. It's a great, exciting experience for them to pay a visit to their capital. And the tourists seem to regard it in the same way. When they come to Samoa, they stay in Apia. And that's the only part of Samoa they see. They visit Vailima, the home of the famous poet Robert Louis Stevenson, which has now been converted into a residence for the New Zealand

High Commissioner. They climb to the top of the Vaea Mountain and feel passionately literary as they place floral bouquets on the master's grave, though most of them, I'm sure, have never even read his books. They drive in taxis out to a small waterfall, so small that it's difficult to find. They buy a few trinkets that are labeled "Souvenir of Samoa" in front and "Made in Japan" on the back. And after three days of expensive touring, which scarcely gets them outside the city limits, they pack up their smart wash-and-wears, smile smugly to one another, and say, "Well, I guess that covers Samoa." But that doesn't cover the island at all. For Apia is not Samoa.

In Apia the white race once more did its best to spoil an unspoiled land. During the war Samoa's capital was treated to a downpour of so-called civilization. The flood consisted of 40,000 American soldiers who had a perfectly marvelous time because the island, in spite of all gloomy predictions, never came within the Japanese danger zone. Apia was turned overnight into the Sodom of the South Seas, and it has never been quite the same since.

As in Tahiti, the idyllic, innocent love life of the Samoan girls became muddied by prostitution. The entrance to the American Army airfield was called the "Gate of Sin," and the town quickly learned to live up to its newly-bestowed name. The Samoans lost no time in learning to convert natural hospitality into dollars and cents. The banana cluster that had formerly cost a few pennies was sold for a dollar: and why not, asked the cheerful Samoans, when the nice American GI's looked so happy and said it was "cheap"? The Samoans who had been living well on seven dollars a month got work from the Americans at three and a half dollars a day. They felt like millionaires, and drove prices sky-high by throwing their cash into circulation with complete lack of restraint. The Polynesians have never been able to grasp the idea of saving. Money is for spending, they think, and the moment they get some they rush out to buy. They acquired tastes for hand-painted Hawaiian shirts covered over with nude ladies, and ready-made violet-blue suits sent direct from New York's Seventh Avenue. And they made money hand over fist through black-market dealings in illegally distilled Samoan wood alcohol, which was called "jungle gin" and sold to good-time American Charlies at exorbitant drunkards' prices.

That all ended long ago, but the scars are still to be seen. And some of the scars are quite pretty. Samoa's chocolate-brown children with blond hair and blue eyes are by far the nicest reminders of all those long-gone days. For extra babies have never been a problem on Samoa. No power on earth can make the Samoans see that some children are more legitimate than others. Each mother cherishes her mixed-blood offspring, and proudly exhibits them as two-legged souvenirs of "Johnny" and "Joe."

A less attractive souvenir of the GI occupation is Apia's addiction to chewing gum. Everyone in Apia chews from morning till night. And the Samoans regard it as an extra pleasure to chew as noisily as they can. Sitting next to an army of loudly chomping Samoan women in a bus or a movie is enough to drive anyone mad. Anyone, that is, but a Samoan.

I was so disgruntled with Apia that I couldn't wait to get out of the hotel and move to one of the villages. I had to wait, however, because the rainy season had arrived at about the same time I did. No one who has lived in the West can imagine how rainy the Samoan rainy season actually is. Day and night, without the slightest interruption, it pours, and pours, and pours. We were rained on from above, below, and sideways, and we were confined to our hotel like the main characters in Somerset Maugham's story. Unfortunately we had no Sadie Thompson to divert us. Come to think of it, we didn't even have a Polly Thompson among us. All we had was our own grumpy selves and—needless to say—the rain.

In the rainy season everything gets wet. It rains through the roof and through the closed windows. The smoke blows down into the kitchen so that you get smoked beef, smoked rice, and smoked caramel pudding on the table. Laundry is hung indoors and never dries. You stick to every chair you sit on. Your clothes get moldy in their closets. Your shoes turn green. And you turn purple while you wait.

So there we sat. We played cards together. We played solitaire alone. We read all the worn-out magazines, which were so old they belonged in a museum. We read the paperback mysteries, and tried to amuse ourselves by guessing what had happened on the missing page 165 of *Murder Comes to a Nudist Colony.* Occasionally we indulged in a bit of stimulating conversation. The following is an excerpt from one of the more witty gambits we attempted:

"Morning, George."

"Morning, Henry."

"See it's still raining, George."

"Yep, still raining, Henry."

"Think it'll ever stop, George?"

"Nope, don't look like it ever will."

"Gosh, this sure is a lot of rain, George."

"Sure is, Henry, sure is."

And to make matters worse, the radio broadcasts always informed us that it was sunny everywhere else.

I will never forget the little Australian businessman who was the most waterlogged of us all. He spent the entire two weeks of his costly Samoan vacation sitting in a wicker chair and trying to dry out. He had invested his life's savings in the trip, but on his first day in Apia he had been attacked by a murderous cloudburst and had come back to the hotel looking as though he had been shrunk in somebody's wash. His only pair of shoes were so wet that he could have kept a couple of live carp in them. His clothes had become two sizes too small, and he had water in his ears. Even the works in his waterproof wrist watch had been drowned in the sudden deluge. While his shoes dripped from the chandelier and his suit dripped in the kitchen, he sat sweating in his wicker chair dressed in a quilted winter bathrobe.

With lips tightly clamped over damp false teeth he sat there and poured all the hatred he could muster into the travel agent who had suggested the trip. It would be a dark day for that travel agent when this wet customer went home.

But the rain did finally let up. And with the sun, I too came out and shone in the Samoan countryside. I prepared to settle myself under a palm-leaf roof as far away from Apia as I could get.

When I went off to live in a village, I wasn't at all sure how I'd manage on an open-air platform. But I was lucky and found a vacant palm hut that had been built by a fellow European. It had a door. Of course the door was a little bit frivolous under the circumstances. The circumstances being an absence of walls. My one-room palm villa consisted of a platform surrounded by a fence, covered by a roof, and decorated with a door. What I had rented was actually no more than a porch without a house. But it had, as I've said, a door. And that pleased me.

"Merciful heavens, are you going to live there all by yourself?" asked an American lady belonging to a South Seas tour group which consisted of twenty wealthy, travel-mad young girls from the States, the youngest being seventy-two.

She did not know Samoa, however much she might think she did after having been there for three days. No matter what other difficulties I might have in my palm hut, loneliness would not be one of them. Nobody lives "all by himself" in Samoa.

I had plenty of uninvited guests once I moved in. One of the first to arrive was a young fish named Oswald. At least I think he was young. He certainly walked up my steps in a more sprightly manner than I ever managed. Yes, I said walked. Oswald was a walking fish. And if you think I'm kidding, just open up your encyclopedia and take a look under "P." There, in all its multisyllabic glory, you will find *Periophthalmus barbarus Linnaeus*. Oswald was one of those. Some people refer to his species as "mud springer" or "mangrove hopper." But whatever you call him, he was the strangest pet I have ever had. I was a little bit startled the first time my walking fish came tiptoeing up to my porch. For no matter what Oswald thought he was, he could not deny that he was a fish. He had scales, gills, fins, and a fish's tail. But he also had a lung. He could breathe both on land and at sea. Whenever he got fed up with life in the lagoon, he would lift up his fins, pull out his legs, and start hopping along the shore. He also liked to vary his diet. His many visits to me were due more to gluttony than personal friendship. Oswald just loved all the tasty insects I kept in my hut. But he was always courteous when he came. Before attacking his food he would always stop to greet me politely with his curious, protruding eyes. If I seemed to be sullen or rude, he would dart off with a sudden skip and then stare at me balefully from a palm. Oswald knew who was boss. Compared to his four inches, my six feet or so of height must have seemed colossal. Small wonder he learned to respect me. Our association prospered and we became fast friends.

I had a few two-legged friends, too, and of those little Simi was my favorite. He was going on five and had the biggest brown eyes I've ever seen. He knew how to use them too. He had a fine talent for getting his hands on every bit of chocolate in my hut. He would never take anything outright. On Samoa that's not necessary. All Simi had to do was present me with the goods and then say, with a pleading, angelic smile, *"Fa'a mole mole."* And then I would invariably melt, just as the chocolate was doing in his fingers. I was obliged to, both because of that irresistible angel smile and because, as a Samoan villager, I had to conform with the unwritten laws of the community. As on Fiji, where the magic formula was *"kere-kere,"* a Samoan can point at anything belonging to a relative and say *"Fa'a mole mole."* This means "hand it over," and hand it over you do. The only recourse a Samoan has to this form of plundering is to make a careful note of the attack, so that he can be sure to *"fa'a mole mole"* something from the other first chance he gets.

Simi was my neighbors' son, and I spent more of my time

with them than I did at home on my one-room porch. My special girl friend was Simi's mother, who was a large woman with an equally large sense of humor. Tulipa was her name, and she was as fat and jolly as Rubina on Tahiti. Tulipa was married to Fapoi, and they had an enormous number of children. But which were whose was something I never found out. Tulipa was sure that some belonged to both of them. She herself had brought a number of illegitimate children into the marriage, but it was all so long ago that she could no longer remember which ones she had had with whom. The arithmetic was just too complicated. She also had no idea of the children's exact ages. She thought Simi was five, and on that basis she was pretty sure that Luina, who had long ago borne her first child, was considerably older. How much older she couldn't tell. She also felt quite sure that two of the younger ones were outsiders her husband had had with other ladies during the marriage. Why didn't they live with their mothers, I asked. Oh, they just hadn't gotten along very well with the mothers she supposed. She didn't really know. One day they had landed with Tulipa and Fapoi, and they had stayed.

This sort of thing is very common on Samoa. Nearly all the villagers are related to one another, and the children circulate freely from one relative to another. They call all uncles and aunts father and mother, and all cousins are brothers and sisters. The children decide for themselves where they want to live. When they are small the mother always leaves them with a woman relative, who passes them on to a couple of other aunts before they return home again. It is an old tradition to teach the children from earliest childhood that they can find love and understanding with more than one person. In Europe mothers are proud when their children are so closely attached to them that they grow hysterical whenever the ties are cut. The Samoan mother regards that sort of feeling as rather sickly. She thinks it healthier for the child not to be too dependent on any one person. It will help the children over many sorrows later in life, when they may be disappointed in friendship or love; for then they will know that substitutes can always be found.

I began to understand a little of my chambermaid's contempt for my addiction to closed doors. I grew up in a world of closed doors. In Europe parents and children live squeezed together in their closed little boxes, and the closed doors are usually opened only for the children to make a solemn exit. That sort of thing is unknown on Samoa. Once when I had seen nothing of Simi for a week I asked Tulipa where he was. "I have no idea," she said. "He disappeared sometime last week, but I think he'll come home again soon. He usually does!" She took it for granted that he had settled with some relatives. And he was welcome to do so if he felt comfortable there.

Does this mean that little Simi will be allowed to go through life without ever learning responsibility? No, not at all. He'll never be allowed to live *off* his relatives when he comes to live with them. Wherever he lives, he'll be given chores to perform. Both boys and girls are expected to help out, and they do so as though it were a game. The boys fish in the lagoon and gather coconuts. They learn to repair fishing nets and build canoes. And they go with the grown men to the plantations and lend a hand there. It's all a game because there's really no such thing to them as work. Their toys are the tools they work with. The girls are brought up in much the same efficient way. They help out in the house, weaving palm mats and beating tapa, the thin cloth-like material hammered out of the bark of the paper-mulberry tree. The girls also look after all their little brothers and sisters. This, by the way, is one of the major reasons Samoan women can have as many children as they please. There's never any problem of getting nurses or baby sitters. The big ones bring up the smaller ones, and the chain goes on as long as the mother does. And the girls make excellent teachers. They spoil their human dolls, but they won't stand for any nonsense.

Well, many Westerners will say, what about the awkward age? They can't avoid that, can they? But they can and do. We have accepted the fact that the awkward age is a physiological phenomenon: the child too suddenly develops into an adult, with new glandular functions, and so on. But the Samoans have demonstrated that what we call the awkward age is caused by social pressure. Our teenagers are not allowed to let their behavior follow their development. The new, awakening emotions are surrounded by taboos and prohibitions. And it's no good saying that this is all due merely to an outmoded moral code. It is also a social and economic necessity in our world of closed doors, where an illegitimate child is both a problem and a burden for the small isolated family and its economy.

On Samoa the climate and the community solve this problem. The food grows on trees, and children are common property. The young ones can be given full erotic freedom, and the consequences will trouble no one. The so-called awkward age vanishes like dew in the sun. It simply doesn't exist on Samoa.

As I've mentioned, Tulipa's oldest daughter, Luina, had already had her first child. And with all the young friends she had, more could be expected. Sometimes when she was not at home in the evening and I asked where she was, Tulipa would say she was "under the palms." Her roguish smile made it clear what she meant. She was quite content with the fact that her young daughter had many lovers. She thought it healthy that the girl should work the desire for casual relationships out of her system. In that way she might learn not to let herself be cheated by physical attraction when, later on, she would have to choose a partner for life. The European girl who has been kept on the leash thinks it's the real thing the first time she is kissed by some carefree Don Juan. The Samoan girl looking for a husband just laughs at her Casanova. No thanks, my friend, she says. I know all about it, and it can be wonderful. But now I want to get married, and that's got to be to a steady, sensible man. Off you go under the palms and carry on playing with the girls. I'm after something else.

Two nice young Samoans often came to visit Luina in Tulipa's hut. One of them always sat down on the straw mat right beside the girl, courting her with wide smiles and burning eyes, while the other sat silent in a corner. I asked Tulipa if the attentive gentleman was a prospective son-in-law. "No," smiled Tulipa, and indicated the silent one in the corner. "That's the one, over there. He's crazy about her. The other one is his *soa*."

This was the same thing I had experienced myself on New Year's Eve, when Miss Luna sent her friend to me as love's ambassador. A *soa* is an emissary of love, who goes on behalf of his friend to the chosen one and presents his friend's case with warm, ardent words. It's not considered proper for the one who is in love to set to work directly himself.

In the village we had a young man whom Tulipa did not like. Luina, too, avoided him when they met. I thought he was a pleasant fellow, and asked Tulipa what was wrong. Was he an enemy of the family? "No," said Tulipa. "But we keep a lookout for him. He's a *moetotolo*."

A *moetotolo* is a "sneak lover." This is a young Samoan who for some reason or other has departed from the rules of the game. Sometimes it begins with the girl he loved and dated "under the palms" deceiving him. One night she doesn't turn up, and leaves him wondering where she is. And next day he hears that she has taken another lover. Most young Samoans take this sort of thing lightly; they simply go out and seek fresh conquests. But with some it sticks. They want to avenge themselves for the insult, and they do so in a strange way. They know the girl has received their rival under the mosquito net in the hut where the whole family sleeps. The family doesn't protest as long as this takes place discreetly. And the *moetotolo* tries to take advantage of this. Cloaked by the darkness he sneaks in under the girl's mosquito net in the hope that she will think he is the other—his rival. Often he succeeds, but if the girl discovers that she has been deceived she shouts and wakens the family. Sometimes the sneak lover escapes unseen. As a rule he strips completely before the assault and rubs himself all over with coconut oil. Then there is no lava-lava left behind to reveal his identity, and the slippery body makes it easier to escape if one of the girl's relatives should be quick and grab him in the darkness. But if he should be caught, then for the rest of his youth he will be left to seek his love as a *moetotolo*. No girl will have him as her lover. He will have to make do with this peculiar sort of rape, exempt from further punishment.

Psychologically the *moetotolo* is hard to explain, but he has no easy time of it. I asked Tulipa if she didn't feel sorry for the nice young man both she and Luina had so brutally rejected. "What's the poor fellow going to do?" I said. "Won't he grow bitter and wicked? Aren't you in danger of his turning into a murderer one day?"

Tulipa just shook her head. But in the evening she called me out in front of the hut and pointed to two young men walking together under the palms.

"Look," she said; "there he is. That's how he finds love. His friend is the eldest son of one of the most distinguished families in the village. He's not a *moetotolo* himself. But he's a clever boy, and he's ambitious. He wants to go to New Zealand to study. He doesn't want to get caught by some girl who may spoil his plans if he marries too early. So he has chosen a *moetotolo* as his friend. It's very common."

"And there's nothing against that?"

Tulipa smiled her most carefree smile.

"No, why should there be?" she said, surprised. "I mean, we don't like men who act like girls. Those who wriggle their bottoms and swing their hips, you know. We laugh at them. But if they behave reasonably, they can play together as much as they like. Why should they bother us . . . ?"

And why should they bother us indeed. In the carefree and doorless life of my Samoan village I had learned more about human privacy than anywhere else in the world. Even I learned that privacy has nothing to do with closed doors. I had long since put aside my precious door, hinges and all, in order to live the open life of reef and lagoon. Through the wall-less walls of my doorless hut I could look out in the evening at a moonlit world that sang and laughed—and loved—on the short of the sea. The whispering palms bent protectively over the carefree people who danced beneath the sky.

I had acquired a new address in Samoa. I lived at Number 1 Happy Lagoon. I had landed in a village of paradise, yet I was a spectator rather than a participant. My past, my upbringing, my traditions, my habits . . . all these created an invisible wall that locked me out of the Samoan paradise. I could never help but cringe inside whenever I heard the children calling, "*Papalangi! Papalangi!*" Literally translated, *papalangi* means "the man who has burst the horizon." It is the Samoan word for a foreigner, a man who doesn't belong and cannot stay.

Those were days of borrowed happiness, and I knew it. I knew, even better than the children, what *papalangi* really meant.

It was some help, when I finally did have to leave, to know that I was on my way to another paradise. I was going to Fiji and from there on to Tonga, and Tonga, I was sure, would bring me new days of borrowed pleasure. I never dreamed that on my way from one earthly paradise to another I would glimpse hell itself.

I sailed from Apia, and two days later I was back again. The shipboard murder which I've already discussed forced us to turn back to shore. I stayed in Apia in an effort to help the arrested steward, but, as you know, I got nothing for my trouble but a lot of heartache and bitterness. The steward committed suicide, and I, in disgust, went down to the harbor and hopped the first schooner in sight. It was that boat that took me to Monuafefafa, where Theophile and Marcelle helped me to peer into a paradise that was far different from the one I had known on Samoa.

When I left Monuafefafa, the only transportation available was a fishing boat sailing to the New Hebrides. Since I had no choice, I took it. From the New Hebrides I might, with luck, be able to get a ship to Fiji; if not, I would have to make the complete detour via Australia and New Zealand in order to catch the monthly boat to Tonga.

On the New Hebrides it turned out that I could get to Suva direct if I waited a month or so for the next ship. It was a relief to save the expensive detour, and the wait, I was sure, would be a pleasant one. I would be staying with my old friends from the *Lalona*, Madeleine and Pastor Veyrier, whose vicarage was on one of the lovely outlying islands of the New Hebrides, with a view of a lagoon and plenty of room.

"Too much room," said Madeleine, after showing me around. "I run a free hotel here for missionaries, and you know how I feel about that. Especially now," she added, as we sat down on the sunlit loggia looking over the lagoon. "Pierre's away, you know, and that's a good thing, for I've something very serious to talk to you about."

I looked at her in some surprise. "What's it about?" I asked.

"Rudy," she answered. "Rudy and 'La Rasputine.' "

"Why don't you tell me the whole thing from the beginning," I suggested.

She leaned back and began. "Rudy came to the New Hebrides —you knew that, didn't you? Yes, I thought so. Well, he came to find his brother. And that's where the trouble began. This brother of his—who's actually only a half-brother—turned out to be one of the worst racketeers in the islands. The man has swindled and defrauded his way from one end of the Pacific to the other. Sometimes he managed to run before a place got too hot for him. But on the Tokelau Islands he was caught redhanded. They kicked him out so fast he didn't know what hit him. And it was lucky for him he did get out in such a hurry. The natives were ready to kill him.

"What does he do? Everything. He swindles them out of their money, their homes, their women. There just aren't any limits. The man's a monster of greed and larceny who ought to be locked up in a prison somewhere. But instead he roams around free, going from island to island and making whatever he can before getting kicked out. Well, he did the same thing when he got to here. Before Rudy had even arrived at the capital of the New Hebrides his brother had been thrown out of there too. Nobody knew where he was, and nobody cared. But Rudy cared —his brother had written that he had lots of money, and Rudy was depending on that to get him through. He came out here without a cent to his name. And with not a penny in his pocket he was stranded on an island where his name was so deeply hated that no one would have anything to do with him. He needed money desperately, but he had no way of getting it. After what his brother had done, they'd have lynched him if he asked to borrow so much as a dime. Well, it finally occurred to him to write to us, and of course we immediately arranged for him to come here. You should have seen him when he arrived. He was half insane. The disappointment had hit him too hard, and he was on the verge of cracking up. I was terribly worried about him, but there was nothing to do about it but keep him here for the time being. He stayed with us for more than a month, and I think that got him back on his feet again. I don't know, though. You could tell he was still hurt, inside and out. And I could understand why. You know how much he had been looking forward to finding some sort of paradise in the South Seas. He expected so much from these islands. And instead, through no fault of his own, he found nothing but hostility and hatred when he got here. It was bound to hurt."

"And where is he now, Madeleine?"

"Pierre got him a job as an English teacher at one of the mission schools here in town. The one where 'La Rasputine' teaches too . . . and there's the trouble again. For she was the one who started the rumors that got him kicked out and sent to another school on one of the small islands up north. Oh, I was terribly angry over it, but I had a guilty conscience as well. We all teased 'La Rasputine' on board the *Lalona*. We really made the trip horrible for her. She was a dreadful woman, of course, but we could have been nice. And none of us were, least of all Rudy. You know how she adored him at first—and he was really quite cruel to her. Well, at any rate," Madeleine pursed her lips and stared angrily out at the reef, "if this trouble was her way of getting revenge, I shall never forgive her."

"But what happened?"

" 'La Rasputine' spread rumors about Rudy."

"What kind of rumors?"

"Oh, just rumors. I'd rather not say. I don't know what was truth and what was gossip. I got so worked up about the whole thing that I behaved too impulsively again. I stormed down to the Headmaster of the school here in town, and demanded the full story. Of course he just put me off with a lot of vague talk. Mr. Missionary had done what he called 'solving the problem without risking a scandal.' I asked him if he had discussed the matter with Rudy. No, he hadn't. The subject was too painful. But—and get this, mind you—he had entrusted the boy to God's mercy and commended to him the power of prayer. Power of prayer, my foot. Our so-called spiritual advisor was too delicate to get his shabby soul smeared.

"Did you speak to 'La Rasputine'?"

"No. Mademoiselle had a headache. And that I could well understand. I asked the headmaster to give her my regards, and say I hoped her head would keep aching for all time to come."

"Well, did you ever find out what it was all about?"

"Oh, there's talk everywhere. You know how rumors fly about in the Pacific. No, I don't think there's any point in my spreading that sort of thing. It's probably not true. And if it is true, then it's really not something for chatting over."

"Did Rudy himself say anything?"

"No, not a thing! He closed up inside himself, just as usual. And that's the worst thing possible for him. Now I'm more worried than ever. I have a feeling he's dreadfully lonely up there. I don't know why we allowed him to leave. When Pierre gets back next week the three of us must hold a conference and see what we can do to help Rudy. We should have done that long ago. The boy needs help desperately, and I only hope that it's not too late."

But by the next morning it was already too late.

It was only half-past five when I heard a knock on my door at the vicarage. I opened the door, and there stood Madeleine in her dressing gown. She was pale and her eyes were full of tears.

"Can I come in?" she said. "I must sit down for a moment. I can't help it. My knees are shaking."

I helped her to the armchair, then waited for her to dry her eyes before going on.

"Pierre just came back. He's here now with Mr. Jones, the Headmaster of Rudy's new school. Rudy . . . Rudy was with them, too. Pierre was just in to say that he had to go, but he'll soon be back with Mr. Jones."

"And Rudy?"

Two large tears rolled down Madeleine's cheeks. She started to speak, but her voice cracked.

"Come now," I said, "it can't be that bad."

"Oh, but it is!" she cried. "Rudy . . . Rudy has been arrested."

"Arrested?" I echoed. "But what on earth for?"

"He . . ." She could scarcely get the words out. "He . . . he's killed a young native up at the school!"

We learned the whole story—or at least as much of it as was then known—when Pastor Veyrier came home with Mr. Jones. I disliked the missionary from the very moment we met. He was a squat, pudgy little man with an unpleasant face and an unctuous voice. His self-righteous smile cast an ugly light in the room. Madeleine and I entered just as Pastor Veyrier and Mr. Jones were in the middle of a heated argument.

"But how in heaven's name could you do anything like that?" Pastor Veyrier was demanding.

The missionary shrugged his shoulders. "A sudden impulse."

Pastor Veyrier turned toward Madeleine and me. "Do you

know what Mr. Jones has done? He's put a match to the hut where Rudy lived up at the school. It's been burnt to the ground."

"As if there hadn't been enough trouble," began Madeleine angrily.

The missionary showed the whites of his eyes. "You must understand, my dear friends, that I could not bear the thought of my school being besmirched with the scene of such a dreadful misdeed. It was my own spontaneous reaction against evil." He smiled and folded his hands piously in his lap.

Pastor Veyrier stretched his arms imploringly toward the ceiling. "Dear God above," he cried, "now we won't be able to find out if Rudy left any letters or notes in his room."

"Rudy himself could tell us that," said Madeleine.

"No, he can't. The boy won't say a word. We can't get a thing out of him to explain why it happened."

"Couldn't we get Mr. Jones to tell us everything, right from the beginning?" I suggested.

"Yes," said Madeleine, "let's hear it. It's so incredible, I just can't believe it. There must be some explanation."

The missionary cleared his throat and put on the solemn air of a clergyman about to deliver a sermon. "Yes, dear Madame Veyrier, there is an explanation, although I'm afraid it's a most unsavory one."

Madeleine interrupted him, and looked at her husband. "Pierre . . . then it's true, what La Ras—— . . . I mean, what Mademoiselle Raspail said?"

Pierre nodded gravely. "Yes . . . or some of it, at any rate."

There were red patches of color on Madeleine's otherwise chalk-white face. "So just send him away, then! Don't speak to him. Don't try to help him. Just give him a kick in the pants like some filthy animal you don't want to dirty your hands with! Do you call that Christian love for one's neighbor, Mr. Jones? Do you?"

Pierre interrupted her. "Please Madeleine," he said reproachfully, then turned back to address the missionary. "You must forgive my wife, Mr. Jones. Naturally she's very upset about the whole thing. She liked Rudy very much."

The missionary nodded forgivingly, and turned his cold eyes back to the ceiling. "Of course, of course, it's quite understandable. My wife and I, we're just as shocked as you people are. We liked Rudy too. Or at least we did in the beginning. But you see he—ah—became more and more reticent as time went on. He sat alone in his room nearly every evening. It seemed to me a rather rude demonstration that he didn't like our company."

"But surely you must have understood that it was only because he was unhappy," Madeleine said.

"Tell me, how did he seem to you on the day that it happened? Was he feeling morbid, or very deeply disturbed?"

"No, not at all. That's just what's so confusing about it. He seemed to be feeling fine. When he had lunch with us he was actually quite cheerful. But he refused to join the pupils who were going out to a plantation on the coast to gather coconuts. He was always trying to get out of duties like that. No sense of responsibility. Did I go myself? No, as it happened I was feeling a little bit under the weather that day, and decided to stay at home. I was sitting in my office when it happened. One of the pupils had come back from the plantation because he felt sick. He stopped in the kitchen and asked for Sister Caroline, our nurse. Why he didn't look for her in her house, I don't know. She was there. It was she who heard Rudy open the door of his hut and call for a boy. The only reason she didn't go out and remind him they were all away was that she was taking a rest and naturally didn't want to get up. The poor child must have heard Rudy calling too, and gone to him without knowing the dreadful fate awaiting him. What's so incredible is that it could have happened without us hearing it. Neither I nor Sister Caroline heard a sound. I knew nothing at all until Rudy came running madly toward my house, shouting my name. When I went outside to see what was the matter, I saw him wandering up and down like a wild animal. He was utterly beside himself. 'What is it?' I asked.

" 'Go down to my hut,' he moaned. 'Go down there quickly. Hurry, please!'

" 'Well, will you please tell me what's happened?' I said. After all, I didn't want to have to walk all that way over if I didn't need to. 'Is something wrong?' I repeated.

" 'Yes,' he said, 'Yes, I've killed him. I've killed that boy.'

"I called Sister Caroline, and we got Rudy into her house. He came willingly. Sister Caroline put him on her bed and gave him a sedative, while I hurried down to Rudy's hut. And there I found the murdered boy. There was a horrible wound in his head, and several deep cuts in his arms. An ax was lying on the ground. I carried him over to Sister Caroline, but there was nothing we could do. The boy was already dead. We couldn't grasp it. It made no sense. The boy was new at the school, and had been there for only a few days. He was fourteen, and not in Rudy's form. I'm almost sure Rudy never had spoken to him and that he didn't know the boy from Adam.

"Of course we sent a telegram to the police, reporting what had happened. And when my wife and children came back from the plantation, I got out my gun and kept guard over the room where Rudy lay. The injection put him to sleep, but my wife was worried because of the children. And in the evening, fortunately, it happened that Pastor Veyrier arrived in his boat and we were able to send a telegram telling the police that we would be coming with Rudy ourselves. He was questioned as soon as we got here, and now he's in jail."

"I'm glad you were there, Pierre," Madeleine said to her husband. "What did Rudy say when he was questioned? Did he give any explanation?"

But Rudy had been silent. He simply confessed to the murder, and would not reply to any other questions. Nor would he have a defending counsel. "I'm guilty," he said. "I have no defense."

But Rudy did have a defending counsel. One of England's

finest lawyers flew out to the New Hebrides, and with him came a famous psychiatrist from London. Rudy's mother was on the plane, too. I had no idea how she'd managed to afford the expenses. Rudy's family had never struck me as well-off. But soon another guest arrived who could explain it. Polly Thompson suddenly appeared, unannounced. She had flown the entire detour via Australia. And when Rudy's mother thanked her, with tears in her eyes, we understood. Polly had paid for it all. Polly Thompson, who was known in Suva as the biggest tightwad on the islands, had forked out for the travel expenses and fees of both the defense counsel and the psychiatrist. It must have cost her a fortune, but she brushed all gratitude aside.

"Stop making such a fuss," she snapped. "I've got enough money left for a decent funeral, and at my age that's all I need to worry about. I just don't get the hang of what's happened here. But I do know one thing—Rudy's been mistreated. Mistreated by life and mistreated by those damned missionaries. That's why I'll help him, even if it costs me my last penny."

"You're a good woman," said Madeleine gently. Polly flared up.

"Me, a good woman? Ha! that's a laugh. No, I'm a disgusting, malicious old bitch, that's what I am. But I love that boy more than anyone else in the world. I understand him. I know what it's like to be mistreated, to be one of the 'half-and-halfs'—one of those who are different and so have to be stamped on by everybody passing by. If we poor souls didn't help each other, I don't know where we'd be."

Rudy's mother was a small, sad, dark woman swaying between sorrow over Rudy and pity for herself.

"Oh, do stop crying so much," Polly said. "What good will it do? If you've neglected your son all your life, then it's high time you started to help him. And tears aren't the way to help."

But nothing else seemed to help Rudy either, for he just didn't want any help. "I'm guilty," he said. "I knew what I was doing. I've nothing to say in my own defense."

On this small island it was not hard to get permission to visit him in the jail. But our meeting with him was sad. He sat for a long time with his head bent low after being led into the room where we were waiting. His mother immediately burst out with a rash "Rudy, how could you do this to me?" Rudy looked at her with despairing eyes, and got up as though he wanted to escape. But Polly—large, multicolored, warmhearted Polly—took him in her arms. "Now . . . now . . . now," she said comfortingly. Rudy lay sobbing against her shoulder, and though Polly herself dissolved into tears, she managed to calm him down. There are so many different kinds of tears. Rudy's mother's tears bordered on the hysterical. She cried over Rudy. But Polly cried with him.

She made Rudy sit down, and once more he stared with remote eyes, not saying anything.

"Don't you even know your own mother?" Mrs. Zellensky wailed.

Polly groaned in despair. But Rudy looked up. "Yes," he said quietly; "yes . . . I know you. You are my mother—and you are my friends. But now it's as though none of you belong to me any more. You did once. Once . . . long, long ago."

He turned his eyes toward the window, where the palms still swayed in the sun.

"Why," he asked plaintively, "why has the world changed so? It's not the same world any more."

He glanced back at us, his guests, and suddenly it was as though he saw only Madame Veyrier. He smiled sadly at her.

"Oh, Madeleine . . . you're here, too. You were always so kind to me. No . . . you mustn't take my hand. Your hands are too pure for that."

I admired Madeleine because she was able to smile. Her eyes were moist, but she held the tears back. She took both Rudy's hands, and kissed him on the cheek.

Rudy held her hands desperately.

"Madeleine, Madeleine . . . the others are so far away, but you're so close to me. You make me remember. Oh, Madeleine . . . do you remember? I thought everything was going to be so good. I thought I was on my way to paradise. And then I landed in hell."

He sprang up from his chair with clenched fists.

"Yes," he shouted, ". . . in hell . . . in hell!"

He staggered as though he were going to faint, but Polly took hold of him and got him to sit down in his chair. His head fell forward and rested on the table.

"Now we must go," said Polly. "He can't take any more."

"But he must tell us why he did it," lamented his mother. "He's got to tell us. Rudy . . . why did you do it?"

Polly flexed her muscles and pushed Mrs. Zellensky out the door as resolutely as she had once thrown the Fijian woman down the stairs of the Blue Lagoon.

"Let him be," she said. "It's no good, anyway. We've got to leave it to Sir Thomas. That's why we brought him here. Only a psychiatrist can help him. If he can't get Rudy to talk, nobody can."

But it was Madeleine who made Rudy talk. When the psychiatrist had spent every day for a whole week in Rudy's cell in vain, Madeleine asked if she might go with him the next day. She went in to Rudy on her own at first, and it was not long before she called the doctor.

"I'll tell you some of it," said Rudy. "I've promised Madeleine I would. I'll answer your questions if I can. But we must be alone."

"Why did you kill the boy?" asked the doctor when Madeleine had left.

Rudy did not reply.

"What were your relations with the boy?"

"I didn't know him. He was new at the school. I'd never spoken to him."

"Did you speak to him before it happened?"

"No."

"Were you particularly depressed that day?"

"I was always depressed."

"Why?"

"Because of what had happened—what led to my being transferred."

"So it was true, what you were accused of?"

"Not all of it. But some of it."

"Were you so depressed that you thought of suicide?"

"Yes! Several times I tried to drown myself in the river. But I didn't succeed. I couldn't take my own life. I didn't have the courage."

"You realize what your punishment will be if you plead guilty in court?"

"Yes . . . death."

"Doesn't that worry you?"

"No, it's nothing but good. I want to die."

"Did you know what you were doing when you killed that boy?"

"Yes."

"Was there a specific reason why you did it?"

"Yes."

"Will you promise to answer my next question honestly?"

"Yes, if I can."

"Did you kill the boy because you thought it was an indirect way of committing suicide?"

It was a long time before Rudy answered. He sat with his eyes closed and waited. Then he raised his head and looked at the doctor.

"Yes," he said. "Yes . . . that's why."

Rudy repeated his explanation in court, and his confession landed in heavy type on the front page of the newspapers.

THE MURDER WAS SUICIDE.

Both the defending counsel and Sir Thomas did their utmost to have Rudy declared insane. But he behaved so sensibly in court that he contradicted the men who were trying most to help him. At the same time there was unrest among the natives. The rumor had spread that the white man would be acquitted. Some months before, two natives had been hanged for the murder of an English plantation owner. Why shouldn't the white man who had murdered a native be hanged, too? There were disturbances on the murdered boy's island. The authorities were afraid that the unrest might spread. An extra police cordon was stationed around the courthouse while the case lasted.

The judges considered their verdict for a long time, and were evidently not in agreement. But the result was that Rudy was sentenced to death.

Polly forked out again, and there was an appeal. She traveled to England, to New Zealand, to Australia. She contacted every politician who had a grudge against the colonial administration. She started an agitated press campaign.

"Political death sentence on Pacific island," wrote one newspaper. "Accused, declared insane by famous neurologist, must be sacrificed to calm the native population which the incompetent civil servants are unable to control."

The result was that the court of appeal squashed the sentence. Rudy was sentenced to detention in an asylum in England for life.

I did not learn this until much, much later, and by then I had long since traveled to Tonga.

Naturally the murder case was discussed on board the ship which took me to Fiji. There was only one other passenger, a small, monkey-faced Spaniard, named Señor Juan Bastante. The captain called him "Don Juan," and the name was reasonably appropriate. By his own testimony, Don Juan's escapades would have made Casanova himself look naïve.

The captain was a big, good-natured blusterer with his own very firm salt-water theories as to how people should behave.

"Nasty business, that murder on the New Hebrides," he growled. "Hope the fellow will be hanged. The sooner we get rid of that sort of character, the better."

On the other hand, the captain was very enthusiastic about "Don Juan."

"Hell, there's good stuff in those Spaniards," he grinned. "Look at that little shrimp of a man. Would you think he could get it wholesale? But you bet he can. You should see him with the girls. He gets them laid every time, that's a fact."

"Don Juan" grew a couple of inches every time the captain praised his hormones. I could well understand his own extravagant praise for the paradise islands. Letting a Spaniard loose in the South Sea Islands is like letting a dog loose in a butcher shop.

Before we left the ship in Suva, "Don Juan" had managed to inform me that he was a very pious Catholic. He never missed Mass, and went regularly to confession.

"Last time my father confessor was very pleased with me," he said proudly.

"Oh? Why?"

Don Juan laughed. "Well, you see, the month before last, I had twenty-two sins to confess. But this month it was only eighteen. 'Ah,' said my father confessor, 'that's good. Now at least we're going in the right direction.'"

We stayed at the same hotel in Suva, and before I continued to Tonga there was no doubt that "Don Juan" was going in the wrong direction again.

It was on Tonga that the news about Rudy caught up with me. Once more I was living in a palm hut, and it was there that I received letters from Polly and Madeleine Veyrier.

"We won and yet we lost . . . ," Polly wrote.

That evening I sat by another happy lagoon.

Around me, carefree brown people played their game with life. If Rudy had been born out here in the world of open doors, he might have been one of them. But now the world of suppression, with all its closed doors, had locked him in behind a door which would never be opened again.

An old man from the village came down to the beach and sat beside me.

"You look sad, my friend," he said. "Is your heart heavy?"

"Yes . . . I've had bad news about a good friend."

The old Polynesian's eyes stared thoughtfully out at the lagoon.

"We must take our sorrows as life's bitter medicine, and learn from them," he said. "Have you seen how beautiful the sea is in the sunset tonight? The sorrows of our friends are like ships that have been wrecked on the ocean. And still we find pleasure in the beauty of the sea, even though we know it hides so many wrecks."

A kingdom for a queen

When I set sail for the Kingdom of Tonga, I knew very little about the place I'd be seeing. I knew that Tonga was the world's smallest kingdom, and I knew that Salote was the world's largest queen. Beyond that, I had just a few dry facts. There are 150 Friendly Islands, of which only thirty-six are inhabited. The total population is estimated at about fifty thousand, although there hasn't been a census since 1939. The capital and chief seaport is called Nuku'alofa, and it was to Nuku'alofa that I had been heading ever since I had turned my back on Denmark and the Western way of life.

Queen Salote's little kingdom is so far off the beaten track that Tonga is rarely visited by tourists. There were no travel brochures to tell me in advance what I should look for on the Friendly Islands. I would have nothing to go by but my own intuition and my own rather nearsighted eyes. But that didn't bother me in the least. On the contrary, I was feeling as excited as an old-time explorer setting out for an unknown land. Captain Cook, I am sure, could not have felt any more curious than I as I stood on deck that morning and waited for Tonga to come rising out of the sea.

It was a Monday morning when my ship sailed into Nuku'-alofa, though the weather felt for all the world like a Sunday. Which in actual fact it was. The date line was up to its old tricks again, making Tongan Sundays into eastern Mondays. The line is drawn on the map between the Fiji Islands and Tonga. But the Friendly Islands were so friendly, they insisted on moving over to the wrong side of the line in order to keep the same time as their neighbors, Fiji and New Zealand. In addition, the Parliament of the Kingdom of Tonga has, in its inscrutable wisdom, resolved by law that the Tongan day must begin twenty minutes before it actually begins anywhere else. So it was an out and out fraud to say that we arrived at seven on a Monday morning; it was really twenty minutes to seven on the morning of the day before.

Seeing Tonga for the first time from a ship's deck is like witnessing a mirage. The island is so flat that it cannot be seen at all until you are nearly on top of it. But when, suddenly, it does appear out of the sleepy blue swells of the sea, it looks like an illustration from a fairy-tale book. All you can see at first are hanging gardens with towering trees, seemingly suspended in mid-air. The trees, I found out, were the "Norfolk pines" which stand like sentries around Queen Salote's miniature castle. The South Sea Queen's palace is situated close to the sea and the port. As I stood on deck, I fancied that perhaps the Friendly Queen was at that moment standing on her balcony, dressed in scarlet slippers and a golden crown, looking out as curiously as the fairy-tale princess who peered out her tower window to see what stranger was arriving in her kingdom.

The island which has been honored with both palace and capital is the largest of the many small ones in the kingdom. The island is called Tongatapu, or "Holy Tonga," and Nuku'alofa, the capital, means "love's place." As we approached the harbor of "Love's Place," slender palms seemed to bow low and bid a romantic welcome to us with drowsy palm-leaf fingers. The skipper, too, waved with his fingers, and his sign language was understood by a group of men waiting for us in canoes. They plunged headlong into the water and swam the hawsers to the mooring buoys with an Olympic, muscular grace. Our human tugboats were magnificent to look at. They may not have been as efficient as their machine-age counterparts, but what they lacked in engine power was more than made up in the sheer beauty of their performance.

The entire town seemed to be down at the dock, celebrating some sort of national holiday. And a national holiday it is, too. "Steamer day" is a big event in Nuku'alofa. It takes place only twice a month in the banana season, and when there are no bananas, the ship stops only once. A seaplane from Fiji used to land on the lagoon once a month, but the route was a complete loss and it's now been closed down. The Tongans are very suspicious of these new-fangled airships. They would rather swim to Fiji than go by air.

So the ships to Tonga are always crowded and mine was no exception. We were jammed to the gills with cheerful Tongans all singing and strumming their Friendly way home. They sang away the last few inches into port, then joined the engines in a quivering sigh that announced that at last we were there. We had arrived, and Nuku'alofa, the little sunshine capital of the Pacific from which the famous South Sea Queen reigns over her 150 Friendly Islands, stood waiting.

There's no problem finding where to stay when you land in Nuku'alofa. There is only one hotel in the entire kingdom. And although Tongan tourists are as rare as Christmas flies, it's a good idea to make your reservations well in advance. Tonga's solitary hotel has a total of only twelve beds, and since at least half of them are always occupied by the residents, the kingdom has a hard time knowing where to put its extra guests. When the tourist invasion soars as high as six, the place is all booked up.

Another bit of friendly advice I should pass along to would-be Friendly Island tourists concerns the matter of visas. Most countries say they either do require one or they don't. Not Tonga. To visit the Friendly Islands, you must send in a written application for a visa. The letter must be a personal one, preferably written by hand, and addressed to the Prime Minister. After a suitable waiting period, His Excellency replies that no visa is required and that you are welcome to come. This letter from the Tongan Government is as cheerful and as informal as an invitation from an uncle in the country. But it is actually as formal as any document you can find; without this letter announcing that no visa is required, no tourist can get in. The letter itself serves as a visa, and nobody outside the Tongan Government knows why.

This flowery invitation, by the way, does not mean that a stay in Tonga is free. No, you will have to pay your hotel bill, just as anywhere else. But it won't make you poor. The hotel is called The Beach House, but in everyday language it's known only as Bella's. Bella, whose proper name is Mrs. Riechelman, is as indispensable to the Friendly Islands as Queen Salote. One of Tonga's great political problems is that each year Bella threatens to retire. Fortunately she's a little bit fonder of reigning than the Duke of Windsor, and so everyone hopes that it will be a long time before she decides to abdicate as hotel queen of Tonga.

The old white judge's residence which Bella rents from the government admittedly doesn't have much in the way of modern conveniences. But the rooms have free air-conditioning from the Pacific, and the windows, thanks to Tonga's eternal summer, are covered only with screens. In spite of the heat I woke up each morning feeling as fresh as a steak in a freezer.

My room was attractively furnished, with plenty of space and beautiful tapa rugs on the walls. And there was even a door. Of course it was a rather restless door, which swung open every time the wind knocked. It swung open every morning at sunrise, as carefully as it had with Tukua, when my delightful Tongan "Rose" woke me up with a cup of tea, two biscuits, and her smile. And here, with my tea every morning I was treated to an unhampered view of the sun rising over the sea. Both tea and sunrise were served to me in bed, and since I'm one of those people who cannot get up with the same effortless pleasure as the sun, the arrangement worked out perfectly.

It wasn't difficult to plan my first excursion into town. Before doing anything else, I would, of course, have to pay a formal visit to Queen Salote's Royal Aide in order to report my arrival and most humbly apply for an audience.

I steered toward the harbor, where the miniature coast road links fingers with the equally tiny main street. At the intersection are both the royal palace and a squat tropical bungalow which, for all its modest proportions, houses the postal service, the customs authority, and the tax department. These institutions, however, are no more formidable than the little bungalow. Nobody takes officialdom too seriously in Tonga. Since these are the Friendly Islands, all business is conducted on a very friendly basis. You pay duty only if you happen to be on unfriendly terms with the post-office or customs officials. Fortunately I was in good standing the day a parcel of film arrived for me from Fiji. In spite of all the customs regulations to the contrary, I was immediately given my parcel duty-free.

Just a few steps across the road from the world's smallest, friendliest customs authority lies a large lawn which is the big meeting-place for all Nuku'alofians. Housewives exchange gossip here, while lovers walk hand in hand along the paths. Children practice their bicycle riding, and in the afternoon everyone gathers around for the daily football or cricket match. If there happens to be a banana boat in town, the village lawn is also the place where the boxes of fruit are packed, with so many breaks for refreshment that the so-called job looks more like a town-sized picnic.

It's all very democratic, for the lawn is Nuku'alofa's *mala'e*—palace square. Behind it, Tonga's large-size queen resides in a small, white-lacquered palace which could easily be mistaken for someone's turreted summer home on the Atlantic coast. And in this toy-sized palace lives one of the largest royal families in the world. There is Queen Salote herself; then her two sons Crown Prince Tungi and Prince Tu'ipelehake; their wives; then the eight little chocolate-brown princes and princesses who are now the pride and future of Tonga's royal family tree. And, as if those weren't enough to fill any small castle, there are also literally dozens and dozens of other relatives who have anchored themselves with Polynesian matter-of-factness to the comfort of life in a palace. The palace is so full of royal and quasi-royal Tongans that even an American housing commission would have to declare the premises dangerously overcrowded. However, nobody in Tonga seems to think overcrowding is dangerous. They are used to doing things on a small scale, and they apparently like being squeezed all together into the smallest spaces conceivable. There were once plans to build a larger, more modern palace outside the town, but nobody seemed to care much for the idea, least of all Queen Salote.

From her waterfront palace Queen Salote smiles out each morning at the sea, and the sea returns her smile. Several times in the past the sea has also mourned with its Queen. When the Queen's sister, Princess Fusipala, died in 1933, and again when the Prince Consort died suddenly in 1941, the sea around Queen Salote's island turned blood-red. No expert has been able to explain the phenomenon. While scientists puzzled over the problem, the Tongans simply accepted it as the sea's expression of sympathy with the Queen's own bleeding heart.

The sea sent another omen shortly before news of the Pacific war reached Tonga. A heavy fog descended over the lagoon. The Tongans wondered about this strange mourning veil hanging ominously over the sea, for it was the first time they had experienced the fog we others know so well. When the radio announced the Japanese attack on Pearl Harbor, nobody doubted that once again the sea had sent an omen of misery and death.

Queen Salote's park stretches down to the sea. Toward the town there are low walls, and fences of the tall "Norfolk pines." But there is no barbed wire around the palace. And the few sentry boxes are usually empty, for the royal sentries are rarely at their posts. The wrought-iron gates form no barrier, either, as they are always wide open to the public. Anyone who feels like it can walk straight in. But nobody ever does so except on legitimate business, for the people's love and respect are sufficient protection for Queen Salote and her palace.

At the palace I also saw another expression of the veneration which the Tongans show their Queen—a ceremonial courtesy which explains why, in spite of the pouring rain, Queen Salote refused to drive in a closed state coach in Queen Elizabeth's Coronation procession through London. At that time the enthusiastic Londoners thought the South Sea queen's water ballet was a heroic performance, staged because she wanted to give all the wet spectators their money's worth of view. But that wasn't her reason at all. When a Tongan wants to pay tribute to his Queen, he waits for a rainy day and then walks past the royal palace with his umbrella folded up. To a Tongan, getting wet while the Queen is dry is a very natural expression of respect. And so it was just as natural that Queen Salote should have gotten *herself* wet when a princess of higher rank, England's soon-to-be-made-Queen Elizabeth, passed by in a closed golden coach. To the British this was courage and a spirit of self-sacrifice. To the Tongans it was simple courtesy and good upbringing.

Naturally I put on my most royal manners when I paid my first visit to the palace. But my courtly approach was as out of place there as it would have been anywhere else. I was received with informal friendliness by the Queen's Royal Aide and nephew, Tu'i Hala Vaea. Young Vaea was as charming as his exalted aunt. On my very first visit he promised me, with one of his most melting South Sea smiles, that he would arrange an audience for me with the Queen. He confirmed the promise, furthermore, by presenting me with three oranges.

I felt reassured and happy as I left the office of the Royal Aide, juggling my three oranges. It's a long way from Copenhagen to Nuku'alofa. I would have been hopelessly downcast if my petition had been refused. But knowing that I could count on meeting the Queen, I went cheerfully out the palace gates intending to take a look at the town.

As I walked through the park, I looked hopefully around for a glimpse of the Queen. At the time I didn't know how much of a recluse Salote actually was. Her few public appearances are made only on state occasions. The rest of the time Queen Salote stays hidden in her palace, and this annoys the New Zealand tourists no end. On their round-trip cruises, they're given only half a day in Nuku'alofa, and the moment they arrive, they rush ashore to look at the Queen. When they learn that Queen Salote does not sit on public exhibition in her park, they grumble indignantly, sounding for all the world like visitors to a zoo complaining that the tiger isn't out. Still grumbling, they walk, disappointed, into the town, and there they grumble even more. Tonga's capital is sad and boring, they say. What's there to see if you can't see the Queen, they ask one another. There's nothing here, absolutely nothing at all.

And the tourists are right. There is nothing to see in Tonga. What the tourists don't know is that therein lies Tonga's great charm. Tonga has nothing to offer but peace—beautiful, idyllic, calm, and entrancing peace—and that, considering the state of the rest of the world, is really quite a lot. No, the nicest thing of all about Tonga (aside from its Queen) is the fact that there's nothing to do. There are no "musts" for you to track down, note, and appreciate. Tonga has no museums, no souvenir shops, no banks, no newspapers, no libraries, no monuments. On the other hand, Tonga also has no unemployment, no strikes, no housing shortages, no hunger, no want, no suicides, no political parties, no high taxes, and no national debt. As a matter of fact, Tonga is probably the only nation in the world with a national surplus. There are, of course, no railways either, even though one of Nuku'alofa's streets has adorned itself with the name "Railway Street." Perhaps the wise fathers of the town thought the name sounded musical.

There's something touching about Tonga's capital, which thinks, with its almost 5,500 inhabitants, that it's a big city. But a big city it is for the Tongans, most of whom have never seen anything bigger. Nuku'alofa has grown so self-conscious about its size that it has acquired a staff of traffic police. There are no less than two of these elegantly uniformed officials in the capital. They sit under corrugated-iron canopies in the main street, and from there they direct the sparse traffic with signs that are much too grand for anything so small. Usually the traffic policemen are lost in their own private thoughts, and need to be jarred awake by a horn or bicycle bell in order to be reminded of the rare and thrilling event of traffic. When they do wake up, they give the road users an exuberant smile and grant them permission to pass along the already quite passable street.

One morning I watched a cyclist come rolling along with a very pretty girl riding on his handlebars. The traffic policemen smiled extra widely and made a formal bow. And no wonder: the girl on the handlebar was one of the Queen's maids of honor, and she was being escorted by one of the knights of the palace as stylishly as though the bicycle were a golden carriage.

This episode inspired me to acquire a bicycle myself. A Westerner on the island of Tongatapu quickly discovers that a bicycle is a useful middle course between Tonga's few, much too expensive taxis and Tonga's numerous, much too cheap buses.

My bicycle and I quickly made friends with the whole of Nuku'alofa, where the dead-straight roads resemble those of New York, in miniature. With the exception of a few skyscrapers two stories high, the houses stay close to the ground. The shops of the capital are all tiny department stores, offering for sale a mixed profusion of all the little necessities stacked up on desks and shelves.

There are a few Indian shops, but Tonga's Indians do not have an easy time. To avoid the problems the English have had with the large Indian population on Fiji, the Friendly Islands have resorted to brutally cruel measures. It was decided long ago that those Indians who had already settled on Tonga might be allowed to stay; but they would under no circumstances be permitted to increase their number. At that time, there were only two dozen or so of them on the islands. And two dozen or so they must remain, regardless of whether the increase threatens from without or within. As a result, the arrival of a newborn child is a far from happy event for an Indian family on Tonga. With each new birth, one of the older relatives must leave.

On a large green common in the middle of Nuku'alofa lie Tonga's royal tombs, where Queen Salote's Prince Consort was laid to rest at his much too early death in 1941. But the royal burial ground has none of the gloomy atmosphere of a cemetery. The Tongans are much too practical and cheerful for that. They have fenced in the pompous grave monuments, and set off the rest of the large area of grass as the local golf club. This is equivalent, more or less, to renting out a part of Arlington National Cemetery to a badminton club. But everyone in Nuku'alofa is pleased with the arrangement. The only drawback is that every now and then a stray golf ball disappears over the royal fence and so ends up as an odd decoration on top of the tombs.

I had no difficulty climbing up to the top of Zion Mountain, which is in the middle of the town and also the highest point on the island. The reason that I refrained, after this monumental ascent, from sending a telegram to Sir Edmund Hillary, was simply that the Everest of Tongatapu is a little bit less than sixty-five feet high. From this peak I had an excellent view of Nuku'alofa's pride, the newly-built Methodist church. The Tongans are terribly proud of their large, stylishly modern house of worship, which happens to have the biggest—and only—tower clock in the kingdom, so big that its scarlet painted hands can be seen from any point on the island. During the entire time I stayed in Nuku'alofa those scarlet hands remained fixed at six minutes to two. But that didn't lessen the natives' pride in their church. Tonga is a kingdom where neither clocks nor people have any idea of time.

All Tongans are Christian, but the religion is a great deal stricter than on Samoa. The Methodist missionaries dominate the little kingdom, and their puritan zeal has meant that, compared with Samoa, Tonga is at best a poor man's paradise. Tonga's Constitution contains a law forbidding all work *and all play* on the sacred Sunday. Even sports like fishing or golfing are considered illegal, and that ruling applies for Westerners too.

The missionaries of Tonga have also turned nakedness into a sin. A stiff fine is levied against any male Tongan appearing in public stripped to the waist after age six.

With so many repressive new laws it seems a wonder that Christianity ever took hold on Tonga at all. But take hold it did, for it had something very valuable to offer. According to the old religion, only Tongans of high rank and class were considered to have an immortal soul. The run-of-the-mill bourgeois Tongan might also have a soul, but his would dissolve into nothingness once he died, while the souls of the socially distinguished would go to eternal salvation on the heavenly island of Pulotu. When the people heard that the missionaries were distributing immortal souls free of charge, they rushed right over to the new temples and enthusiastically joined the ranks.

Aside from souls, the church also distributes a few other things. One of them happens to be haloes. Tonga's streets are full of angels. You can recognize them without any trouble. They're usually large-size matrons who go marching off to church in their wildest warpaint, armed with the dignity of a maharajah's favorite elephant. They walk as though they're among God's chosen. And so they are. For these are the ladies who, as a result of energetic churchgoing and zealous appearance at Bible lessons, have been awarded the church's highest distinction, the honorary title of "Angel."

The week on Tonga has seven days like ours. But the main difference between Sunday and a weekday on Tonga is that there the day of rest is the busiest of all, thanks to the vigorous church activity into which the Methodist missionaries have thrust the Tongans. If the Tongans don't find their playless Sundays too boring, it's because with their cheerful sense of practicality they have seen to it that there is not much Methodism in the madness. Churchgoing is considered a welcome entertainment in a country offering few things to do. The churches have become popular clubs, where everybody can get together in his Sunday best and join in a community sing. Like the Samoans, the Tongans are heaven-inspired singers whose musical vocal chords can outdo even the strongest organ. Their talent for choral singing is so fantastic that they can improvise in four parts after hearing a tune played only once.

Another reason why Tonga tolerates a too-blue Sunday is that Saturday is celebrated in just the opposite way. The Tongans make an effort to do everything on Saturday that they know they can't do Sunday. The main public event is the weekly football match, in which the entire population gathers for massive American-style football battles on the grass. The great event of each season is the game between Suva and Nuku'alofa. This test is carried out with a bloodthirsty fierceness which recalls the old pagan days of bloody wars between Fiji's cannibals and Tonga's famous, unflinching warriors.

Among other entertainments, Nuku'alofa has two movie theaters, called "Finau's" and "Mrs. Mann's," in honor of their respective owners. Mrs. Mann's is actually Mr. Mann's, but nobody seems to care. Mrs. Mann (or Mr.) has alluringly called her temple of art the "Come-Again-Cinema," though—to be very frank—one would really rather come again to Finau's because the seats there are much more comfortable. At Mrs. Mann's, the come again audience is obliged to settle hard and fast on benches made of old American railroad ties. Nowadays, however, it's possible for us commoners to sit in the stiff dining-room chairs of the former royal box. The royal family now has its own theater, where the more select films are shown for the Queen and her court.

The American movies shown at the plebeian theaters are considerably less select. The loudspeakers are so asthmatic that it sounds as though the Hollywood stars are speaking Tongan instead of English. But they're not, since the Tongans can't understand a word either. To make up for this, they supplement the inarticulate loudspeakers with very articulate enthusiasm every time they're presented with America's wildest West or Chicago's most cutthroat gangsters. Like the Samoans, they want shooting and murder for their money, and they're not satisfied unless they're served up with at least three or four full-length features and five or six supporting items. The shows usually last from seven until well after midnight, and what more could any Tongan want for the price of a quarter? That the programs are rarely changed doesn't matter in the slightest. Seeing the same films several times over is always quite an experience, since the operators generally ignore the numbers on the reels and show the films each time in a new and thrillingly different sequence. The Tongans don't give a damn if the screen hero dies before he is born, just as long as the guns bang merrily away from end to end.

In spite of the lack of modern conveniences in Tonga, you can call in advance to reserve the royal box at Mrs. Mann's. Nuku'alofa has a modern telephone system, even though it may not have very much else. Electric lights didn't appear until 1951, and by 1956 the power plant was so overworked from producing all this unaccustomed energy that it had a nervous breakdown and had to take a two months' vacation. Nuku'alofa has no waterworks, but that can be explained by the fact that there is no water anyway. Everyone manages by collecting rain water, except during the dry season, which is the time each year when everyone in Nuku'alofa begins to wonder why there isn't a waterworks.

Speaking of telephones reminds me of the Dane, Viggo Petersen, who left the Copenhagen Telephone Company and wound up, through fate's inscrutable ways, as Telephone Director of the Kingdom of Tonga. Naturally I had to pay a visit to my countryman. I was delighted with the Petersens' roomy tropical villa—so roomy that the distance between kitchen and dining room could be covered in no less than five minutes—and I was even more delighted to meet their two little Tongan-born daughters. Two-year-old Jenny was at that time becoming especially talkative, though I couldn't figure out whether she was speaking Danish, English, or Tongan. It sounded like all three at once. But I knew it would be a long time before Jenny learned to pronounce the name she was given as a christening gift by her royal godmother, Queen Salote. Even her parents had to pull out the birth certificate before they could announce that their daughter's full name was "Jenny Ulukilipetea Petersen." They knew that the middle name meant "the white dove." But the dove herself had no idea what fun her name would give her later on in school lists, registration offices, and passport departments.

On Tonga they bend over backward for unusual Christian names. At Bella's, for example, we had a chambermaid who was called Waitemata. Charming, isn't it? Very Polynesian? Not at all. Waitemata is New Zealand's most popular beer. This is like an American family choosing to call their daughter "Miss Reingold." Which my spies tell me is actually being done.

All over the Pacific islands you will find sweet little South Sea girls who, without any sign of a smile or a sneer, have been christened "Major" or "Sergeant." In most cases the inspiration came from this being, by and large, all that the mother knew about the father.

Most Polynesian names are quite delightful, but I must confess I was a little disturbed by one highly respected chief who, in all seriousness, had been christened "The Old Pig," and who had been called this since he was a very young pig. But it's just as honorable a name as those with which two of Queen Salote's grandchildren have been blessed. The little Princess "Fusipala" would in English be known as Princess "Rotten Banana," and her brother, the little busybody Prince "Uluvalu," is quite normal in spite of the fact that his name means Prince "Eight Heads."

The Tongans must regard the figure eight as a lucky number, for nothing else could explain the great popularity of all sorts of eight-figure names. The plump Speaker of the Tongan Parliament would be welcomed by bartenders all over the world, since "Mr. Kalaniuvalu" is actually "Mr. Eight Gallons." And then there was the very peaceful, gentlemanly assistant on the state experimental farm who, without in the least deserving it, had to put up with the name "Henelivalu," or "Henry the Eighth." He was not even the eighth Henry in his family, so make something of that if you can.

In all likelihood my visit to Tonga will produce some startling suprises for anyone visiting Queen Salote's kingdom in a few years' time. Our future traveler will probably run into several light-brown toddlers who will be introduced as "Dagens Nyheder" —the Danish newspaper I work for—or maybe even as "Little Wonderful Copenhagen." Now don't misinterpret me and start counting on your fingers. The names will only be the result of the Tongans' fondness for using children as walking calendars. As I've mentioned, on Tonga they have very little conception of time. But if, one day, there should be some question about how long ago that Danish fellow was here, they need only turn to little "Dagens Nyheder" and figure out when he was born. Look, they will say, he's just three years and seventeen days old; it says so here on his birth certificate. But that means it's over three years now since the tall man from Denmark was here. How time flies!

When Nuku'alofa's brand-new church was first built, the event was commemorated throughout the land by saddling newborn infants with the incongruous name of "Tower Clock." "Tower Clock" was a distinctly male name; don't ask me why. And it was just as natural that the twins with which one Tongan woman celebrated Queen Elizabeth's and Prince Philip's visit to Tonga should have been named "Elisapesi" and "Filipe." Fortunately, the twins were of opposite sexes. But even if they hadn't been, it wouldn't have made any difference. The Tongans don't fuss about technicalities.

All sorts of events are commemorated in names. If Mama happens to be sick just before she gives birth, baby may wind up with a name like "Pneumonia." Papa's homecoming from the United States will be recorded in a child named "Fokimeiamelika" (Back from America), and there are even some children on Tonga who have been aptly christened "Warm-on-a-Cold-Rainy-Night."

While I was on Tonga, we received an official visit from the British submarine *Telemachus*, and this event, too, was commemorated in the church books. Little "Telemachus" arrived before he was expected, but he got there just in time to hear the welcoming salute of guns. Actually he was lucky to have been called "Telemachus"; he could well have gone through life as "Submarine."

"Telemachus" aside, the British naval visit produced a number of festive celebrations. Queen Salote announced a grand ball in the town, and the submarine responded with a cocktail party to be held afterward, below sea level.

I was invited to the Queen's ball, and was convinced that this meant I had won her favor. I was also sure in advance that Tonga's Queen would be a brilliant hostess, and on this point, at least, I was right. The party was splendid, and spirits were much higher than is usual at court balls. Only one thing was missing, and that was the Queen herself. When Her Majesty announces a court ball, she is both the perfect—and the invisible—hostess.

She never appears at her own parties, but stays instead in the palace and lets her two sons represent the throne.

And both Crown Prince Tungi and Prince Tu'ipelehake represent it so it can be seen. They are both as tall as their mother, and both, I am sure, are heavier. The Crown Prince is in his early thirties, and his younger brother in the late twenties. But in spite of their youth they have filled out so much that they must weigh about three hundred pounds apiece. Like all members of the Tongan royal house, they were born big. But a very royal appetite has helped. At any celebration Prince Tu'ipelehake can manage a whole barbecued pig on his own. A European woman on Fiji once told me what happened when Tonga's Crown Prince one day came to lunch without advance warning. She didn't think she had quite enough to set a royal table, so she borrowed twenty eggs from one of her neighbors. The eggs were turned into a huge omelette garnished with all sorts of things, and the Crown Prince was naturally served first. His hostess asked him to take potluck with what little she had in the house. Crown Prince Tungi smiled and said that was quite all right, he was on a diet and only too glad to have a light snack instead of a lunch. He thereupon took the dish from the servant and devoured all on his own the light little egg dish made from twenty eggs.

Crown Prince Tungi of Tonga is an intelligent young man, but he is nowhere near as popular as his younger brother. Prince Tu'ipelehake is the very image of Queen Salote, while the Crown Prince doesn't resemble his mother at all. He has neither her looks nor her smiling charm, and those are the requisites for public success in the Kingdom of Tonga. The Crown Prince, who studied law in New Zealand, has been the country's Prime Minister since 1939. Tonga's main source of income comes from exporting copra and bananas, and the New Zealand Union Steamship Line makes a lot of money out of its monopoly on transport facilities. The Crown Prince's great dream is to put the New Zealand firm out of business by establishing Tonga's own merchant marine. With this aim in mind he went to Europe a few years ago to look at ships. He stopped in Holland, ordered one made-to-order copra boat, bought two piccolos, and came home. He also brought home with him a pair of enormous Dutch wooden shoes, which some people on Tonga insist were built at the shipyard along with the boat.

Nearly all of Queen Salote's economy-sized family is connected in some way or other with the government. Prince Tu'ipelehake is Minister of Agriculture, and most of his cousins, uncles, and great-uncles hold similarly important posts. Both young princes are married to ladies who were chosen by Salote from among Tonga's most distinguished families. Tonga has a peerage consisting of about thirty-five titled lines, but since all of the titles can be removed by the royal family, the Tongan elite is not as rigid a class as is the nobility elsewhere. Members of the peerage are forced to toe the line if they want to have any rank left to pass on to their children.

The princesses also represent the royal house at parties. Both are as small as their husbands are large, and both were on hand at the submarine reception, where we all gathered round to see whether Crown Prince Tungi would be able to squeeze himself down the hatch. His Royal Highness filled the narrow vertical entrance like a cork in the neck of a bottle, and it looked for a while as though some of the sailors would be forced to pitch in and act as corkscrews.

The underwater reception drew a huge crowd, which included every V.I.P. in Tonga except, of course, for the Queen. Her few public appearances are usually made on Sundays, when she arrives without ceremony at the new Methodist church and sits in her own pew at a suitably elevated distance from the people. She doesn't sit anywhere near as high up, however, as did her great-grandfather, George the First, who was the first Christian king of Tonga. Now George the First was delighted to become a Christian. But when his newly converted Majesty went to church for the first time and saw the English minister climb high up into the pulpit, King George grew angry. Whoever heard of a commoner rising higher than a king, he thundered. He immediately ordered his carpenters to build a pew raised on stilts, and there, on the following Sunday, sat King George, singing piously over the heads of all and sundry, including the overly-presumptuous British minister.

Queen Salote sits closer to her people than George did, but she's no more easy to approach than he. People who want to learn anything about the Queen have to watch and listen for a long time, for hers is a difficult jigsaw puzzle to put together. The complete picture can be constructed only by fitting the pieces together, bit by bit.

There is a serious Queen Salote, a devout Methodist who sees to it that all the strict demands of the missionaries are met both by herself and by her subjects. There is a sorrowful Salote, who carries about with her the memories of too many members of her own family who have passed away before their time. There is a smiling Queen, who waves through the windows of her car as she rides through town, and there is even, I am told, a laughing Queen, although she, I suppose, is kept locked up inside the palace.

There is also a walking Queen, but she, as it happens, is invisible. All of Nuku'alofa knows that the Queen likes her evening stroll along the beach. But they also know that she does not like to be recognized while she walks. Even queens must go out for a bit of exercise, and queens, more than anybody else, like having their privacy undisturbed. And so it is customary on Tonga, when passing the Queen on her walk, to pass right by without so much as a bow or a curtsy in her direction. Several times during my stay I met the Queen out on her walks. And although I was growing increasingly anxious to speak with her, I never once dared break the important unwritten rule. Pretending she was a ghost—and a very tall ghost, at that—I sailed right by, hoping my repeated display of good Tongan manners would endear me to her heart.

I managed both to see and hear Queen Salote at close range a few days after I received a very elegant invitation from the

Queen's Royal Aide. The invitation was a printed card which read as follows:

'Ofisi 'o e Palemia
Nuku'alofa

Kia Mr Andersen
   'Oku fakaafe'i heni ke ke (ke mo) me'a mai
     ki he Huufi 'o e Fale Alea
   'e he 'Ene 'Afio ko-Kuini Salote Tupou
     'i hono 'aho 14 'o Sune, 1956,
     'i he taimi 10.30 Pongipongi.
Ke he 'atu 'eni ki he tangata le'o matapa

I realized at once that this was an invitation. I could also interpret, on my own, *'Ofisi 'o e Palemia* as being bound to mean "Office of the Premier." With a bit of study, I managed to figure out that *Kuini Salote* (Queen Salote) wanted to see me about something on 14 *Sune* (June) at 10:30 *Pongipongi* (in the morning). The bottom line of thirty letters I took to mean "R.S.V.P." But having gone that far, I had to seek outside help in order to find out what it was that *Kuini Salote* was inviting me to on 14 *Sune* at 10:30 *Pongipongi*.

The Tongan language is a very complicated one, outside of those words like *kuini* which have simply been taken over from English. Queen Salote's own name sounds very Polynesian, but it's only the Tongans' version of "Charlotte." Queen Salote is actually Queen Charlotte of Tonga, named after her great-grandmother queen, who brought the name over from England where it was then the name of the wife of King George the Third.

Tonga's royal family is one of the oldest dynasties in the world, and the history of the islands is a quaint mixture of legend and fact. The first account of a Tongan king dates back to about the year 950, when the King of Tonga bore the impressive title of *Tu'i Tonga*. But kings will be kings, and as the years went by, most of them felt less and less like defending their thrones against would-be rulers. By the time of the twenty-third *Tu'i Tonga*, being a king was more trouble than it was worth, and this august ruler therefore handed his secular power over to a co-regent, who was given the title of *Tu'i Ha'atakalaua*. The old *Tu'i Tonga* retired but retained for himself the dignified station of the country's religious figurehead, thereby winning the public esteem without fear of assassination. His retirement was made more interesting by a divinely beautiful woman he discovered on the island of Ata. She was so beautiful that when the king first saw her he danced a dance of joy and, in a fit of sheer delight, hit himself over the head with a pair of drumsticks. His son and successor, King Kau'-ulufonua, was less poetic. He celebrated his victory over a group of political opponents by cutting his dead enemies into small pieces and distributing the parts as souvenirs to all his warriors.

But sooner or later, even the *Tu'i Ha'atakalaus*—the secular kings—grew tired of fending off enemies. King Mo'ugatonga, the sixth in the newly established line of co-regents, decided to lighten his burden even further by creating a third branch of royal power, which was given the title of *Tu'i Kanokubolu*.

Tonga was ruled by this triumvirate of kings until Queen Salote's great-grandfather, George the First, gathered the powers of office into his own capable hands and restored the single monarchy. As a result of careful intermarrying, all three of the formerly royal lines are now combined in Tonga's present ruling family.

In 1875 Tonga set up its first parliament and drafted a democratic constitution; and in 1900 the King of Tonga signed a treaty putting the country under British protection. This "protection," however, does not affect Tonga's national independence. Great Britain simply guarantees the currency and promises protection in the event of an enemy attack.

After paying a visit to my friend the Royal Aide, I found that what Queen Salote had invited me to on the 14 *Sune* was the great celebration in honor of the opening of Parliament. Tonga's House of Parliament is about the size of a small night club, but its annual opening ceremony is performed with great dignity. I promptly R.S.V.P.'d, and at 10:30 *Pongipongi* on the appointed day, I stood solemnly among the ranks of loyal Tongans. The entire police force of Nuku'alofa was on hand; both members were wearing their full-dress uniforms, and both were energetically blowing their whistles in all directions. The whistles were necessary, because the kingdom's standing army—forty men and one tank—was holding its annual parade through the main street. The men are fine soldiers, but the tank is rather an embarrassment to the country. On its first day of maneuvers, it broke down and had to be towed back to the garage by an ordinary tractor. After the army had gone by, there was another procession, this time a highly spirited and colorful one. All the students of Nuku'alofa's surprisingly numerous schools had turned out, and they marched briskly down the streets dressed in their school uniforms of red, white, and blue.

The processions were only a build-up, however, to the solemn moment when the guns of the harbor announced the arrival of Queen Salote. In days gone by, the Queen of Tonga used to walk the short distance from palace to Parliament, dressed in the ermine-bordered robe of state and accompanied by the entire court. But she has grown more shy nowadays, and insists instead on driving to Parliament in a closed car, wearing only her everyday best. When she climbed out of the small black car, I could see why the additional pomp and ceremony had been dropped. Standing at her full height—which is a good deal taller than nearly anyone else in Tonga—the stately Queen looked more majestic than all the crowned heads of Europe put together.

After the singing of the national anthem—a triumphal song composed to order by a German composer whose name no one on Tonga can remember—Queen Salote entered the halls of Parliament, where she left her royal crown, said to be the heaviest in the world, on a red velvet cushion while she read her speech from the throne. Although I sat rapt through the entire thing, I must confess that I cannot remember a single word of that speech. The fact that it was delivered in Tongan may have something to do with it, but I rather think my lapse of memory was caused, instead, by the lady's charm; I was oblivious to all but her beautiful smile. I could not take my eyes off her from the moment she arrived.

I learned afterward from Vaea, the Royal Aide, that Queen Salote had also noticed me. When the Queen started back to the palace, her chauffeur began driving so fast that I and my cameras were forced to race breathlessly against the car. My headlong marathon through the Tongan street led the Queen to peer out the window and then turn to Vaea to ask, "Who on earth is that galloping European?"

"That's the Danish journalist," Vaea answered.

"Good heavens," said the Queen, "the poor man will have a heart attack from running so fast. Ask the driver to slow down, please."

I got this from Vaea himself, whom I'd come to know almost too well during the course of my stay in Nuku'alofa. I was in to see him so often that most people seemed to think I'd been hired as his assistant. Which in a way I was. My careful inquiries about an audience with the Queen were always answered with a smile and an encouraging nod. "Just wait!" he would say cheerfully. "You know how these things are, it takes time, only time, the Queen will see you soon!" Vaea grew even more cheerful when I began to help him with his work. The Queen received letters from all over the world, written in every conceivable language; but as her Royal Aide could manage only English, everything else was simply put aside, or answered with a polite "Just wait!" in either English or Tongan. I offered my services as unpaid official translator, and Vaea accepted them with gratitude. Letters had poured in particularly since the Coronation. Suddenly everybody felt impelled to correspond with the heretofore unheard-of Queen of Tonga. Some of the letter writers were just friendly admirers. But most of them were stamp collectors. They wrote asking for Tongan stamps, and they received them, free of charge, together with greetings from the Queen.

My new job kept me busy. In what spare time I had left I worked equally hard trying to build up a solid front of noble behavior with which to win the respect and confidence of the Queen. But in spite of all my efforts to acquire a halo and keep it well polished, nothing happened. There was still no word from Salote.

I brooded on what I could do about it. I had contacted every influential person I knew. If none of them could be of help, it looked as though I would have to contact a sorcerer.

I mentioned this to Bella, and sure enough, she produced one for me. His name was Mr. Butkuso, and he arrived a few days later as a new guest at the hotel.

Mr. Butkuso was a professional wizard. He had come from Australia in order to give performances at the local theaters. He could make ladies float on thin air, he could pull handkerchiefs out of the sky and rabbits out of hats. He ate fire and swallowed swords. Truly, he was a man of many talents. Too many. The Tongans were frightened to death of his magic, and refused to come within fifty feet of the theater where he was playing. Poor Mr. Butkuso. After playing to nothing but empty houses for two weeks, he was forced to take the next banana boat back to Australia. He left Nuku'alofa disappointed, convinced that even the primitive Tongans had failed to appreciate his magic.

But he was far wrong, as I found out later when I went to live in the village of Houma. I was chatting one evening with Ofa Hafoka, an eighteen-year-old village boy who had been educated in the mission schools of Nuku'alofa. Ofa had been to see Mr. Butkuso's tricks. "And didn't you like them?" I asked.

"Like them?" replied Ofa, staring at me in wonder as though I'd just revealed a second head. "How could anyone like such tricks as those? The man was a devil, that I know," he added, shaking his head.

Ofa's village contained barely two hundred souls and seven

churches. All seven churches fought valiantly for the possession of Houma's souls. Ofa was a Mormon, and he went to church three times every Sunday and sometimes on Tuesdays as well. He feared both God and his missionary, but secretly he had more respect for the numerous demons and evil spirits which he knew still haunted his district. The missionaries never got rid of the old gods of pagan Tonga. The Tongans downgraded them to demons, and thereby managed to keep them alive.

One night we sat by the ocean discussing deviltry. "Do you know," he said, pointing fearfully to a spot where moonbeams danced on the waves, "that right here where we're sitting a demon sometimes appears from the sea? A huge, horrible sea demon with evil eyes and many arms. I haven't seen him myself, but plenty of those in the village have."

I could have asked Ofa if he had ever heard of giant octopuses, but I didn't. I much preferred hearing about demons.

"Have you ever seen a demon, Ofa?" I asked.

"Oh, yes," he answered. "One night, right here in the palm scrub."

"How did you know it was a demon?"

"He took his head in both hands and lifted it off."

"Were you afraid?"

"Yes." Ofa ran his hands through his hair. "But if I saw him again, I wouldn't be afraid. I'd go right up to him."

"Why?"

"So I could touch him. Then I could go back and tell those who don't believe in demons that I had felt one and he was real."

A shadow appeared out of the darkness and loomed before us. But it was no demon. It was only Ofa's horse, Sharp Knife, come to tell us it was time we were started home.

It was pitch dark as we set out for the village, and naturally we cut a wide detour around the local cemetery. No Tongan would dare walk past a graveyard after nightfall. That's when the ghosts get out of their graves and go walking, although nowadays they're not anywhere near so dangerous as they used to be.

In the old days, no Tongan would dare set foot outside his house after sundown. The ghosts used to wander right through the middle of town, threatening the lives of any living souls who might happen to cross their paths. But these are modern times, and now there are only two ghosts to be found in the village proper. One is Feluhuni, a she-demon, and the other, her male counterpart, is a ghost whose name I never quite caught.

Feluhuni, the she-devil, steals around in the dark disguised as a beautiful girl. She tempts men beyond their power to resist, and she haunts many a dream of young boys who ought to know nothing and old boys who ought to know better. The he-devil practices the same dark deeds on women. And he is a very useful demon for any small mission-bound village to have. For how can the missionaries blame an innocent young girl who has been lured into sin by such a dreadful devil as he? This nameless demon is, of course, held responsible for every fatherless baby born to the good Christian girls of Houma. Fortunately, the half-demon children look just alike all the others, and they grow up to be just as normal. Some of them, in addition, bear a striking resemblance to the most handsome young men of the town. But that, of course, is just another of the terrible demon's wicked tricks.

From Ofa I learned a great deal about life in the little kingdom in the South Seas. Ofa himself had been to school. He knew how to read and write but had neither the opportunity nor the inclination to indulge in either. He had never seen a newspaper or a magazine in his entire life. And as the two major achievements of printed Tongan literature are the Bible and the telephone directory, he had little to look for in the way of books.

The Tongan brings all his problems and letters to the village elder, who is local representative of the Government and also postmaster. On the rare occasions when mail arrives, the elder takes up a position in the center of the village and there recites the names of those lucky ones who, if they have the time and feel in the mood, can come and get something as strange as a sealed-up message sent from a faraway place.

Telegrams never get farther than the capital. The telegraph station in Nuku'alofa, called *Makoni* (after Marconi; the "r" is missing because the Tongan alphabet has none), has a blackboard outside the office on which the names of addressees are written in chalk. Years may go by before recipients of wires will happen to pass by the blackboard and see their names.

Like the cannibal king of Fiji, Queen Salote owns all the land —150 islands worth—in her kingdom. But unlike Fiji, Tonga's islands cannot be bought or sold. The land is rented out, at the modest price of $4.50 per year for about ten acres, to any male Tongan who has reached his sixteenth birthday. The only condition attached to the arrangement is that each Tongan is obliged to plant his area with at least two hundred coconut trees. Of course, he may grow anything else he cares to. But if he decides he's content with the bare minimum of coconuts, he can still be sure of a good annual income over and above the tax for his land.

In spite of its feudal ownership, the Queen's kingdom is actually the most perfect Communist state in the world. The inexpensive land tax has virtually abolished private property on Tonga, even though the Queen, in fact, actually owns all the land. The economy is an exclusively agrarian one, and so Tonga, with all her prosperity, has managed to avoid the blemishes that scar other, less prosperous, industrialized societies. With neither factories nor merchants, Tonga has no middle or working classes. Her nobility is honored by titles, but except for the honor, Tonga's "distinguished families" live in the exact same style as everyone else.

The Tongan village is an economically and socially self-sufficient unit that would come close to perfection were it not for the increasingly strong tendency—spurred on by the missionaries—to "modernize." Slowly but surely, the idyllic beauty of the airy palm huts is being exchanged for so-called modern houses, which are considered much finer because they have windows and corrugated-iron roofs. Windows and roofs are not only unnecessary in the Tongan climate, they are downright ugly. These tinfoil houses are springing up all over the island like weeds, and like weeds, they threaten to strangle the buoyant palm-like life of the little kingdom in the sea.

But life in the village is still, for the time being, safe. Everyone strolls along at half speed, stopping every few steps to appreciate the view or play a new game. Even the chickens on Tonga seem to have invented better games than the old dull one of laying eggs. The ratio of chickens to eggs is so off-balanced that I am firmly convinced that Tonga's chickens have invented a brand-new method of propagation. And I hope that if anyone ever finds out what it is, he will have the good grace not to tell me.

I would have preferred staying in the villages all the time, but I was forced to keep one foot in the capital in order to find out what was happening to my audience with the Queen. Time after time I inquired as tactfully as I could. But to all intents and purposes, the only thing that was happening was that nothing was happening at all.

Apparently my shares stood high. At Nuku'alofa's big social event of the season, the hospital ball, it was traditional for Tonga's elite to waltz around the hall one at a time in carefully prearranged order. First came the young Prince with his Princess, then Her Britannic Majesty's Consul with the Counsul-ess, and, third in line—to my own utter amazement—came I, pirouetting gaily about with the stately Head Nurse of Tonga. At the time, I flattered myself that this honor indicated the Queen's respect for my noble behavior. In retrospect, however, I am forced to admit that I was probably chosen only because I was the sole gentleman in the kingdom tall enough to dance with the giant Head Nurse.

While wandering back and forth between the villages and the town, I had an opportunity to look in on the royal grandchildren. I was pleased to find that they were not weighed down by their royal dignity, no matter what else might have caused their royal plumpness. At the express wish of their grandmother, they are allowed to play their way through childhood like perfectly ordinary Tongan children. They go to the public schools, and the teachers have strict instructions to forget titles and treat the prince-lings just like all the other children. And the royal grandchildren are allowed to choose their own playmates, without regard for rank or class.

Back home in the royal park, Tonga's royal children have a playmate unlike any other in the world. This playmate is a highly respected member of the royal household who demonstrates his own importance by not giving way even before the Queen. When these two meet on the same garden path, it is the Queen who must step aside, not the other way around.

This august member of the royal household is also the oldest of the family. His exact age is not known, but it is estimated at about two hundred years. At any rate, there is no doubt that "Tu'i Malila"—the Prince of Malila—is the oldest citizen in the king-dom. The fact that he crawls through life in slow-motion is not due merely to his advanced age. In his youth he was slow-footed too, for the Prince of Malila is a tortoise.

The prince is one of the treasures of history. When the famous English explorer Captain James Cook stepped ashore on the Friendly Islands for the first time, he presented the then-King of Tonga with two tortoises, one male and one female. Unfortu-nately, the wife passed away in her girlhood, about a hundred years ago, and the noble tortoise Tu'i Malila has been a widower ever since.

Although scarred by the ravages of time, he is still active and insatiably curious. His curiosity has led him into dangerous waters though. Once he absent-mindedly crawled into the middle of a forest fire, and saved his life only by withdrawing into his shell. His private air-raid shelter has been considerably scorched since, and its condition was anything but improved when, some years later, the tortoise happened to be run over by a truck. The acci-dent was unavoidable, though, because the Prince of Malila can-not look before he crosses the streets. Tu'i Malila is almost totally blind. But in spite of his failing sight, he still rallies to the call of adventure and travel, and often needs to be brought home by the police whenever he ventures so far away from home that he cannot find his way back.

Although the Prince of Malila is older than the Queen, he is easier to approach. I had had several audiences with the tortoise, but still not a single word from Queen Salote. The three oranges I had been given by the Royal Aide were slowly rotting in my drawer. Withering away with them was my faith in the promises of Vaea. It may seem naïve, but it took me a long time to discover that when a Tongan keeps on saying "yes" without anything happening, it is actually just a polite way of saying "no."

For a long time I tried to figure out for myself what was wrong. Had I committed some grave Tongan *faux pax?* Did the Queen think I was a spy or, worse yet, a would-be assassinator? Was there something suspicious about my frequent disappearances into the villages? Did she think, because of my brief association with Mr. Butkuso, that I too was a devil in Danish disguise? I simply couldn't understand it. After all, I wanted nothing more than a brief audience with Salote. And since I had heard that she was as friendly as her islands, I had assumed that meeting her in person would be a relatively simple feat to accomplish. But I was mistaken. The explanation came, finally, from the Queen herself. One of her close friends at last informed me that Queen Salote simply did not allow interviews with the press. She had received too many insults from passing journalists, whose stories had depicted her as nothing but a crowned fat lady in a royal side show. The queen had washed her hands of newspapermen for good.

Now, it is true that Tonga's Queen is large. But her weight and girth are the least important of her queen-sized attributes. Salote is as bighearted and broad-minded as she is wide. Unlike other reigning monarchs, who choose their closest friends exclusively from the stiff precedence of the peerage, Queen Salote respects only the aristocracy of mind and soul. Although her front door is ostensibly open only to the Government and the peerage, some of her closest friends are commoners, and she often relies on them as her most trusted advisors.

When I discovered at last that the Queen's front door was closed to me, I realized that I would have to go around to the back. I enlisted the help of three of the queen's "back-door friends," and, under their guidance, began my campaign.

All three ladies were members of the newly formed Tongan Society for the Advancement of Woman, the *Langa Fonua ae Fefine Tonga*. This new project was one of Queen Salote's major interests. She had worked all her life at trying to broaden the interests and capabilities of Tonga's women, and my fellow conspirators were sure that if I were to work earnestly at spreading the Cause, I could not fail to melt the heart of the hardhearted queen. And so it was that I, Jørgen Andersen-Rosendal, embarked upon a lecture tour of all the women's groups in Tonga.

My speeches turned out to be far different from what I had expected. The Tongan ladies did not want to hear about the equality of women; they wanted only to be told about eskimoes and icebergs. Naturally, this caused my interpreters a great deal of trouble; the Tongan language, in addition to all its other peculiarities, has no words to express cold, ice, or snow. What the ladies of Tonga now think of Eskimoes, igloos, and icebergs is something I cannot even imagine. One of my best lecture series was given at the Queen Salote School, where the Tongan Women's Society taught courses in modern pre- and post-natal child care. The school was very well equipped; its main equipment consisted of a caretaker's wife who helped out the Society by producing a fresh infant model each year. In between lectures, I judged competitions for preserves and distributed prizes for the best gardens. It was as perplexing a job for me as it was a new one. Never before had I been forced to judge fifty layer cakes in order to choose the one most deserving of Tonga's regal blue ribbon.

One of my three allies was Nuku'alofa's leading lady, the half-Tongan Mrs. Protheroe. She looked like a miniature edition of Madame Chiang Kai-shek, and she wielded about as much power. Mrs. Protheroe was the highly esteemed Chairman of the kingdom-wide women's organization. Tonga's Madame Chiang Kai-shek had wisely joined arms with Queen Salote's closest "back-door friend," Nanisi. Nanisi was an unpedigreed Tongan whose innate blue blood shone through her noble soul. Each evening Nanisi was known to slip in through the back door of the palace to discuss the day's pleasures and problems with the Queen.

Last of the "big three" was old Sivi Tongileva, an old Tongan woman who, without effort, had gained the name "Queen of the People." Sivi became a good friend of mine because of "the Rose of Denmark," Queen Alexandra of England. Old Sivi still remembered the days when the Danish rose had sat regally on the British throne. The old lady's sight could not have been very good, for she declared, remembering Prince Philip's Danish ancestry, that I looked the image of the Prince himself. This comment went racing around the island even faster that I did, and sure enough, at my next preserves competition, I was introduced as a close relative of England's Prince Consort. When this happened, to the tune of roaring applause and a bombardment of gifts and good wishes to Elizabeth, I turned to Madame Chiang Kai-shek and said, "Dear God, don't you think I ought to tell them it's a mistake?"

But Madame would not let me. "It's too late," she said. "You'd only bring them a terribly painful disappointment. They're feeling so excited by it all, it would be a shame to let them down."

By the time I arrived at the next village, my status had been raised from relative of the Prince to the Prince himself. Every resident of the village presented me with a gift, and during the day I was obliged to be guest of honor at no less than eight luxurious banquets. Since my appetite dwindled as the day wore on, the kind villagers insisted on stowing all their extra food into the trunk of my car. I returned from this excursion with enough fruit and vegetables to feed a town for a week. In addition, I had been given a dozen fried whole pigs and five still-cackling chickens. And when I complimented one village woman on her table linen, I found that tablecloths, napkins, and all were being duly

loaded into the car. I might warn you here and now that com-
plimenting a Tongan woman is a very risky thing to do. One old
Tongan woman was all dressed up for the occasion in a multicolored skirt, and when I told her how pretty it was, she tore the
thing off and wound it around me, overjoyed at her chance to
give me a gift she was sure I wanted. I also made the mistake of
admiring a Tongan baby who was sitting on the floor of a palm
hut, all wrapped up in a beautiful piece of tapa that could easily
have covered the whole family. The baby's owner immediately
stripped the infant and handed over the tapa, placing it expertly
around my waist like a sort of Tongan crinoline. It went perfectly
with the skirt I was already wearing, but still I felt I could do
without it. I had begun to give the tapa rug back, when Madame
Chiang Kai-shek quickly stopped me and said, "You've got to
keep it, it's yours now." For the rest of the day, including my lecture appearance, I had to walk around like a Polynesian lady in
evening dress, carefully lifting my skirts every time I took a step.
The little brown baby smiled as happily as its parents, feeling apparently not in the least bit robbed, even though it was sitting in
stark naked splendor on the floor. The Tongan baby was beautiful, but I dared not say so out loud. I might have been offered it
as a present, along with the rest of the goods I had thoughtlessly
plundered in my effort to apply Western good manners to the
traditions of Tonga.

Fortunately, all this reached the ears of the Queen. She was
both amused and pleased, and that was just what I wanted. My
three allies had set me on the right path. Thanks to their guarantees, plus those of the Duke of Edinburgh and the late Queen
Alexandra, I finally—after two months of waiting—received my
invitation through the back door. There was to be a royally intimate tea party, with the three back-door friends acting as chaper-
ones, and instead of a formal ten-minute audience I was to have
an entire, very informal evening with Queen Salote.

Queen Salote's palace struck me as one of the most pleasantly unostentatious castles in the world. The throne room on the first floor was no larger than a fair-sized dining room, and the state-room, where all the ministers of State gathered each week, was about the size of a small study. The Queen's private apartments were on the second floor, and it was to the royal inner sanctum that I had been invited.

The royal tea party began with a black cat. The cat, Tomui—meaning "Came-too-late," which was what, I was told, she did —walked across the room with her tail standing up and bade a blasé good-evening to the Queen. Then she turned her back on Her Majesty and began investigating my newly pressed trousers. Tomui was a cat who dared not only to smile at a queen, but who insisted, in addition, on having a daily audience with her in order to show off her brand-new litter of kittens. But since I represented a new and unexplored territory, the cat was willing to forego her evening exhibit for Salote.

Tonga's Queen sat stiff as a royal poker on a sofa just opposite me. The sofa was green, and the Queen was lavender blue. Her dress was straight out of Paris, but the straw mat around her waist, symbolizing humility and modesty, was purely Tongan. She wore a single strand of pearls and a pair of tastefully small diamond earrings. As for her area and bulk, there are no words to describe them. Queen Salote's size is so royal that it lifts her above run-of-the-mill definitions of dimension. I can only say that she was a princess born to be a queen, and that she was therefore drawn on a royal scale, in larger proportions than we ordinary mortals are.

It was during our tea party that I discovered how shy the Polynesian Queen actually is. It required all my most diplomatic inter-viewing techniques to bring her to say anything at all. But the Queen had broken a principle; she had decided never to speak with another journalist, yet she was sitting across from me. Under the circumstances, she could not help but put aside much of her normal reserve and capitulate both gracefully and with humor.

And once she got started, our formal conversation quickly turned into an informal chat, with both of us laughing comfortably together and delighting each other in turn with the best of our stories.

Now who, for example, would have believed that the Queen of the Kingdom of Tonga was an expert shark hunter? And who would have believed that anyone in the world might have enjoyed the famous London fog? Yet the Queen of Tonga did. She had never seen fog except for that ominous day before the bombing of Pearl Harbor. It amazed her that there were some cities that remained cloaked in this ghostly shadow year in and year out. When I asked her for further reactions to London weather, she simply laughed and announced that the place was very wet. But she had seen snow for the first time in her life, and that had been a very exciting experience.

She refused to elaborate on the long sea voyage which had taken her to and from Europe. "I'm anything but a good sailor," she said.

Queen Salote also told me about her life during the Pacific war. She spent the war years in hiding, secluded out in the country in a "war palace" completely hidden by palms so that it could not be seen from the air. Below the houses there was an air-raid shelter in a cave. It was a good hiding place, but not a cheerful one. Even in the middle of the day the rooms were so dark that the Queen gave her wartime residence the name of *Ahononou*, "The Short Day." Trees grew out of the floor and up through the roof. And all the furniture had to be arranged around the pillar-like trunks. "We were able to hang pictures on the trees, so it was really very handy." Queen Salote smiled.

"The boys were in New Zealand during the war," she added. By "the boys," she meant the two princes, who will probably continue to remain "the boys" no matter how old or wide they grow.

Before the tea party was over, Queen Salote asked me how I

had liked the buffet at the submarine ball. "Why, it was just marvelous," I said.

"And did you try the pickled fish salad boiled in banana leaves?"

"Yes, I did," I answered.

"And what did you think of the baked fish?"

"Why, it was delicious," I smiled, growing more and more baffled by her interest in my taste buds.

But Queen Salote simply smiled one of her wonderful smiles. "I cooked them myself," she said proudly.

Just as I was leaving Tonga, two ladies of the court arrived to bring me Queen Salote's farewell gifts. One was a gay palm carpet with colorful fringes, and the other was a wonderful piece of tapa covered with all the royal symbols. These treasures are now at home in Denmark, where they decorate my rooms and remind me of an unforgettable evening spent with the Queen of Tonga.

Before my departure I attended one more court party in Nuku'alofa. Like the others it lacked only one thing; the beautiful, lonely, motherly Queen was in her palace. Yet I knew that from the solitude of her castle, Queen Salote could hear the music of the party and so take part in it without being present. She knew and loved the songs of her kingdom. The orchestra consisted of a group of lovely brown maidens, called "the Palace Girls," who had been lent, in honor of the occasion, by the Queen. The Palace Girls Orchestra is often called to play for the Queen, especially in the evenings. When the burden of royal power seems too heavy, and when personal sorrow seems to weigh too much, it comforts Queen Salote to have the Palace Girls distract her thoughts with their songs of the Friendly Islands.

When I think of Queen Salote now, I like to imagine her in her bedchamber, lying on an enormous pile of the finest, softest palm mats in the kingdom. There she rests like the princess in the story of the pea, often sleepless because even the pea of a small Tongan worry can trouble her sensitive soul.

But from a chamber nearby, soft melodies float in to the Queen. The brown girls play and sing their Queen to sleep. And when the ladies-in-waiting tell them that Her Majesty has gone to a far-off place on the wings of their South Sea music, the door to the bedchamber is carefully closed. The girls and their ukuleles whisper their way home in the warm night. A great stillness falls on the palace under the diamond-studded crown of the Southern Cross.

The South Sea Queen is asleep.

My desert island dream

Once upon a time there was a Danish ballad opera about a South Sea Queen and a little desert island. The opera gave no address, but with diligence you can find them. I have. The Queen, as you know, is Salote. And my desert island, which is part of the Queen's little kingdom, is called Lifuka.

I discovered my desert island when I set off to see the rest of Queen Salote's kingdom. Although Tonga's territory is small, it covers great distances, and the islands are like miniature towns spread out across a watery continent. In the south of the kingdom is Tongatapu, largest and most queenly of all the islands, surrounded by its cluster of ladies-in-waiting. Tongatapu and its auxiliary islands are set in a sea so calm-looking that one would never suspect it of concealing the most dangerous depths in the world. But the Pacific is never the same in any two places. In the Ha'apai Islands, which are situated in the middle of the kingdom, you can have the extraordinary experience of watching a man walk on the water all the way out to sea. And this is no miracle: the Pacific around Ha'apai is as shallow as a country creek. Further to the north are the rocky islands of the Vava'u group, which stand huddled together around the nooks and corners of a Norwegian-style fiord, creating a natural harbor nearly as good as the one at Pago. In northeasterly solitude the two islands of Niuatoputapu and Tafahi form their own little group. And in the west, completely isolated from all the other islands, stands the majestic volcano island of Niuafo'ou.

Niuafo'ou is better known to most people as Tin Can Island because of the unique way in which the inhabitants received their mail. This island is completely enclosed by coral reefs, and only the very smallest boats can pass through the reefs into shore. Naturally, the large mail steamers were never able to drop off their bundles. The inhabitants of Niuafo'ou were forced to stand helplessly on shore while their letters, papers, and supplies went sailing by. The problem was solved, however, when the German-Tongan family of Quensell invented the "swimming mailman." This invention consisted of having one of the Quensell sons swim the mail out to the ship in securely sealed tin cans. The ship would wait for the swimming mailman, then haul in the cans while dropping over other tin cans containing the mail destined for Niuafo'ou. It was dangerous because of the sharks, but the Quensells managed to operate their service without loss of either letters or lives. The venture was a profitable one, for stamp collectors all over the world fought to get envelopes with the rare postmark reading "Tin Can Mail."

Not to be outdone by the Quensells, Captain Newton of the steamer *Horoto* once decided to try an invention of his own. He tried sending the mail ashore by rocket. On the day that the new system was to be launched, Captain Newton fired his mail rocket toward the town, where it landed, to everyone's surprise, on the roof of a church holding its Sunday-morning service. The rocket exploded and set fire to the whole building, forcing all the parishioners to stop their hymn-singing and run for their lives. The new system was abandoned, and that was the first and only time that Niuafo'ou ever had airmail.

Tin Can Island is an almost circular volcanic island with a large lake in the middle. In the middle of the lake is another island with a lake, which is thus the lake on the island in the lake on the island in the sea.

In spite of the frequent volcanic explosions, Niuafo'ou's inhabitants were happy on their island. They refused to consider moving until one day in September of 1946, when the volcano went just a bit too far. It erupted sideways and demolished half the island. Queen Salote decided that the nonsense had gone on long enough, and decreed an immediate evacuation. Only a handful of men were left behind, in order to look after the profitable copra plantations. All the others were sent to the practically empty island of Eua in the remote southern part of the kingdom. The exiled Tin Can Islanders were pleased with their new home, but still they missed their old volcano. And nobody missed it more than the island's Protestants. They never tired of rejoicing in the fact that when the big eruption took place, the Catholic church was completely destroyed while the Protestant one was not even slightly singed. The Protestants were convinced that it was a miracle, and many of the Catholics on the island seemed to think so too. Following the volcanic disaster, most of the Catholics of Niuafo'ou decided to change over to the apparently safer harbor of Protestantism.

Another now-evacuated volcanic island is Fonualei, in the Vava'u group. This island behaves very strangely. In addition to its frequent eruptions, Fonualei keeps increasing its size. It expands several feet each year, and no one has ventured to guess when, if ever, it will reach its full growth.

But the strangest and most famous of all Queen Salote's islands is Fonuafo'ou, or Falcon Island. It's a place I would have liked to visit, but couldn't. It simply wasn't there at the time.

Nor was Falcon Island "there" in the middle of the last century. It did not exist. And so it was rather odd when, some time later, skippers began talking about a dangerous reef which was not marked on any chart. In 1865 the English ship *Falcon* discovered that the said reef was no reef at all, but was actually an island. The ship's captain reported his find, and the British sent out an expedition to explore the new land. But when the explorers arrived, they found nothing but sea water marking the spot where the island had been. Falcon Island, it seemed, had disappeared as mysteriously as it had come. But it was not gone for good. In 1877 the English ship *Sappho* observed strange doings in the water near where the island had disappeared. Smoke and steam rose from a seething, pitch-black sea. This disturbance went on for a couple of years, until it appeared that the vacillating island had decided to come up again for a bit of fresh air. This time it pulled itself together and shot right up as though never to sink again. It heaved itself up into a volcanic island over thirty-five feet high, complete with a steaming crater in the middle. Geographers all over the world carefully marked the new island on their maps, and assumed that the fickle volcano had come to stay. But they failed to reckon on the power of the Pacific's surf. An island built of volcanic ash and unprotected by coral reefs cannot survive in the struggle against the sea. By 1884 the island had been reduced to a poor, flat little pancake, and, overcome with embarrassment, it quickly drew back into the oblivion of the sea.

For more than a quarter of a century Fonuafo'ou was missing again. Then in 1927 it launched a new drive, this time more savagely determined than ever. The birth pangs were so violent that the enormous columns of steam rising from the procreating sea could be seen as far away as Nuku'alofa. After this dramatic overture, a solid circular volcanic island appeared from the sea, and all the experts were convinced that this time the island had *certainly* come up for good.

In May 1927 a group of scientists set out to study the reluctant island. With them came Tonga's Prime Minister, the Prince Consort Tungi, who annexed the reincarnated Fonuafo'ou in the name of the Queen. The Prince planted a flag in the volcanic soil, but the flag didn't flutter very long. Within less than a year, the submarine powers had begun pressing the elevator buttons again, and the island slowly started to sink. In the end it disappeared so completely that not even a drop of ash is left to indicate the place where the one-time island had so often played jack-in-the-box with itself and the Pacific.

And that is why, on my trips around the Tongan kingdom, I could not visit the strangest island in the world. I tried. But the island was not at home.

The Tongan sea is full of treacherous coral reefs. Navigating through them is so difficult that ships never attempt to sail at night. When I took the boat from Tonga's capital to the little Ha'apai Islands, the trip lasted as long as a journey twice its size. We were forced to put up overnight at a tiny island called Nomuka.

Nomuka is famous because it was the first of the Friendly Islands found by the English seafarer, Captain Cook; and it was there that the famous mutiny on the *Bounty* took place. Nomuka is also the place where two European copra exporters, who had been in deadly competition with each other for years, decided to meet one day for a friendly two-man convention. Their meeting was the result of mutual anxiety over the news that England had gone off the gold standard. What this actually meant, neither man knew. But after a careful estimate of the gold they them-selves had stacked up, they solemnly decided that Nomuka would stick to her guns and remain on the gold standard no matter what any other nation did.

The Tongan smack which took us from Nuku'alofa to Nomuka boxed itself dizzy in the stormy crests of the sea. My fellow pas-sengers looked convinced that they, too, would have liked to sink, like Falcon Island, to the bottom of the sea. Strangely enough the people of the Pacific are poor sailors, and the Tongans are no exception. I tried to count the number of passengers on deck, but it was as hopeless as trying to count the shrimps in a well-made salad. The *Hifofua* always carried at least twice as many passengers as it had room for. There were only two small lifeboats, and if anything disastrous had happened, we would have been forced to split up into a ratio of approximately one for the land and four for the sharks.

The *Hifofua* calmed down considerably when we approached the bay between Nomuka and its sister island, Nomuka-iki. We were paddled in to shore in a small red rowboat, and before the evening was over I had become a popular hero whom Nomuka will never forget. They may even erect a statue in my memory. There would be a plaque below, reading *Siana lo'loa o Tennima'ake* —"the tall man from Denmark"—and the statue itself would, no doubt, be placed on the sacred spot where his unforgettable landing took place.

My heroism, in this case, consisted of simple foresight. I had heard in advance that the Friendly Island to which I was headed was considered a paradise primarily for mosquitoes. Nomuka happens to be one of the two Tongan islands with a fresh-water lagoon on its premises. The lagoon provides plenty of the drinking water that's so scarce on the other islands, but unfortunately it also provides whole armies of mosquitoes who seem to be born, like the old-time Fijis, with an insatiable taste for human blood. I had taken the sensible precaution of buying myself a bottle of insect repellent. Before leaving the ship, I had smeared both myself and all my companions with the stuff. None of us found the smell of Mysol too pleasant, but our reaction was nothing compared to that of the mosquitoes. They drew back in fury and began to attack the islanders with double their normal amount of vigor. But when our Tongan hosts had also been smeared with the lotion, the mosquitoes were forced to beat a bloodless retreat. They retired in rage and began, I assume, to lay plans for a general transfer to another, more nourishing island.

I solemnly presented the bottle of precious fluid as a gift from the Kingdom of Denmark to the island of Nomuka. A great dance was held in my honor, and I graciously accepted the new-found prestige. I had become a hero of the people, and all because of a bottle of Mysol that cost me exactly twenty-nine cents. The mosquitoes may try to forget me, but the Nomukans never will. Nor will, I trust, the New Zealand manufacturer who from that day on had an entire lotion-hungry island to supply.

After liberating Nomuka from the mosquitoes we set sail again and steered toward the coral island of Lifuka, the capital of the Ha'apai group. It was on Lifuka that Captain Cook received such a rousing reception from the natives that he decided henceforth to call the Tongan territory the Friendly Islands.

And the friendliness has not grown dusty in the two hundred years since then. The little tourist-free island has, of course, neither hotels nor restaurants. But I was immediately shared out and adopted like a holiday child by the entire Friendly island. And I, in turn, decided to adopt Lifuka for my own.

Let me describe to you something about my own private desert island.

It is so small that the entire island, from the lagoon in the east to the bay in the west, can be crossed by foot in fifteen minutes. The walk from south to north takes a little bit longer, but it's a more adventurous journey. The sea surrounding the northern tip of the island is decorated with a necklace of miniature islands strung together with bridges built by the coral polyps. These bridges are passable only at low tide, and even then, they are restricted to pedestrians. The polyps have painted their handmade bridges in all the colors of the rainbow, and the pavements themselves have been designed as beautiful mosaics. If you feel hungry while you are crossing these coral bridges, you need only dip your hand halfway into the shallow water to pick tiny light green clusters of grapes. This delicacy is called *limu*, and it can best be described as a cross between grapes and caviar. The sea around Lifuka is as good as a delicatessen. Its well-stocked shelves offer a wide variety of edible foods.

The capital of Lifuka is called Pangai. It consists of a narrow strip of houses, all standing proudly in a row and trying for all the world to look like a village street. The sidewalks are made of sand, and the roads are upholstered with grass.

Tonga has only two seasons: a warm winter and a slightly warmer summer. And in the soothing stillness of this centrally heated luxuriance, the little palm huts grow in such perfect harmony with their surroundings that they might have been grown from a package of seed labeled "South Sea Huts—Perennial."

That's what my desert island looks like. Life there is surely as close to nature as it can come. The sunrise serves as an alarm clock, and the birds perform evensong. The bird choir of Tonga is not, however, a noisy one. Since there is a scarcity of fresh water on most of Tonga, only a few land birds can survive. There are sea birds galore on the Friendly Islands, but only a fool of a land bird would think of settling there.

To make up for the scarce bird life, Tonga's only mammal has been equipped with wings. The sky is filled every evening with hordes of flying beasts who glide by on web-thin bat's wings. These are the "flying foxes" of the South Seas. Fortunately they are vegetarians and use their sharp teeth only for attacks on fruit and coconuts.

The flying foxes sleep by day and are up at night. Unlike human beings they are very noisy when they sleep, but make not a sound when they're awake. When they followed me on my evening walks, I minded not at all. They preserved the silence I'd come looking for, and that was all that mattered. As the only European on the island, it was a bit difficult for me to be left alone now and then with my thoughts. There was only one place where nobody dared disturb me, and that was the coral cemetery by the sea. No Tongan dares go near a graveyard after sundown; they are afraid of ghosts. And one evening even I thought I was having visions from the dead. I came across a grave that had been neatly bordered with empty beer bottles, placed bottoms up and stuck in the sand. And when, out of curiosity, I picked up one of the bottles, I found myself staring in disbelief at a genuine Schlitz label in my hands. How that empty Schlitz bottle wound up as a tombstone on a desert island I do not know. I don't know, either, whether it was meant as a touching farewell to some dear deceased who had drunk his last glassful of beer, but that's what I'd like to think. It would be as suitable a decoration as a worn gilt cup and a blue coffee pot would be on the grave of Denmark's Mrs. Hanson.

Mrs. Hanson! Ah, yes, do you remember her? Katrine Hanson, the good Danish matron who sat opposite me on the train from Copenhagen to Esbjerg. Mrs. Hanson, who felt so sorry for me because I was going all the way off to the South Pacific. "Oh my God," she had said. "Do you really have to . . . ?"

I met her again on my desert island, and, just like a woman, she turned right around and felt sorry for me because I would soon have to go all the way back to Denmark. "Oh my God," said the second Mrs. Hanson, "do you really have to . . . ?"

I met the second Mrs. Hanson on the island of Lifuka. It happened shortly after my arrival, when Pangai's copra manager offered me a bottle of fresher beer than the one I had found in the cemetery. The beer was served by the manager's wife, and although she was as heavy and brown as any Tongan matron, I felt there was something decidedly Danish about her. I couldn't put my finger on it, but I knew there was something familiar about the lady. I mentioned this to the manager's wife, and she quickly provided the explanation: before she was married, her name had been Katrine Hanson!

"My father was the Danish sailor, Hans Jørgen Hanson," she explained. He had come to Tonga once, long, long ago, and there he had collided with a South Sea girl so beautiful he forgot to rejoin his ship before it sailed. When his South Sea Mrs. Hanson died at an early age, he turned right around and discovered the same virtues in one of her sisters. He married his sister-in-law, and continued living happily from then on. We Danes are in many ways very practically inclined.

And "Mrs. Hanson" of Lifuka was certainly very practical herself. She noticed that the Tongans, after selling their copra crops each month, would always take their large sums of money and march right into one of Pangai's shops where they would spend it all as quickly as it had been paid. Well, thought Mrs. Hanson, no sense letting a good opportunity pass by. She opened her *own* well-stocked shop right next to the copra office, and so solved the problem in a most profitable way. Copra money in Pangai now circulates with admirable expediency: the copra manager hands over a fat bundle of cash to a Tongan; the Tongan hands most of the bundle over to Mrs. Hanson, and she, in turn, passes the money back to her husband at the end of each day. It all works out splendidly, and there's only a minimum of bookkeeping involved.

From her shop Mrs. Hanson-Hapai had a view of Queen Salote's summer palace. I could see that the Pangai palace was undergoing some kind of repair. "What are they doing?" I asked.

"Oh, just putting on new doors," she answered.

"But what happened to the old ones?"

She smiled with only a hint of embarrassment and said, "I think they were stolen."

And "stolen" they were, although the Tongan thief was probably not aware that his removal of the doors was actually stealing. The Tongans have only the vaguest notions about private property. For years they believed that "yours" and "mine" meant "ours," and they lived in this state of perfect community for so long that the concept of theft as a crime is still beyond their limits of comprehension. Tonga's criminal code is probably the only one in the world which has had to define theft as "that which occurs when a citizen converts to his own use property belonging to others, *including relatives and close friends*." The law adds, however, that this conversion of goods is theft only if it was the taker's intention to keep the property permanently. Moreover, the law does not even call the offense "theft" outright, but simply ordains that such action "will be punished as though it were theft."

One day, for want of other entertainment, I decided to look in at Lifuka's city court. There I met a typical example of the Tongan who has never grasped the idea of private property. The prisoner, who was accused of theft, was a Polynesian Romeo whose bronzed muscles were casually draped with a ragged shirt. He leaned against the stand with the weary elegance of a born charmer, and looked as though he were bored to death with the entire proceedings.

He was such an undangerous-looking criminal that I was rather shocked to see his ankles fastened with chains. I had never before seen anything like that in Tonga. But this, I found, was an extraordinary case. Romeo was a jailbreaker. He had been put into jail about a week before, and there he had apparently decided that a few conveniences would be useful in his cell. One night he simply broke out of jail, strolled down to one of Pangai's shops, looted it of what he needed, and then returned, just as casually, to the jail and locked himself in again. The prisoner thought he'd behaved admirably about the whole thing. After all, he explained to the judge, he could easily have run away. But the judge did not seem to appreciate Romeo's behavior at all. He tried very hard to explain to the prisoner that it was really all very dishonest. But the judge's angry words made not the slightest impression on Romeo. He listened with a contented little smile, and seemed to think he had actually done rather well.

Romeo was sentenced with drums beating and flags flying, and he was sent to serve his time in the more solid prison of Nuku'alofa. When he sailed from Pangai, he went as an ordinary passenger on an ordinary boat, without police escort, but wearing handcuffs. I went down to the harbor to say good-by, and Romeo waved to me with the Bible he held in his chained hands. Since my visit to the court, he had regarded me as a personal friend. The fact that he was on his way to serve out a prison term didn't spoil his pleasure over the anticipated trip. He had been to Nuku'-alofa before, and he was delighted with the opportunity to visit there again, free of charge.

Tonga's main prison lies a little way outside Nuku'alofa, set in one of the most beautiful sites on the island. The prison does not look like a prison at all. Instead of bars, there are only bits of barbed wire strung around the huts where the prisoners live. They serve no purpose, however, and seem no more formidable than a white picket fence. In the old days, prison life on Tonga was so idyllic that most of the prisoners regarded it as a paid-for summer's vacation. They were free to come and go as they pleased, provided only that they obeyed the instructions posted at the entrance. This list of rules simply warned them that if they wished to be let in again, they would have to be back by 6:00 P.M. And the prisoners always made it their business to return before closing time. After all they did not want to miss the free supper and the equally free and comfortable bed for the night. Most prisoners on Tonga are considered lucky because they are given free room and board by the government. The governor of a small South Sea island was once given such an ample budget for his newly erected prison that he immediately arrested all his relatives in order that they too might enjoy the benefits of this splendid free hotel.

There is no stigma attached to imprisonment on the Friendly Islands. At worst the prisoner is regarded as a man who has been "unfortunate." When he is released, he's welcomed by family and friends with a lively home-coming party. Afterward he resumes his role in society just as though the "misfortune" had never taken place.

Prisoners in Nuku'alofa's prison have the special honor of being gardeners to the Queen. They look after the royal park without supervision, and when the day's work is done they report to the prison officials—if they can find them. Then they march back to the prison, where they end the day with evensong in front of the barbed-wire gates.

Only on rare occasions does Nuku'alofa's prison have the grim atmosphere that fills most prisons elsewhere in the world. In 1955 peaceful Tonga was shaken by an exceptionally brutal murder committed by two teenage Tongans. The crime was so outrageous that even the Queen of the Friendly Islands decided that an example ought to be made of it, and the two murderers were brusquely sentenced to death. The only problem was how to get them hanged, since the kingdom had, of course, neither a scaffold nor a skilled hangman. The problem was solved, at last, by building an exact copy of an English gallows, complete with scaffold and trap door. But when it was all finished, still another problem arose. How could they find out whether or not the newly built gallows would work? They obviously could not hold a dress rehearsal. All went well, however, for the contrivance worked on its first try, and the two murderers were hanged on schedule. The friendly but also practical Tongans thus made sure that the brutal killings were both the beginning and end of any outbreak of juvenile delinquency on Tonga. The method they used would not have been approved by our social workers, but it achieved its purpose. It is fairly certain that there will be no more gang murders in the peaceful Kingdom of Tonga.

The event reached the world's press, and as I was functioning at the time as Nuku'alofa's voluntary translator to the Royal Aide, I came across a letter concerning the matter from a gentleman in West Germany. In his letter the old German described the sad and bitter life he and his family had led since the end of the war. He had learned through the newspapers that the Kingdom of Tonga wanted a hangman, and he wished to apply for the job. His past experience had not been precisely in hanging, but it was close enough for him to promise excellent service in the position. If Queen Salote would hire him, he wrote, he would be able to spend the twilight of his life in happiness and peace.

Mrs. Hanson-Hapai did not think I should apply for the hangman's job, but she did suggest that I remain on the Friendly Islands. "You might as well," she said. "All you need for your job is a typewriter, and you can sit and type just as easily here as you could in that cold, dark place up north."

"But I've got to return to Denmark," I tried to explain.

"Do you really have to?" she asked again.

And did I really have to after all? I had asked myself that question many times since my arrival in the South Seas. And I thought I saw an opportunity for finding the answer when I heard that Tavi had moved to the nearby island of Tungua. I borrowed the governor's motorboat and went chugging off across the bay in search of the fellow Westerner who had turned his back on civilization and who thought he had found happiness in the South Seas.

His full name was Preben Viggo Heinrich Kauffmann, and he was born on June 11, 1923, in Fredericia, Denmark. He attended the public schools in Copenhagen, and was graduated from the Polytechnic College. He became an engineer. With his diploma, he received a family dinner and speeches wishing him success of every kind: a good position, a bank account, a villa, and a car. And since he was a very industrious young man, he soon began acquiring all those luxuries that had been wished upon him.

But something was wrong. Beneath those layers of hard-earned success very different dreams were whispering, and their whispers turned into shouts when the young engineer went vacationing on the island of Bornholm, off the Danish coast. On Bornholm, he found, he could have lived as carefree and happy a life as that of a wild gull in the sky; he could have, that is, if only the weather on Bornholm had been a little bit warmer.

He became restless, and the migratory birds who were his friends on Bornholm showed him the way out into the wide world. He began on a small scale by hopping across the Sound to Sweden, and he finished up by landing in far-off San Francisco. Finished, for it was there that he finally decided to follow his deepest yearnings. He sold all his belongings and invested the money in a sailboat called *L'Hirondelle—The Swallow*. And on the canvas wings of his swallow he sailed out across the great Pacific.

Preben Viggo Heinrich Kauffmann joined the brigade of the many paradise seekers of the South Seas. He became a *raireva*, a restless soul who sails like a cloud on the wind from one island to another.

But he found his paradise. He said so himself, and his eyes told me it was true when we sat talking in front of his palm hut on a desert island. There he found the totally different world he had always dreamed of. There he wanted to live, and there he hoped to die.

The Swallow took him across the Pacific to Tahiti and from there on to the Cook Islands, Fiji, and at last to Tonga. In Nuku'-alofa he found an understanding friend in Queen Salote's Minister of Public Works, the large, rather sad-eyed nobleman Tu'i Havea Ha'ateiho. This distinguished Tongan had been punished by the gods for an offense committed when he was a young man. He had refused to marry Queen Salote's younger sister, and had chosen instead a beautiful Samoan girl named Leafa'a. But he and Leafa'a had been cursed with a childless marriage, and to make up for this painful emptiness in their lives, they had opened their doors and their hearts to every homeless youngster who passed their way. Preben Viggo Heinrich Kauffmann was one of these.

Havea looked upon the young Dane as a new-found son. He established Kauffmann in his own home, and found him a high-paying job as a government engineer in Nuku'alofa. But that was not what the young Westerner wanted. He had traveled to Tonga in search of something quite different, and not until he came across the lonely rock island of Hunga Tonga did he feel he had found it. There his dream of a tropical Bornholm could come true.

He left his job. He gave Havea all his worldly belongings and all his cash. He gave his bird-winged boat to the Crown Prince. He knew he would need none of those things any longer.

The engineer Preben Viggo Heinrich Kauffmann, born on June 11, 1923, in Fredericia, Denmark, died and was buried in the city of Nuku'alofa some years ago. He was reborn on the rocky island of Hunga Tonga as the nature man Tavi. His new name was taken from Tongan mythology; nothing less than the name of a god would do.

When I met him, Tavi Kauffmann was not living in his self-appointed paradise. He had left the rocks of Hunga Tonga in order to find something new, and on the island of Tungua—where we met—he had found it. The object of his later search turned out to be a beautiful South Sea maiden who promised to return with him to his lonely rock-bound island. Her name was Ofa, and *ofa*, in Tongan, means "love." Together Tavi, the Dane turned Tongan god, and Ofa, the human symbol of South Sea love, would live as Adam and Eve in their own secluded little world.

I arrived on Tungua without advance warning, and immediately presented myself to my host. In honor of the occasion I whipped out my most impeccable Danish, and announced, with extended hand, "Mr. Kauffmann, I presume?"

He welcomed me with a warm handshake and a smile. "Only a Dane could pronounce it that way," he said. "What part of Denmark are you from?"

"Roskilde," I said, choosing to give him the name of the small Danish city where I was born in order to make our Stanley-and-Livingstone meeting in the middle of the Pacific even more outlandish than it was.

"Don't tell me you've come all the way from Roskilde to Tungua to see me," he laughed.

"No," I assured him, "I had to make a few stops along the way."

He no longer looked the least bit Danish. His hair was shoulder-length and his face was framed with a wildly growing beard. His skin was bronzed by the South Sea sun, and he wore nothing but a lava-lava wrapped around his waist. He had become a vegetarian, and lived on the fruits of the island itself. "It's not the most satisfying diet," he admitted, "but then I don't need much energy out here. I make do with whatever Nature has to offer. The only things I need to buy are soap, matches, and a few snatches of cotton."

I asked him about the world he had left behind. "That," he said bitterly, and looked away. "They can keep it, their so-called civilization that's headed straight for annihilation. What is it? Nothing but a batch of machines battering humanity to pieces, and all of it run by people who, in their race for more and more money, never have any time left at all for living."

No time for living in the way *you* would like to live, I thought. Aloud, I asked, "Are you happy?—Or maybe I should choose another word."

"You should," he answered, "but the perfect word for it doesn't exist. Let's say I've found what I was looking for."

"And don't you ever miss what you've left behind?"

"No, no, never!" he shouted, as though the question were one he had been waiting for for a long time.

I decided to change the subject. "How did you happen to choose Tonga?"

"Pure accident," he explained. "I happened to find what I was looking for here. I'm happy, but I don't think most of the natives are. The Tongans are still struggling with the new religion, and I think it makes too many harsh demands on them, demands that are contrary to their nature."

Unlike the Tongans, Tavi was struggling with neither himself nor life. In many ways he was a fanatic, but his fanaticism was too mild and peaceful to be offensive. He found happiness, I suppose, in his own melancholy way. There was something rather bleak and cheerless in the peace he had found, and that cheerlessness, I suspect, came from his knowing that the happiness he had found had brought nothing but grief into the lives of those he once loved. He was caught, as so many of us are, in the eternal conflict caused by the close family group on which our society is based. We are, nearly all of us, so closely tied to those immediately around us that we can rarely seek our private satisfactions without inflicting pain on others. In the Polynesian world there is no such conflict; the family unit is replaced by the all-embracing life of the community. There is a freedom in solidarity that we, in our close-knit little groups, can scarcely comprehend. Yet Tavi

Kauffmann had not found his way into that solidarity. He was not part of the Polynesian world, nor would he ever be. He went his own way, a lone wolf wherever he walked.

No, Tavi Kauffmann did not prove to me that a Westerner can become a carefree South Sea Islander. He had changed his address, but he himself was still the same. The invisible wall created by his different culture and background had cut him off as effectively as the Pacific had cut his island off from the mainland. Tavï was still, like me, a *papalangi*, a man who had burst the horizon, but who had wound up in a world which would never be his.

When I left the island, he knew that I would one day be returning to the little country in Europe that he had left behind. But he had no regrets; or none, at any rate, that I could see. It was not until the very last moment that he seemed suddenly to recall a bit of his past. I was already speeding away when I heard him call out a last message. "In Havea's house there's an album of photographs from my home in Skelskør," he shouted. "I'd like to . . ."

But his last words were drowned in the surf of the coral reef.

I thought of him again when, on my last morning before leaving Lifuka, I handed my Polynesian soul back to the desert island. I wanted to say "thanks for the loan," and I went down to the lagoon at sunrise to make my farewells.

After a quick swim in the dawn-lighted water, I stretched out on the warm sand and looked out over the sea. It was the same Pacific I had seen so often. The same, yet always different, for the changing moods of the ocean are like the patterns in a kaleidoscope. The Pacific is sometimes an innocent blue, and other times it's a stormy gray. For me it had been the peaceful sea of Tavi Kauffmann and the boisterous sea of Polly Thompson; the superstitious sea of Tukua and the bitter sea around the island of lepers; it had been the joyous sea of Moana; and it had been the storm-tossed sea that had washed over Rudy's life. But always it had been the sea, and always it had been the same sea. *And still*

*we take pleasure in its beauty, even when we know it hides so
many wrecks.*

By now I knew my Pacific quite well. I had traveled its surface,
and I had glimpsed into its depths. But what about my own surface and my own depths? Was I still the same? Or had I, like the
Pacific, changed faces and hearts during the course of one brief
journey? On that last morning, as I lay on the sand, I wondered
how many of my dreams would be left behind in the South Seas.
One of them, I knew, would be left with an island beauty, a creature so ravishing that I scarcely know how to describe her. And
describe her I should, for in all my rambling stories I've told you
nothing about my own love.

Unfortunately, I never knew her name. We did not understand
each other's language, although our level of communication was
sublime. I called her Ophelia simply because I sensed that she
called me Hamlet. After all, I am a Dane. However, I had no fear
that when I left my Ophelia would drown herself in grief; not at
all. I knew she couldn't drown, for the sea was her home. She
lived at the bottom of my last happy lagoon.

A mermaid you say? No, don't be silly. Ophelia was no mermaid; she was something ever so much nicer. Indeed, my Ophelia
was the most charming pink sea anemone I have ever known.

Although she had a fixed abode, I often had difficulty finding
her. She kept herself well-hidden in the colorful tangle of that
fantastic submarine world of the coral reef.

Ophelia and her friends lived in an exquisite coral garden
which looked as though it had been planted by water fairies and
sea nymphs. Coral trees like finest porcelain rose from the sea bed,
flowering all year round with fossilized lace leaves in gold, rose,
and pastel blue. Between the trees there were Capri-blue grottoes,
China-red pagodas, desert-gold minarets, and towering Buddhist
temples. And swimming in and out of this subterranean splendor
were all the inhabitants of the coral city: sky-blue sardines,
golden-tailed little sea virgins, and piquantly spotted courtesans

with come-hither looks in their eyes. There were the hungry giant starfish who ate with their feet and were so greedy that they could put down delicacies twice their size simply by slinging out their stomachs and digesting their banquets externally. There was the unhappy soft-tailed hermit crab, who kept outgrowing his apartments and who, every time I saw him, seemed to be wandering around looking for a new conch flat that would be big enough to last. There was the spider crab, who planted decorative gardens as camouflage on its shell, and who carefully weeded the roof whenever it began growing over the sides. There were giant clams, octopuses, toadfish. There was the archerfish, which killed by spitting with as sure an aim as any first-class marksman. There was the cowfish, with its four horns, and there was the cofferfish, which looked very tempting to eat, but was actually as hard as a water-soaked nail.

And, finally, there were the great beauties of the reef, the prima donnas of the sea—the veil-dancing anemones. And my Ophelia was the most beautiful of them all. Each time I came calling, she blushed a coquettish shade of pink and bid me an amorous welcome with her dainty veil-like arms. In spite of her flowery looks, my Ophelia was a living creature. She was vain, and never ate while I was looking, possibly so that I might think she was so ethereal that she could live on love alone. I never had the heart to tell her that I knew she did eat after all. I had seen her sisters being fed in the acquarium in Noumea. At the time I had envied the Noumean sea-anemone keeper; his is probably the easiest job in the world, for these delicate creatures eat only once a week.

My affair with Ophelia was not entirely without drama. There were a few rough spots in the course of our romance, and nearly all of them caused by a jealous rival. The eternal triangle, you know; but I think I came off rather well. Like all sea anemones, Ophelia had a boarder. And this gentleman, who was, as you will see, no gentleman at all, seemed to think he had the right to get fresh just because he was renting a room. Of course this attitude of his was pure nonsense, for I'm sure he knew as well as I did that theirs was a purely physical relationship. This business of apartment-sharing is always like that. No real feeling in the thing at all. And among sea anemones, the situation is even worse; the relationship is as cut-and-dried as can be. The tenant fish has access to the sea anemone's poison barbels. He invites unsuspecting guests home, whereupon the hostess immediately paralyzes them. It is then a simple matter to murder the victim, and the boarder shares his freshly-killed meal with his delicately constituted landlady. She, in return, gives him free room and board, provided, of course, that he remembers to clean up the bones.

Now, Ophelia's boarder, as I've said, was an extremely jealous young man. He insisted on sticking around nearly every time I came along with my goggles to have a rendezvous with my little pink mistress. He would place himself threateningly just outside the front door, and curse me up and down with his stupid fish mouth.

Fortunately, he was not at home when I went out that last day to bid a sad farewell to my Ophelia. We were alone, and she blushed a more seductive pink than ever. Just as I was on the point of leaving—never to see my fair maiden again—she tried to tell me something with her veil-like arms. I think I understood what she said.

"Why don't you stay out here with us?" she asked. "Why do you want to leave us and paradise?"

And there was only one thing for me to answer. "Ophelia," I said, "it would be blissful to stay here with you. But I can't. I'm a European. I breathe through different gills."

It was only natural that my eyes should be wet when I left Ophelia. I had been lying with my entire face down in the water. But I don't think she wondered about it, for I don't suppose fish can weep.

My eyes were slightly moist again that day when, later on in the afternoon, I crossed the polyp bridge to the neighboring island of Foa. There I wanted once more to hide in the grass-soft stillness beneath the dreaming shadows of the palms. There I planned to say my last good-by to the desert island. But it was the desert island which said good-by to me.

I saw a young Tongan come riding toward me through an avenue lined with palms. The slender columns of the trees bent gently over him, creating a cathedral built of leaves beneath the shining dome of the sky. He rode half-naked, handsome and golden-brown. Like a prince of the sun, he danced his golden horse across the turf without holding the reins. His head was tilted back, and his eyes were so distantly turned toward God's great sea that he never noticed me there. He seemed neither to see nor hear; he only sang. And his song was a joyous, earth-shaking, wordless serenade to the land, the sea, and the palms, to life, to himself, and to the sun.

And his was the sky-blue song of the South Sea Islands.